FOR THE *Love* of a CHILD

FOR THE *Love* *of a* CHILD

THE JOURNEY OF ADOPTION

MONICA L. BLUME, L.C.S.W. & GIDEON O. BURTON, PH.D.

with an introduction by BONNIE D. PARKIN

DESERET BOOK

SALT LAKE CITY, UTAH

If you would like more information about free counseling for an unwed pregnancy, please visit ItsAboutLove.org, a Website sponsored by LDS Family Services. This private, nonprofit organization was established by The Church of Jesus Christ of Latter-day Saints to provide licensed adoption services and to strengthen individuals and families. There are also many other reliable adoption agencies and adoption lawyers who can assist unwed parents with information about adoption.

Library of Congress Cataloging-in-Publication Data

Blume, Monica L.
  For the love of a child : the journey of adoption / Monica L. Blume,
Gideon O. Burton.
    p. cm.
  Includes index.
  ISBN 1-59038-440-7 (pbk.)
    1. Adoption.   2. Adoption—Religious aspects—Church of Jesus Christ of
Latter-day Saints.   3. Birthmothers.   4. Adoptive parents.   5. Pregnancy,
Unwanted.   I. Burton, Gideon O.   II. Title.
  HV875.B595   2005
  248.4—dc22   2005007045

Printed in the United States of America   72076
Publishers Printing, Salt Lake City, Utah

10   9   8   7   6   5   4   3   2   1

To our spouses, Dennis Blume and Karen Burton,

for their patience and unflagging support of this project,

and to the many birth parents—past, present, and future—

who act so courageously for the love of a child

Contents

PART 2

STORIES OF ADOPTION

FOREWORD

Fred M. Riley
COMMISSIONER, LDS FAMILY SERVICES

Adoption has been a part of the tapestry of society and culture since the beginning of time. It is the process whereby children are taken into loving homes as a way for society to protect its own. Adoption allows those who are childless to become parents, providing children with love, nurturing, and security.

Perhaps the best-known example of adoption is Moses, whose mother saved his life by arranging for him to be cared for by another loving parent. That unselfish act, involving two loving mothers, established the great heritage of love that is evident in so many adoptive placements that have occurred since then.

Adoption is not simply a legal function—it is a process of the heart, in which caring, willing birth parents and adoptive parents make loving decisions in the best interest of the child. In the media, unfortunately, adoption has often been portrayed unfavorably. Stories of pain among adoptees, birth parents, and adoptive parents have been highlighted for sensational purposes, giving an unrealistic depiction of adoption that can discourage some from considering its great blessings.

This is why now is such an appropriate time for this book, *For the Love of a Child,* to be written. In my thirty years of professional work, I've not seen another book that portrays so well the true nature of adoption. Monica Blume and Gideon Burton show great insight into all of the intricacies of the adoption process. Most important, through reading this book one becomes aware of the great good that adoption can be for society, families, and individuals. Adoption is a loving choice both by the birth mother, who desires to give her child more than she is able to, and the adopting couple, who desire to give a safe, nurturing home to a child.

In the pages of this book, one comes to understand the emotions of the parties involved in adoption. Compelling stories of the best of what humans have to offer one another can help readers understand the great sacrifice made by the birth mother so that her child might have a better life. The emotion involved in that sacrifice is hard to imagine, but it is portrayed within these pages in a better light than I have ever seen.

I encourage all who desire to understand the true nature of adoption to read this book. As they do, their understanding, intellect, and emotions will be touched, and they will gain a greater understanding of the intense power for good that adoption has in the lives of individuals and in society as a whole.

ACKNOWLEDGMENTS

We wish to acknowledge Bonnie Parkin, general president of the Relief Society of The Church of Jesus Christ of Latter-day Saints, for her ongoing support of adoption and for her enthusiastic commitment to this publication. We are likewise grateful to Daniel K Judd of the Sunday School General Presidency for his support from early on, and the professional and spiritual perspectives he contributed.

This project would not have been realized without the cooperation and guidance of LDS Family Services. In particular we wish to thank Steve Sunday, assistant commissioner, Fred Riley, commissioner, and the many readers at LDSFS headquarters who critiqued the manuscript and provided invaluable guiding suggestions. We thank Jerry Harris, director of the Provo LDSFS agency, for the research and writing he contributed. Caseworkers from all across LDSFS prepared and submitted client stories and secured permissions from contributors. We thank them for assisting in and promoting this project and for their significant ongoing work with birth parents and adoptive families.

We acknowledge Sheri Dew and Jana Erickson of Deseret Book for their commitment to the importance of this subject and editor Suzanne Brady for ably and cheerfully seeing the project through to completion.

For their substantial feedback on the entire manuscript, we gratefully acknowledge Valerie Holladay and Heather Burton, who saved us from many misdirections and refined our vision. To the following individuals we also express gratitude for their helpful suggestions or for editing or copyediting parts of the manuscript: Brittany Jones Beahm, Julie Haupt, Wendy Fullmer, Sharolyn Blume, Karen Burton, Dennis Blume, and Corey Hansen.

We thank Jennifer Liu Ng for providing her beautiful Chinese calligraphy within the book and Charlotte Mortimer for providing illustrations for promotional materials.

Special thanks go to Becca Knapp for the central role she played.

Finally, we especially wish to acknowledge our many contributors—both those represented here and those whose accounts could not be included for lack of space—for offering to share these powerful and personal stories for the benefit of those readers whom they will surely inspire.

Introduction

THE ETERNAL NATURE
OF ADOPTION

Bonnie D. Parkin
RELIEF SOCIETY GENERAL PRESIDENT

I hold a special love for all those immersed in the miraculous experience of adoption. I have many dear friends who have adopted children. I've witnessed their heart wrenchings before adopting as they tried to determine *Why us?*—as they watched friends and siblings give birth to small wards while they remained with empty, aching arms; as they sought inspiration about bringing children into their lives; as they went through the interviews and screening processes; and then, as they waited—waited to be chosen by a birth mother, waited to meet her, and most exciting (yet harrowing), as they waited to meet their new child. I've seen their great rewards as they've raised their children, wrestled with teenagers (and lived to tell about it), and, most wonderful of all, became eternal families around a temple altar.

I have friends with daughters who got pregnant before marriage. I've witnessed their heart wrenchings as they tried to determine *Why them?*—as they've watched the daughters of friends and family marry in the temple; as they've sought inspiration about the baby's best interests. I've seen them make a sacrifice—not unlike our Father's—that changed and blessed the lives of parents sealed to children for time and all eternity.

My testimony of adoption has been strengthened as I've served on the LDS Family Services board and witnessed close up the Church's efforts at facilitating eternal families. The Brethren feel very strongly about the fruits of adoption and have asked that I share those feelings with the Saints wherever I go. My tender feelings for all of you involved in adoption come from

1

such personal experiences. And through such experiences, I've come to realize that the adoptive experience is not unique to you, your situations, or to the thousands like you. Adoption is, in fact, a principle of eternity that affects every one of us.

Adoption is an eternal principle on many levels, but maybe chief among them is the way it reveals the Lord's love for every single one of His children. Adoption makes manifest the love of the Lord in our lives. As Sister Blume shared with me: "You cannot go through an adoption without realizing that Heavenly Father loves you and is aware of the tiniest details of your life. There are no coincidences in adoption." One of those friends I mentioned earlier wrote:

> The very moment we had our first child placed in our arms at the adoption agency, I knew it was the will of the Almighty that this child be raised by us. We had prayed and pleaded, promised and reasoned. And here we were at last, with a son that our Father had so lovingly sent to be a part of our eternal family. Later, He sent another wonderful son and then a beautiful daughter. Each time we had the undeniable witness that the children were special children meant to be raised by us. (Personal correspondence)

Besides the obvious reason, that we create eternal families, there may be another reason why we feel the love of the Lord when we witness adoption. You see, upon our baptism, and then through keeping our progressive covenants, each of us is grafted, or adopted, into the house of Israel. We become the children of Moses and Abraham (see D&C 84:34). Further, we literally become the children of Christ. Listen to King Benjamin:

> And now, because of the covenant which ye have made ye shall be called the children of Christ, his sons, and his daughters; for behold, this day he hath spiritually begotten you; for ye say that your hearts are changed through faith on his name; therefore, ye are born of him and have become his sons and his daughters. (Mosiah 5:7)

And then, just as in an earthly adoption, we take upon us the name of Him who adopts us and we are "called by the name of Christ" (Mosiah 5:9). It is an eternal principle that *all of us* must be adopted into the family of Christ.

Our mortal sojourn is full of hard things—it's what we signed up for. And facing an out-of-wedlock pregnancy or being childless are incredibly hard things! On a fundamental level—like all tests—it challenges our view of who we are and who we're supposed to be; it strains our marriages, our families—even our relationship with God.

What if you're pregnant and unwed? Here are a few of my thoughts. First, remember that you can be forgiven! You can, and you must, move forward and receive *every* blessing promised by the Lord to His faithful children. Then seek for the Lord's sweet forgiveness. It will be difficult, it will be painful, but *forgiveness will come.* Keeping a baby is *not* a penance to make wrong choices right—only the Atonement can do that. In the First Presidency's words:

> Birth parents who do not marry should not be counseled to keep the infant as a condition of repentance or out of a sense of obligation to care for one's own. Unwed parents are not able to provide the blessings of the sealing covenant. Further, they are generally unable to provide a stable, nurturing environment which is so essential for the baby's well-being. (First Presidency Letter, 19 July 2002)

Remember your child's future—both here and in the eternities—and ask yourself, "What is best for this baby?" One thing we know is that it is best to be part of an eternal family:

> When a man and woman conceive a child out of wedlock, every effort should be made to encourage them to marry. When the probability of a successful marriage is unlikely due to age or other circumstances, unwed parents should be counseled to place the child for adoption through LDS Family Services to ensure that the baby will be sealed to temple-worthy parents. Adoption is an unselfish, loving decision that blesses both the birth parents and the child in this life and in eternity. (First Presidency Letter, 19 July 2002)

What if your daughter or granddaughter, or a member of your ward or stake, is pregnant and unwed? I have some thoughts for you as well. Honor her agency. Apply the following wise (but very difficult) counsel to your relationship with her. I'm going to adapt it for parents—but it applies to all who are concerned for the mother:

No power or influence can or ought to be maintained by virtue of [your role as parent], only by persuasion, by long-suffering, by gentleness and meekness, and by love unfeigned;

By kindness, and pure knowledge, which shall greatly enlarge the soul without hypocrisy, and without guile—

Reproving betimes [meaning quickly but infrequently] with sharpness, when moved upon by the Holy Ghost; and then showing forth afterwards an increase of love toward [her] whom thou hast reproved, lest [she] esteem thee to be [her] enemy;

That [she] may know that thy faithfulness is stronger than the cords of death.

Let thy bowels also be full of charity towards [your daughter]. (D&C 121:41–45, adapted)

We never progress spiritually when we yield our agency to others. Thus, if the birth mother is not allowed to choose the fate of her child, how can she grow out of a bad choice by making a better choice?

Something else to remember is that you, too, like the mother, must consider the child's future.

Practice the inspired counsel of the First Presidency, who said, "Unmarried parents should give prayerful consideration to the best interests of the child and the blessings that can come to an infant who is sealed to a mother and father" (First Presidency Letter, 19 July 2002).

While our trials are unique, our charge is the same: we must all deepen our faith in the Lord and His promises. Whether we are childless parents, or unwed mothers, or concerned grandparents, or caring Church leaders, we must seek His ways—not ours—and "cast [our] burden upon the Lord, and *he* shall sustain [us]" (Psalm 55:22; emphasis added). The promises that await such faith are invaluable: "Therefore, he giveth this promise unto you, with an immutable covenant that they shall be fulfilled; and all things wherewith you have been afflicted shall work together for your good, and to my name's glory, saith the Lord" (D&C 98:3).

Adoption starts from hard things—an unwed mother and a childless couple. But the good news is that it does not have to end in hard things! Why? Because of the Atonement. Through the Atonement, sorrow is turned into joy (see John 16:20) and "lamentations into the praise and thanksgiving unto the Lord Jesus Christ, [our] Redeemer" (3 Nephi 10:10). Through the Atonement, the bitter things of adoption are made sweet as families become eternal.

As you struggle with deciding whether to adopt, support an adoption, or place a child for adoption, remember that adoption is an eternal principle. It is endorsed by the Brethren. It testifies of the Savior's Atonement by making the bitter sweet. And ultimately, we must all be adopted by the Holy One of Israel, to be born again and become His children. Of this I so testify, in the name by which we shall be known, even the name of Jesus Christ, amen.

PART 1
THE JOURNEY

INTRODUCTION

Monica L. Blume

Some years ago a young woman was sitting in the office of LDS Family Services watching the movie *Adoption and Unwed Parents*. She was with her mother, by whom she had been adopted many years before.

As she watched a very touching scene of a young unwed mother saying good-bye to her baby to place him with loving parents, tears streamed down her own face. She turned to her mother with a newfound realization: "I never knew that my birth mother loved me."

How moving this experience was to see that this young girl had mistakenly thought for so many years that she was placed for adoption because she was *not* loved. Her comment was particularly poignant to me because I had spent the several previous years working with unwed mothers. Those young women, who had made grave mistakes early in their lives, had found the courage somewhere inside themselves to do the unimaginable: to place their newborn babies for adoption. What made this particular young woman's comment so lamentable was that it showed she had held a painful misconception throughout her life, an idea that her birth mother had not wanted her and had, because of this lack of love, chosen to place her for adoption.

I knew this was almost certainly not true. I have seen too many young mothers who love their babies beyond their ability to express it. I have seen too many young women and young men say good-bye to a baby *because* they loved the baby so much. And there is no one, I am certain, who wants that baby more than the young parents who choose to say good-bye. Equal to that

9

love is the love I have seen from those who have become parents through adoption. To anyone placed for adoption by a mother unprepared to care for a baby, and for anyone who has asked, "How could someone who loves me ever say good-bye and walk away?" I hope this book shows with resounding emphasis: You were placed for adoption *because* you were loved.

Working in the field of adoption has been an eye-opening experience for me. When I began so many years ago, I had no idea of the level of emotion involved. And I had no idea of the degree to which I would come to respect those young women and young men who have the courage to make such a difficult decision. I began in the field so that I could be a counselor and guide for those struggling with out-of-wedlock pregnancy. But the past ten years have also been a great opportunity for me to experience the ways God works in the lives of so many people through one tiny child.

When a young man and woman find that the decisions they have made have led to a pregnancy outside of the bonds of marriage, they are faced with the devastating consequences of their actions. They not only have to face what they have done but must broadcast it to others. They will, over the course of the following months, come to find who they really are and of what they are truly capable. They will have to seek counsel from others along the way, finding those who can be most helpful in the coming decisions they will face. They will make possibly the most difficult decisions of their young lives: choosing whether to marry, raise their child alone, or place their baby for adoption. For those who ultimately choose to place the baby for adoption, other decisions will follow. These are not simple decisions, and they are certainly not easy ones.

After all of the counsel, choices, and preparation, the time will come for those choosing adoption when the final good-byes are made. When a baby is placed for adoption, there is much to consider. It is an experience witnessed only with humility at the magnitude of it and with respect for those able to love a child enough to say good-bye. Many lives will be affected by the experience. And the lives of the birth mother and birth father can be changed forever.

Their lives *will* be changed. I think no one would disagree about this single point. But that change, I would strongly add, can be for the better. Adoption is not just an opportunity to better the life of the child involved. It is an opportunity to better the lives of everyone involved, not the least of which are the lives of the young mother and father who place their child for adoption.

My client Amanda is one whose life has changed in a wonderful way. Opening the wedding announcement from Amanda was a high point of my career. It was wonderful to read that she was going to be married in the Salt Lake Temple; I was happy for her and her new husband and hopeful about people in general and their tremendous ability to change. Amanda certainly had a great deal of room for change when I first met her. She was unmarried and pregnant. But since that day some years ago, she has transformed her life and her relationship with God. Her story is one of great hope, and it is one that (with her permission) I have shared throughout this book.

Beyond everything else, this is a book of great hope.

In sharing these stories and celebrating adoption I do not desire to condone transgression of the law of chastity or to suggest that anything less than the most serious consequences result from immorality. In fact, this book shows the very painful and destructive effects of moral sin and of bad choices. If I could say anything to young people, based on my experience in working with so many who have conceived a child out of wedlock, it would be, Stay morally clean, have high standards, be strong.

I have collaborated in my writing with Dr. Gideon O. Burton of the English department of Brigham Young University. Along with his literary expertise, he brings to this project his experience as a bishop. Together we have written this book in two parts.

The first part shares the experience of adoption through my own personal and professional perspectives, providing information for readers to better educate themselves about the subject. In addressing many of the questions and concerns about adoption, I recount various experiences I have had with clients over the years. It has been my earnest desire to share these experiences in the hope of helping others going through similar experiences. Nonetheless, loyalty and respect for my clients does not allow me to share their stories in their entirety. To make my desired points, as well as to protect the privacy of those who had these experiences, all of the names and many of the details in the stories have been changed. A few of the stories are compilations of experiences, combined to make the necessary points while keeping the retelling of the experience free of unnecessary details. The young women and young men in this book are some of the most incredible people I have known, people who have shown great spirituality and faith. These are stories of courageous young people who had the strength to do what they believed was the right thing, even when the right thing was also the most difficult.

The second part of the book is a compilation of personal accounts written by those whose lives have been touched by adoption. We have included stories and letters from birth parents and adoptive parents, stories from individuals adopted years ago, and stories from many others affected by adoption. Gideon has used his writing talents to organize these heartfelt experiences and present them in an appropriate and accessible form.

Although Part One is written in my voice, Gideon helped to conceptualize and write this book as a whole, and I feel the warmest gratitude for the experience and knowledge he has brought to this project. His interest in the redeeming power of personal writing, his ecclesiastical work with individuals struggling with these issues, and his belief that candid accounts of the adoption experience could positively affect the lives of others have led us to this collaborative effort. His own introduction precedes the stories in Part Two.

It is my hope that this book will be useful to many people for different reasons. Whether the reader is a young unwed parent struggling to decide what is best for his or her child, a family member or friend struggling alongside that parent, or an ecclesiastical leader guiding a beloved family through this situation, the experiences shared in this book offer information, perspective, and hope. Although readers may not always agree with the decisions made in each story, they can benefit from seeing how those decisions played out for the people involved. I believe that the experiences shared in this book can provide not only useful information about the process of adoption but, maybe more importantly, the knowledge that good can come through it.

This book is also for couples struggling with the tremendous heartache of infertility who are considering building their families through adoption. It is also for parents who have adopted a child, to help them gain further insight for themselves and their children as they convey to them the precious gift adoption has been in bringing their family together.

This book is for the many who have grown up, having been raised by loving parents who chose them to be in their families through adoption. And it is for anyone who has asked, "How could someone who loves a child ever say good-bye and walk away?"

Through this project, Gideon and I have become ever more dedicated to the journey of adoption. There is no doubt in my mind that it is for the love of a child that a young mother chooses adoption. It is my hope that by the end of this book there will be no doubt in yours.

Chapter One

OFF THE PATH

AUGUST 29—

The pregnancy test was positive. It was as clear as it could be, but as I held it I just stared, hoping that the results might change. I don't know what I'm going to do. I went into a crisis pregnancy clinic to take the test, and I left the place sobbing. I can't believe I am pregnant.

Me. Pregnant. I'm not one of those kind of girls! I'm going places, finishing school, actively attending church, waiting to marry my missionary.

Or at least I was.

I feel like my world is falling apart. How could I have done this? How did I get myself into this situation? I feel like I have ruined my life.

My parents are never going to forgive me. My whole family will be so disappointed in me. I am so disappointed in me. I wonder if I will ever be happy again.

The first time I spoke with Amanda was on the day she discovered she was pregnant, and she was crying. Amanda, the girl with the long straight hair and intelligent, strong mind, felt as if she was about to lose everything. She realized what was at stake. At the time she discovered her pregnancy, Amanda was in her final year at the local university, one semester away from graduating. She was planning to marry her long-time boyfriend who was currently serving a mission, having kept in close contact with his family while he was away. She had been through the repentance process before in her life, owing to a weakness for not keeping firm boundaries in physical relationships with men. She had completed her repentance long before her relationship with this missionary, only to fall back into old patterns with a young man she had recently been dating. Amanda knew everything she had been working for could be lost.

I thought about Amanda after she left that afternoon. Her situation was not unique, and I felt a pang of sadness for her, knowing that she was probably still crying and would be for some time. Amanda's situation is characteristic of so many young men and women who find themselves in this situation. Pregnancy outside of marriage is a devastating experience—painful for the young woman or man involved as well as for parents and family members. It is a tremendous burden of responsibility placed upon the shoulders of those who are often very young and unprepared to carry it. It can seem completely overwhelming.

LOSING A DREAM

I've been hearing stories from young women and men in Amanda's situation for some time. While working with unwed parents as a therapist over the past ten years, I have heard countless experiences from those directly and indirectly affected by an out-of-wedlock pregnancy. I have heard from mothers who, distraught after discovering a daughter's pregnancy, feel their lives are crumbling. I have worked with bishops who, faced with the pregnancy of a young unwed ward member, are looking for ways to help, guide, and support. I have heard from young men and their parents, struggling to find their role while also feeling a lack of control over the situation. And I have listened to leaders of the Church who express their continuing concern for those struggling in these situations and who offer guidance and counsel.

It is because of these experiences that I am an advocate of adoption. Over the next twelve months, more than one million teenaged girls in the United States will become pregnant (one-third of all births), presenting serious consequences for our society as a whole and for those children (see *Trends in Pregnancy Rates for the United States, 1976–97: An Update* [Hyattsville, Md.: National Center for Health Statistics, 2001; available online).

Latter-day Saints are not immune to the problem of unwed pregnancies. It is estimated that there is an average of one out-of-wedlock pregnancy per ward or branch of the Church per year. Each one of these unwed parents and each of the children involved will be seriously affected by what the birth parents choose to do, what path they follow. There is never a pain-free solution to unwed pregnancy. Nor is every situation the same. I can say, however, that after seeing the outcome in so many cases, I have become deeply committed to the belief that the journey of adoption, although not easy, is a journey toward greater happiness.

Adoption is not the only choice open to unwed parents, but it should always be one of the choices. I challenge the reader to openly consider and understand the reasons a young man or woman might consider adoption and to recognize how that coming child can affect so many lives for good. The beauty of adoption is that it can transform the devastation felt both by the birth parents and by the adoptive parents. The journey of adoption is not painless, but it is one of love and growth that can be powerfully redemptive.

I know this is true because I've seen it happen. While counseling those affected by an out-of-wedlock pregnancy, I have developed a great deal of respect for the clients I have seen. I am aware with every new client that the process of adoption is not an easy one, nor is it simple in any way. Still, I have seen it work out beautifully for all involved.

AMANDA'S STORY: OFF THE PATH

I came to know Amanda quite well over the next two months. She was a remarkable girl. But she was dealing with possibly the most difficult experience of her life. For some time, she found it easy to ignore the fact that she was pregnant. While she wasn't the type of girl to put things off or avoid responsibility, it took her some time to really accept the fact of her pregnancy. She felt normal physically and looked the same as always, and sometimes it must have seemed to her that there was nothing different about her life. But she knew, of course, that there was.

She met with me a great deal during this time. She was scared, very scared, and she had no family nearby. They lived out of state and weren't sure quite how to help her from so far away. The fact that their daughter had become pregnant out of wedlock was difficult for them to handle themselves, and I knew they were also in a great deal of pain. They were hardly able to acknowledge the pregnancy when they spoke with her on the telephone, which scared Amanda even more. Still, I found her to be remarkably strong given the circumstances she was facing virtually alone.

She did, however, rely a great deal on the baby's father for emotional support. Ian was kind to her and concerned about both her and the baby. And although she reported to me that she did not feel love for him, she often thought of giving in to his pleas to marry him and raise the child together. But she could see many obstacles to their future, specifically that Ian was not a member of the Church and was from a different country, with views very different from her own about marriage, family, and religion.

By the time Amanda was three and a half months along, she was perfectly confused about what she should do with her life and the life of her child. She was, however, working closely with a very loving bishop. She was beginning to feel better about herself and more hopeful about her life. And she was beginning to take control of her situation, finding a doctor and building a support system for herself. The choices she was making now would lay the foundation for further good choices as she continued in her pregnancy.

Discovering an out-of-wedlock pregnancy is a very painful thing. Particularly within our church, it represents a great diversion from the preferred path of waiting till age sixteen to date, remaining morally clean while working towards missions and schooling, and ultimately marrying a worthy partner in the temple. Such a pregnancy can therefore feel like an overwhelming detour to those involved. Discovering the pregnancy is the beginning of a set of experiences that will involve pain and humility but also possibilities for tremendous personal change and growth. I will return to Amanda's story throughout the course of the book, but let me now share an example of a girl humbled by the realization of just how many people were affected by her decisions.

CHRISTIE'S STORY: THE RIPPLING EFFECTS

Christie had never felt more alone. As she lay on her bed, she looked around her room at the life she had earlier taken so much for granted. She looked at the corkboard dotted with swimming ribbons she had earned during the past year. She glanced at the college poster on her wall, the one that shouted "Enjoy Stanford!" and thought of the hours of study she had logged in hopes of getting a scholarship to go there. But her eyes lingered most on the family photograph sitting on her dresser.

She saw her mother, always her cheerleader at the swim meets. She looked so hopeful sitting in that photograph, knowing nothing of what was about to happen in their lives. Christie looked at her father next. He had one hand on her shoulder in the picture and looked very serious, but she knew he was a big teddy bear inside. She thought of how proud he had always been of her accomplishments, of her grades, of her spirit of determination. She knew he loved her very much, and she smiled for a moment as she thought of his overprotective nature towards her, always trying to protect her from danger. Her smile faded quickly as she looked into his eyes in the photo and imagined the disappointment she would see in those same eyes when she told him she was pregnant.

But that wasn't the worst of it for Christie. She felt the most pain as she looked at her three younger sisters in the picture. They were so innocent, so trusting. They looked up to her. And as she thought of how painful it would be to tell them that their big sister had completely messed up her life, she found herself aware for the first time of the pain she would cause these people she loved and who loved her.

Christie knew she needed to talk with her mother. She could see her mother was already worried about her. Her parents had expressed concern about her current lifestyle, about her slipping grades and less than humble attitude. Mostly, they felt strongly that she was spending too much time with her boyfriend, Jed. She felt a pang of shame as she realized how right her parents had been and how dangerous her situation had become. And she knew that the information she would soon share would be devastating to them all.

As she thought of Jed, she trembled slightly. He would have to be told, too. How would she begin a conversation that would mean the end of his dreams as well? As she thought of his family, of how kind and trusting they had been, she again felt sharp pangs of sadness and shame. Jed had already applied to several universities and was preparing to move into an apartment for a year to attend school before putting in his papers for a mission. For a mission! She hadn't thought of this before, and the realization made her feel like a boulder was lodged in the bottom of her stomach.

He wouldn't be going on a mission now. No opportunity for Jed to serve the Lord for two years of his life as a full-time missionary. No mission experiences to build his testimony and strengthen his future family. No silly pictures of life at the Missionary Training Center or stories of mistakes in a foreign language for him. He was going to be a young father instead. Everything would be different now for all of them.

So Christie's thoughts must have been. She came to meet with me on the referral of her bishop a few weeks before she told anyone else she was pregnant. It was a heavy burden on her to know about the pregnancy while keeping it from others. She became increasingly aware of the tremendous pain this pregnancy would cause her loved ones, family members, and friends. What she didn't yet know, and wouldn't come to realize fully until long after her baby was born, was the love her family would feel both for her and for her unborn baby, the opportunities for growth and strength that those around her would experience, and the unimaginable degree of pain she and her loved ones would feel throughout this process. The many people whose lives would be affected by the conception of this one tiny child was something she was only beginning to realize and would continue to understand more each day as her pregnancy progressed. She related to me how she told her parents about the pregnancy.

"I finally decided I just needed to say it. So one day while I was driving to the store with my mom, I blurted it out. 'Mom, I'm pregnant.' She didn't say anything for such a long time that I started to wonder if she heard me. And then, finally, she looked at me. And all she did was cry. She just pulled over onto the side of the road and cried. And I just cried with her.

"When she could finally talk, she told me we needed to tell my dad. I've never felt sicker to my stomach than I did while we were driving over to my dad's office, and I've never felt so ashamed. But there was a small part in me that wanted so badly to lean on my parents for help, at least to feel their strength in dealing with this problem, that I was almost relieved as well.

"Well, that feeling of relief left me fast as we walked into my dad's office. He took one look at our tear-streaked faces and said, 'What is it? What's wrong?'" Christie looked very small and scared to me as she related this story. I could see that her parents meant everything to her, whether she had realized it over the past year or not, and letting them down was one of the most painful things she had experienced so far in her young life.

"I've only seen my father cry one other time in my life. It was when his brother was dying. But he cried that day in his office. And I felt he must be so disappointed and ashamed of me. I had let him and my mother down so much. But all he did was hug me tight. I don't know if I ever needed a hug more than I did when he gave me that one, and I just hugged him back while we all cried together.

"It was so hard seeing my parents feel so bad. It still is hard watching them face so much pain and worry because of something I've done. When we told my three sisters, though, I thought my heart would break." Christie's sisters were sixteen, fourteen, and eleven years old. She and her parents decided to keep everything in the open so there would be no family secrets. But they were also aware that this pregnancy and Christie's decision to place the baby for adoption would be formative and life-changing for these three young girls.

"My oldest younger sister was angry with me. Really angry. I don't blame her—I was pretty angry with myself. But it still hurt a lot to hear what she had to say. She told me I was ruining *her* life. My fourteen-year-old sister didn't say much; she was just very quiet. My youngest sister was actually excited at first. She thought it would be fun to be an aunt and have a baby around the house. She has such a soft spot in her heart for babies. So when I told her I was going to place the baby with another family to raise, she looked as if I had just punched her in the stomach. And then she was more upset than anybody and ran from the room. I never realized how much my decisions affected others around me."

Telling her parents and sisters was only the beginning. During this same time, Christie told Jed about the pregnancy. Jed was very upset, of course, and he in turn added many ripples to the situation. He told his parents, who were both devastated. His siblings and extended family members were affected just as Christie's were, as were other loved ones and friends who cared about them and their families. They both spoke with their bishops. The effects continued to spread.

As I watched Christie navigate through these experiences, I couldn't help but feel compassion for the many people whose lives were taking sharp turns in this new direction. Jed and his parents were being affected, and although I had never met them, I was keenly aware that they, too, were experiencing loss in a number of ways. Both Christie's and Jed's grandparents, aunt, uncles, and cousins would learn of this pregnancy and be challenged in choosing how they would handle the information. Family members would have many opinions and feelings about the choices to be made, and each would feel sad not only for their own losses but for the pain being experienced by Christie and Jed.

Their ecclesiastical leaders would be affected. Working with bishops over the years has given me a great respect for their position and a sincere empathy for their concern in shouldering the problems of their ward members. I always feel tremendous gratitude towards those bishops and other leaders who are willing to step into a young woman's or young man's life and share the burden of an out-of-wedlock pregnancy. They will feel pain and sadness as well.

But there would be an even wider circle of those who would be affected by this pregnancy because of the decision to place the child for adoption. Somewhere out there was a family whose own trials were running parallel to those of the birth parents as they struggled with the pain of infertility. Somewhere a couple was praying fervently for their Father in Heaven to send them a child. That couple had parents, siblings, friends, maybe even other children, who were all praying for a child to be sent to their family. These were the people who for the moment did not know that a child growing inside a birth mother would come into their lives as a gift beyond their own understanding. People's lives would be changed by this experience. Many, many people's lives would be affected.

When Christie and Jed placed their baby in the arms of that couple several months later, I marveled again at the extent to which this one child had touched so many. As I observed Christie and Jed's many family members kissing their baby with heartfelt good-byes, watched the nurses wipe tears from their eyes, and wiped a few from my own, I could only imagine the new family members who would be kissing this baby their hellos.

A pregnancy affects so many people. And a child goes on to affect many more. This is why it is so important to separate the sin associated with premarital sex from the pregnancy and the child.

JILL'S STORY: WHAT WENT WRONG?

"We have done everything we could do to help Jill make the right decisions and have a good life. We are far from perfect, but we couldn't have loved her or prayed for her any more fervently. What did we do wrong?" Jill's mom shared her feelings while Jill sat in the waiting room. I believed her when she told me how much she and her husband loved this daughter.

It had only been a few minutes since I had met and talked with Jill for the first time, learning about her feelings, her desires, her seemingly lost hopes and dreams. I heard both Jill and her parents express sadness that her life had taken such a dramatic turn from the way she had been taught and the goals she had been striving to reach for so many years. I also heard Jill share how loving and supportive her parents had been throughout her life and how sad she felt that her decisions were causing them to feel they had not done enough.

Jill's father was a quiet man who clearly held strong feeling of tenderness for his daughter. She was the only daughter he had—in fact, the only living child he had. A son had died some years earlier, and this devastating loss for the family had brought them a greater appreciation for one another. Jill's father was a spiritual man. He, like so many of us, was trying to do what he could to lead his family in the principles of the gospel. And he and his wife were deeply concerned about this detour Jill had taken.

As I visited with Jill and her parents, I was impressed by their desire not only to realize the problems that existed but to change the things that weren't working. In one sense this is very admirable, but upon learning of an out-of-wedlock pregnancy, how much effort should be spent on thinking through what went wrong? Over and over during the early months of such a pregnancy, I hear the question *What went wrong?* Sometimes it is the birth parent who asks it, sometimes the bishop, sometimes a family member. Most often, I hear the question from the parents of the young man and woman who are responsible for the pregnancy.

I'd like to use an analogy in addressing this question. If someone fell from a building and was injured, it would be natural to ask, "What happened?" At that moment, however, it is far less important to answer this question than it is to consider what can be done for the injured person. Although a knowledge of what caused the problem is useful, the more immediate concern is to address the results of the fall rather than its causes.

With out-of-wedlock pregnancies, questions immediately arise about why sexual behavior has occurred outside of marriage, and this concern certainly should be addressed at some point. Indeed, recognizing the factors contributing to the pregnancy can be helpful in preventing further mistakes from being made (common factors contributing to promiscuity are discussed in Chapter 5). But when a pregnancy is first disclosed, it is more useful at this point to recognize what might cause those who are off the path to stray further away or to become stuck in their attempts to return to the plan of happiness.

Here are several factors to consider immediately upon learning of an out-of-wedlock pregnancy. These ideas can prevent further deviation from the path and promote a prompt return to the best course forward.

RESPONDING TO THE CRISIS

Become aware of what went wrong so it does not continue to cause problems. As in the analogy of the falling victim, it is useful to be aware of what caused the problem in order to prevent it from continuing to cause harm. It is important not to focus so much on the cause, however, that progress in seeking a solution is hindered. In Jill's situation, for instance, she recognized some things she should change immediately.

"I knew I needed to stay away from Trevor." She had known this for some time. "Not that Trevor was a bad guy—he wasn't. It's just that we had been involved physically in the past, and I knew my resistance was weak around him. We had both been through the repentance process before after becoming involved. He knew he was weak around me, too, so when we became involved again, we both knew we were taking very big risks and playing with fire."

She went on. "I also know I have a more difficult time making good choices when I'm around friends who are making bad ones. I was struggling personally and got careless about who I was hanging out with. I know I'm probably just rationalizing, but it's really hard to choose being alone rather than being with friends that aren't the best influence on you." Jill had a good deal of maturity. Not all who are struggling with an out-of-wedlock pregnancy can or will look at their own situation so candidly, but their parents or others around them might be able to help.

Jill hit on a strong point and a major contributing factor to early sexual involvement. She said that even though she knew there were some things she *should* do, her insecurities and shaky self-esteem made her struggle in choosing those right things. If an issue of self-esteem leads a young man or woman to make poor choices in morality, it will likely also be a factor in making poor decisions for a baby. The issue of self-esteem is an important one, one that can be altered and improved. Self-esteem can be acknowledged and addressed early and should be further repaired after the crisis of the pregnancy has passed. It can be a key factor in regaining control and finding hope, as discussed in Chapter 5.

Be open, honest, and humble. Frankness and humility can prevent those who have made mistakes from making more. Jill's parents, for example, admitted that they had failed in taking a moral stand with her. Jill's mother commented that they had tried to stay out of the decisions Jill was making in her life because she was twenty-two years old and wanted her independence. They now knew, however, that they needed to be more clear with her about their own and Heavenly Father's expectations of her. While they would continue to support her right to make choices in her life, they would choose to "draw their line in the sand," as it were, so she was clearly reminded of the values with which she had grown up.

Openness and honesty with ourselves and others is necessary to prevent us from becoming stuck in the grieving process. Anger and fear eliminate the open communication that is so much needed. Blaming each other or someone else for the problems we are facing only closes off the opportunity for humility, repentance, and forgiveness. It can cripple opportunities to build empathy and understanding and to recognize the great blessings of the Atonement for all those involved.

There can be tragic results when those dealing with a pregnancy get stuck in the process of grief and loss. For instance, a girl in denial about the pregnancy cannot begin to address the concerns that arise. A parent who is stuck in anger towards their son's girlfriend might miss out on an opportunity to see their grandchild or grow through the process of forgiveness and understanding. Jill was fortunate. Her parents certainly felt anger, but they did not get stuck in their anger. They ultimately chose to be respectful of her ability to make good decisions again rather than seizing control. Sadly, it is sometimes the case that rather than helping their loved one onto a better path, family members and others who should be supporting the birth mother actually become obstacles to her progress. This problem is addressed more fully in Chapter 2. Being open, honest, and humble in dealing with an out-of-wedlock pregnancy can help avoid these additional problems.

Be careful to make decisions or draw conclusions based on real information. When a young man or woman is in the crisis of dealing with a pregnancy they feel unprepared to handle, he or she may be prone to making rash decisions to solve the problem. Even parents, upon learning of a pregnancy, may rationalize choices or behaviors they would normally not believe are right. Taking the time necessary to realize and accept the problem can prevent getting further off the path towards happiness. During a crisis, it may feel as if there is no time for making well thought-out decisions and indeed, in some crises, there is not. However, in the case of a pregnancy out of wed-lock, the decisions that need to be made are important enough to be made completely and rationally, in a clear frame of mind and with all of the resources and information possible. Before developing strong opinions about how choices should be made, it is vital to obtain correct information from reliable sources, take the time necessary to evaluate the facts, and act wisely on this knowledge.

Be forgiving of yourself and others in dealing with an out-of-wedlock pregnancy. Mistakes have been made, and others will likely be made in the future, but dwelling on them is not helpful. For example, tak-ing all the blame on ourselves can lead to unhealthy patterns, such as over-compensating and preventing others from progressing through the process themselves. A mother who decides it is her fault that her daughter is preg-nant because she wasn't a good enough parent might not allow her daughter to carry the responsibility that she should in an effort to protect her child from further pain. Natural consequences can be a powerful teaching tool, one that Heavenly Father uses often. And sometimes the desire to protect those we care about from seeing those consequences can lead to protecting them from learning what they might have learned through the pain. Chapter 3 includes the story of Shauna, a very sad example of how parents "protected" their daughter from what could have been the most valuable and moving les-son of her life and instead taught her a most useless one.

Discovering a pregnancy is only the beginning of a process. Poorly dealt with, it can be a devastating and tragic process of further poor decisions that can damage the relationships of those involved. But when a young woman handles her pregnancy in a healthy manner, it can be a process where all involved find understanding and peace in themselves, in their relationships with others, and in their relationship with God.

I was very hopeful for Jill as she spoke about staying away from people who allowed her to be weak, but she had a long way to go. Not only did she need to continue examining what changes she would have to make in her life to get back on the right path but she also had to seriously evaluate after her pregnancy what would lead her to where she wanted to go. Jill was a remark-able person, she *became* a remarkable person, as she faced her trials. And placing her baby girl in the arms of two parents (who were themselves on a journey of becoming incredible people) was only one stop for her in her pursuit of a healthy, happy, eternal life. Adversity affects us, changes us. It is up to us to determine in what ways we will be changed.

MAINTAINING HOPE

"Sometimes I feel like if I have to deal with one more problem, any problem, in addition to this pregnancy, I won't be able to handle it," said a woman one afternoon in the support group for parents of unwed pregnant teens. She was facing the devastating pain of a daughter pregnant out of wedlock immediately after her recent divorce, a cross-country move, and an ensuing job search. She was talking openly, and though she was dealing with so much, she maintained a positive perspective about her situation. She listened empathetically as other parents shared their concerns and added, "As difficult as it feels to face everything I am facing right now, I know my problems, and I wouldn't want to trade them for anyone else's."

She made a good point. As the parents shared their experiences, trials, and struggles with the other members of the group, I could see why I might not want to choose any of them. One parent struggled financially, another was dealing with disputes with extended family members, and still other parents worried about their other children besides the one who was pregnant. And each agreed that yes, they would rather deal with the problems they had than exchange them.

Such a response might be from an attachment to the familiar, wanting to choose the door behind which we know what awaits. It may be that we would choose our own set of problems rather than someone else's because we have already begun to learn how to manage them. Whatever the reason, getting to this point is a sign that we are moving toward resolution of the problems. An out-of-wedlock pregnancy is a loss, and those involved may experience feelings of shock, denial, anger, acceptance, and resolution, feelings that are experienced by those affected by other types of loss and grief. Possibly the best step towards acceptance is the realization and acknowledgment that all is not lost.

The hopefulness of their situation is easier for me to see than it is for those in the early months of an out-of-wedlock pregnancy. While they are facing one of the most painful trials they can imagine, a trial they feel may result in perpetual and permanent unhappiness, I have seen from experience that they still have much to hope for in their lives and in the life of that unborn child. For a time, it may seem that there are no good choices and not even any lingering opportunities for hope. But I have been watching people go through these experiences for years, and I know they still have many opportunities for hopefulness because I have seen the entire process: the pregnancy, birth, and subsequent follow-through of whatever decision they have made for the sake of the child. I have seen people be happy again.

I think Heavenly Father must feel the hope we often do not as He watches our lives, knows what lies ahead, and realizes our true potential. It may be like watching a child go through the pain and discouragement of learning to ride a bicycle. We watch him get on with high hopes, pedal, and then fall and skin his knee. We reassure him that he will get over the pain, learn to ride, and be happy when he flies down the street without training wheels to hold him back. But while he is lying on the ground, looking at the newly scraped knee, he may find it hard to believe he should get up and get back on the bicycle; it is even harder for him to imagine that he will be better off for having gone through these experiences. Upon learning of an out-of-wedlock pregnancy, those whose lives have been eternally and irreversibly affected can feel that all they have ever hoped for and dreamed about is gone.

But all is not lost. For a young woman who had plans to seek an education, have adventures, marry in the temple, and live a long and prosperous life, hope still exists. For the young man who dreamed about having those same experiences, his choices do not need to include avoiding the situation in order to fulfill those plans. While there are serious and painful consequences for the choices made resulting in the conception of this child, there is also an opportunity for both the young man and the young woman to become someone who they would not have become through any other process.

NATASHA'S STORY: HOLDING ONTO HOPE

One great family I came to know included Natasha, a young girl dealing with pregnancy during her senior year of high school. Theirs was a strong family, but when they first came to me they were fighting one of the most discouraging battles of their lives, a battle to save their daughter.

Natasha had been through a couple of rocky years, years when she had become involved with a boyfriend whom she followed away from school, church, and her family towards other dangerous and destructive choices. Her parents had been fighting hard to redirect her from the path she had been choosing, and they had been hopeful that she might change her course if she could graduate from high school, move in with a family member in another state, and begin college in a new place with new friends and new opportunities. When they learned their daughter was pregnant, however, their hope diminished. Natasha herself hadn't had much hope to begin with, and her family expressed feelings that the pregnancy might be the proverbial nail in the coffin for Natasha's chances at a happy life.

Learning of an out-of-wedlock pregnancy no doubt results in feelings of pain, sadness, and disappointment. As I said earlier, young men and women and their loved ones will likely experience feelings consistent with other types of loss. They may feel shock at the discovery of a pregnancy and disbelief that it may actually be happening to them. They will likely experience anger towards themselves, the other birth parent involved, God, or someone else. But they can get to a point where they meet the problem with some level of acceptance, where they focus less on blaming and pitying and more on seeking a resolution. And just as in other experiences of loss, there is hope as well. Maintaining hope is a key factor in progressing physically and spiritually. The way with which the loss is handled is important and can lead to further strengthening both individually and as a family.

The important thing about Natasha was that her family, particularly her mother, never gave up hope for her. Natasha's mother kept on fighting until Natasha herself had the will to fight alongside her for her life and the life of her unborn son.

Natasha took a while to finally come in and meet with me. I first knew of her circumstances through her sister, who called inquiring about her options and for advice on how to help her. I later spoke with her mother on the telephone several times, as well as her sister and bishop, until finally she trusted me enough to come to my office. It can be scary to meet with someone you feel might influence your thinking if you are already questioning what your thinking is in the first place. Natasha didn't know what to do about the pregnancy, and it took her some time to trust that I wasn't going to tell her.

I liked Natasha instantly. She was candid and open, and I could see why she waited to come in. She seemed afraid to allow herself to be influenced by just anyone. She wasn't yet at the point of trusting her own judgment again.

And though Natasha and her family might have felt she was very near the edge of losing everything, she had in her a glimmer of the abounding potential for which her mother had been battling, she had everything to lose and everything to gain. And to begin with, she needed to find some hope that she could have a good life and be happy again. Today, she is a strong member of the Church, sealed in the temple to a worthy priesthood holder and raising a family of her own. I will share more about Natasha in Chapter 5.

If the challenge of an unwed pregnancy is handled in a healthy and loving manner, relationships can be strengthened and the self-esteem of those involved can grow rather than diminish. True, a grave mistake has been made in participating in sex outside the bonds of marriage. Consequences will result because of this. But the resulting pregnancy itself is not the sin, nor is the child who is conceived. And growth and learning *can* come through this experience. Unfortunately, the fear of having to go through this type of pain again in the future can lead to painful and unhealthy ways of handling the situation. Some people miss out on the learning and growth that can result as the experience progresses. Let me illustrate this point.

Imagine that in a private moment a young girl shares with her mother that she has become involved with someone and is now pregnant. The mother, being human, will likely react with sadness, disappointment, even anger. But at some point the mother must bring her emotions under control and pay attention to the effect her reaction will have on her daughter's life. If the mother, in her anger and disappointment, blurts out, "You are just so stupid. You are ruining your life and my life, too!" she can lay a foundation for her daughter to feel worse about her own ability to do anything right, and the daughter may decide to no longer confide in her for support. The daughter may then turn to someone more accepting, such as a reckless group of friends (people who will not judge her because they have done wrong things themselves) or to the boyfriend with whom she has gotten into trouble in the first place. While her parents may feel she should consider adoption, giving her baby and herself a better opportunity at a successful and happy life, her boyfriend may wish her to keep the baby and to move in together instead. If the mother, instead of focusing on the negative points when she learns of the pregnancy, could convey to her daughter that all is not lost, that they are strong in their family, and that they will be able to get through this crisis together, then her reaction not only can build the daughter's feelings of hopefulness but also can build their relationship and deepen trust.

Of course, we all say and do things we wish we could take back. My husband is fond of saying to me in mock criticism, "Honey, you are a therapist. You know better than to say something like that." I generally respond with mock professionalism, "I do know better. I'm just *choosing* to say it anyway." When I suggest that the way we handle such a situation can dramatically affect the outcome later on, I mean how we handle *all* of the choices throughout the entire situation. When we are willing to learn and grow as we face the problems laid out for us, we open ourselves to opportunities both personally and with our family members to become stronger and, yes, even happier.

Natasha's family made some mistakes in painful moments, but ultimately they helped her learn some valuable lessons about herself and her life here on this earth. Natasha developed a testimony of her value and potential in her Heavenly Father's eyes. She shared with me what she had come to realize, which was that although at times she doubted her own strength to do what she felt best, she was coming to believe in her own ability to do the right thing. And she had come to know a feeling of love from her Father in Heaven, a love that existed even though she had committed serious sins. Despite that, she had to trust in her belief that she could still be loved by Him. She had to continue to believe that He would be there for her and that she would have the strength to do what was right for her own life and the life of her baby.

Possibly most importantly, Natasha had to cling to faith. She had to hold fast to the belief that her Heavenly Father not only loved her baby but He loved her also and wanted her to be happy. It took faith to believe that after the pain of struggling with her decisions and placing her baby in the arms of another mother to raise, she would have peace. Though she might not always feel free from the burdens of pain and sadness in the months following her decision, she could still have peace and hope throughout.

Would she make other mistakes in her life? Undoubtedly so. Though these would not be the same ones she had made before, there would continue to be sin and adversity in her life. Was she still entitled to the love and guidance of her Heavenly Father? Most assuredly, for she would continue to be a daughter with divine heritage, a child of a loving God who would continue to care for her happiness and safe return home. But would she ever be happy again? That is the most important point of all. Heavenly Father loves each of us and wants us to be happy. Happiness is an eternal principle laid out by our Father for each of us. And when a child is placed for adoption, especially when adoption is sanctioned by the Brethren as what is best for that baby, it is also ultimately best for the parent who sacrificed to place the child as well. Our Father loves them both, and beyond everything else, there is the hope of forgiveness, love, and, without a doubt, happiness again.

People have said to me many times, upon learning that I work with birth parents throughout the process of adoption, "That must be so sad." Then they often add, "Well, it's happy for the adoptive couple but sad for the girl who is giving up her baby." I do not believe that Heavenly Father would sacrifice one for the sake of the other, and I always add, "It is possibly the most difficult and painful thing she has ever done. But it is happy for her, too." Heavenly Father loves each of us and has a divine interest in the outcome of our existence. And for the birth parents, as well as for the baby, happiness can come again.

Chapter Two

FINDING YOUR BEARINGS

OCTOBER 14—

My head is spinning. Everything that used to feel solid and secure in my life feels very shaky now that I'm pregnant. It's like none of this is really happening. I wish I could just close my eyes and it would all go away!

My parents seem to be handling everything okay. They don't talk about the pregnancy at all, but they are trying to sound hopeful on the telephone when we talk. Will things ever be normal between us again?

I've begun meeting with Bishop Taylor. For an old guy, he sure does understand how I'm feeling. I think he will be a great support for me.

Ian has been talking more about getting married. Should we? In some ways it would just make everything so much easier. But marriage is such a big decision! I don't want to rush into that or anything else right now. It feels like everything I do these days is either putting off what I need to face or rushing into something I need to take slowly. I'm not sure I can trust Ian or even myself. I think I can trust Bishop Taylor, though. He listens, and really wants to help me. Maybe he can.

What happens after the initial shock of discovering an out-of wedlock pregnancy? There can be a period of time after realizing the problem when you don't know which way is up. It is natural to put off dealing with the problem or even to deny that there is a problem. Obviously a pregnant woman can ignore her own situation only for a limited time. (I have been surprised, though, at how often and how long many pregnant girls will do just that!)

Those struggling with the shock of such a pregnancy are often vulnerable and may act irrationally or allow themselves to be directed by strong opinions that can be biased or misinformed. The decisions to be made about the coming child have eternal consequences, and they deserve to be thoroughly considered. Rather than denying the problem or chasing down the quickest solution, it is important to sit down, assess the situation fully, remember one's principles, examine the resources that are at hand, and then act with a cool head. Even if it feels like the roof has caved in on your family's dreams, repairs can be made. Everyone can survive. But it takes both a rational and a spiritual approach. It takes patience and a willingness to listen to those who have the expertise and wisdom to guide well.

I've found a helpful analogy to describe the best approach to take following the shock of out-of-wedlock pregnancy—the idea of orienteering. In orienteering, you learn methods for finding your bearings. If you are out in the wilderness, you must know the lay of the land before attempting to cross it. That's why you take a map. And even if you lose your map or get confused and disoriented as you travel, there are still many ways to get your bearings. Boy Scouts learn to find north by identifying the North Star in the Little Dipper constellation. But what if it isn't night? By measuring the shadow of a stick in the ground as the sun travels for an hour, you can also find north. And if that fails, north can be found by checking where moss grows near trees. If you are unsure about any one of these ways being accurate, combine as many of them as you can. With so many confirmations of true direction, you can trust you have found your bearings and can confidently proceed on your way.

People in the situation of an unwed pregnancy need reliable guidance. There will be people trying to tell them what to do, and they will need to find and follow stable points of reference to find their way out of the woods. Trustworthy guides will not rush decisions. They will help those involved to find their bearings and take the time needed to check their new surroundings thoroughly—as confusing and difficult as these may appear. And just like the Boy Scout who isn't sure if his compass is working right and so looks for the North Star as well, those involved with an out-of-wedlock pregnancy can feel ready to make sound decisions and walk confidently forward in their journey if their direction is confirmed by more than one trustworthy guide.

Various people are involved with the decisions to be made when pregnancy occurs outside of marriage, beginning with the mother and the father of the unborn child. The parents of these young parents are crucial influences as well. But other guides can also play a role in directing the future of those young parents and their baby, including extended family members, professional counselors, and ecclesiastical leaders. All of these guiding voices can help, especially as they map out the possible roads ahead. Which guides are able to offer correct advice and trustworthy information in this journey? How much should any of these guides be involved in the pressing decisions to be made? Throughout the experience the decision-making process should be centered on divine guidance and spirituality, deferring to God as our ultimate guide.

THE DECISION MAKERS

The decision makers are those who direct the ultimate choices to be made when an out-of-wedlock pregnancy occurs. (These choices are discussed in detail in Chapter 3.) Who will make the final decisions? Who gets to say what will be done? These questions are not as simple as they sound. For example, is the birth mother the decision maker? It may seem an obvious question, and yet I point it out precisely because I have repeatedly seen people trying to step in and make decisions for the very person most affected by the pregnancy—the mother herself. She needs to be primarily involved in making decisions about the baby she is carrying. And what of the baby's father? Should he be involved in decisions about the child? Some would say he is obviously involved; others would say he should not be or that involving him would only complicate matters.

And what about all the others? Who *does* have a say, and who *should* have a say, in deciding what's to be done? Both unwed pregnancy and adoption tend to be topics about which people have very strong opinions, and they tend to express them forcefully on the subject. Even those quite removed from the birth parents may try to exercise whatever control or influence they can to direct the outcome they believe is right. It can happen that someone who should be serving as a guide to the birth parents can actually lead them onto a detour.

In an out-of-wedlock pregnancy, the primary decision makers are and must be the parents of the unborn child. Often, by default, the decision is left to the birth mother alone when the birth father doesn't want to be involved. If the baby's father does wish to be part of the decision, however, it is important that both of the child's parents try to arrive at a harmonious decision, even when it is hard to achieve. Despite the fact that these birth parents may be immature and emotional, and even though they may have exercised the worst judgment possible in the circumstances leading to the pregnancy, there are compelling practical, legal, and spiritual reasons confirming that *they* be the ones to decide the future of their child.

I have found that allowing this decision-making responsibility is especially difficult for the grandparents of the baby—especially when their unmarried child is young and immature. It is also hard for other guides involved. They may feel it is their duty to take charge of an unpleasant situation and to resolve it; and frankly, those confused young people they are trying to help often wish to be told exactly what to do! It may feel natural for the young woman to yield decision making to her parents for a number of reasons, not the least of which is that she doesn't feel she can carry the burden of the decision herself.

I cannot overstate the importance of allowing the birth parents to make their own decisions while receiving informed and loving guidance. If parents or counselors do not respect the birth parents as decision makers—even when the best decision is very obvious to parents or counselors—there can be harmful consequences in the future. The right decision is not the right decision if the birth parents do not feel it is *their* decision, as Sheila's situation sadly illustrates.

SHEILA'S STORY: WHEN OTHERS DECIDE FOR THE BIRTH MOTHER

Sheila came to see me for counseling when she was twenty-four years old, pregnant and unwed. She was planning to place her baby for adoption. But Sheila's story went deeper—this was her second child conceived out of wedlock. As I came to know Sheila I became convinced that she might never have had this second unfortunate pregnancy if the first one had been handled more carefully.

Sheila was sixteen years old when she became pregnant the first time. Her parents were strong members of the Church and concerned for her welfare.

Being well-known in their ward and community, they decided she should go out of state until she had her baby and then place the baby for adoption. She obediently lived out of state and then placed her baby with new parents. All went as planned, and her parents likely believed their daughter was back on track to regain her testimony of the gospel and work towards temple marriage in the future. But Sheila did not follow this course. When I met her, she was not active in the Church and did not even express a belief in the gospel. She was living with a boyfriend off and on and had a very poor relationship with her family. She did not blame her parents for her lifestyle, and neither do I. But I did observe a clearly missed opportunity by Sheila's parents during her first pregnancy that might have headed her in a better direction.

Sheila's first baby, now an eight-year-old child, was doing well. Sheila told me several times that she knew it was the right decision to place her first baby for adoption; however, she did not for a minute think the decision to relinquish the child had been *her* decision—it had been her parents' choice. Of course her parents had made many right decisions on her behalf, which Sheila was able to recognize. But she had very painful feelings of resentment towards her parents for making *that* decision for her, and she still felt guilty that she could not make it herself. Her parents had sent the message strongly that she could not be trusted to make decisions and needed to relinquish control to someone else. And her baby, with whom she was still in contact, was a reminder of her failure. She also struggled in her relationship with God, feeling she was a bad person who had not been blessed with the strong ability to choose the right, as others had been, and therefore was not loved as much by her Father in Heaven.

Sheila made her own choices to create her unhappy lifestyle. She had been taught to believe in a loving Father in Heaven, in the power of repentance, and in her own divine worth. But she had been protected from experiencing these things for herself. Sheila likely would have chosen adoption with her first child had she been given the choice and the opportunity to believe in herself. But because she was not given the opportunity to choose, she did not experience the difficult but necessary spiritual growth that comes in making such decisions—decisions that could have strengthened her for the future.

Had she gone through the process of making a decision herself and following through with that decision, she could have learned several things she still did not know. She could have come to realize that her parents believed in her and that they had faith in God's willingness to answer her prayers about her unborn child. She could have come to realize that her Heavenly Father loved her as much as he loved her child, realizing her own worth in the sight of God and developing a strong testimony of the gospel and of personal inspiration. She could have come to realize that she was a strong person who *could* make the right decision. She could have *become* a strong person. She could have developed a more secure relationship with her parents and family members as she came to see that her family was strong together and supportive of each other.

Certainly Sheila's parents were trying to do what they felt was best by taking the decision out of her hands. But their determination may have been short-sighted, protecting her in the immediate future but weakening her ability to thrive in the long term.

Those who try to take control may be motivated by very good intentions, but when the young people are centrally involved in making choices, they have the opportunity to remake their own lives, to exchange bad decisions in their past with sound decisions for the future. That does not mean the birth parents should not listen to counsel—indeed, much good counsel and information is available to help them make choices, and they should be open to it. But when the birth parents' agency is truly respected, they can begin using eternal principles in their own lives. In years to come, it will be important for those birth parents to accept responsibility for the consequences of their actions, both the negative and the positive results of their choices. There will be difficulties along whatever road they will travel, and that out-of-wedlock pregnancy can be a defining experience for each of their lives. Allowing unwed parents to be the decision makers is enormously difficult. But parents are the decision makers regarding the children they create, whether those parents are young or old, married or not. Everyone else in the decision-making process—*everyone else*—is secondary.

A main reason that parents of unwed parents are unwilling to trust their children to make these life-changing decisions is that the pregnancy provides obvious proof of their lack of good judgment and of their unworthiness. Can those who have been both foolish and sinful decide what is best for a coming baby? After all, they have proven they cannot choose well regarding their own lives. Shouldn't the birth parents defer to the decisions of those who are more wise or worthy?

Brother Daniel K Judd has commented on the issue of whether unwed parents are able to make spiritually sound decisions given their situation. Brother Judd, a member of the Sunday School General Presidency, has long served as a bishop and stake president and has worked with unwed parents both professionally and ecclesiastically. He provided the following insight:

> Several years ago a colleague was asked to speak to a group of unwed mothers about their "religious questions." During their discussion one of the young women made the following statement and asked an important question: "I know that by doing the things that I have done, my worthiness and ability to receive answers to my prayers are in question. At what point can I trust my feelings to know if they are from God or not?"
>
> My colleague responded by explaining that spiritual gifts, including revelation, are given by the Lord to those who love Him and who, even though they may have sinned in the past, are sincerely striving to keep His commandments in the present. My colleague then read the following from the Doctrine and Covenants (paying particular attention to the words I have italicized):
>
> "Wherefore, beware lest ye are deceived; and that ye may not be deceived seek ye earnestly the best gifts, always remembering for what they are given;
>
> "For verily I say unto you, they are given for the benefit of those who love me and keep all my commandments, *and him that seeketh so to do;* that all may be benefited that seek or that ask of me, that ask and not for a sign that they may consume it upon their lusts" (D&C 46:8–9; italics added).
>
> Even though this young woman had been involved in serious sin, if she was sincere in her attempt to repent and make her life right with her Father in Heaven, she could have access to revelation as she sought answers to the questions she was facing. (Personal correspondence)

We must believe that revelation and divine guidance are available to all those who are repentant. Moments of crisis are not times to back away from these gospel principles but rather to rely upon them. Unwed parents can discover that God loves them enough, even in their present state, to reveal to them what to do, provided they are humble enough to seek that guidance.

And of course God does provide His direction by means of loving and wise guides. Revelation is often in the form of the Holy Ghost confirming the guidance given by parents or Church leaders. It is just as foolish to ignore good counsel or to avoid getting correct information as it is to yield decisions entirely to someone else. Part of the humility that is necessary for being able to receive divine guidance is admitting that we may lack sufficient information about the options available to make an informed choice. I have found that many who first try to resolve these problems alone are often relying on false assumptions or unfounded biases regarding the choices ahead of them. Also, the emotions stirred up by an out-of-wedlock pregnancy can cloud judgment and lead those involved to find quick solutions that heal a present pain but do not ultimately consider the best interests of themselves or the baby.

We never have to face any difficulties on our own. Fortunately, within the Church our belief in God and in His willingness to reveal His will to His children makes Him our primary guide. He *does* love His children, particularly as we suffer (whether from our own choices or not), and He *will* give both comfort and divine direction. And just as God established His Church so that He could work through each of us to accomplish His will, so He has made available many different people who can appropriately inform and guide us. We are foolish not to take our bearings from those trusted sources. While each of us in this life has a personal trek to make through our own wilderness, we usually do not find our bearings all by ourselves.

Once we are committed to seeking God's will and are willing to follow God's mouthpieces, the prophets, then the advice and counsel of those guiding our way will be put in perspective. This divine centering will make us sensitive to the real possibility that some well-meaning guides might lead us off the best path forward. This is the paradox: It is not merely a matter of finding trustworthy guides but of finding trustworthy guidance. The same sources of advice and counseling can either help or hurt, as the following stories illustrate.

After discussing in the next few pages the relationship between the birth parents who are making the decisions, I will discuss the various guides: close family members, especially the parents of unwed mothers but also extended family members; formal and professional counselors, such as social workers; and ecclesiastical counselors, specifically bishops and stake presidents. Finally, I will return to our primary guide, our Heavenly Father, and to the challenges and blessings that exist in trying to find and keep a spiritual orientation to the issues of unwed pregnancy and adoption.

BIRTH MOTHER VS. BIRTH FATHER?

Ideally the parents of a child conceived out of wedlock will be able to proceed peacefully through their difficult journey, working together toward the best decisions for themselves and their coming child; however, relationships that produce children outside of marriage are often not healthy ones. The birth father may simply choose not to be involved, and in cases where the birth father maintains interest in what happens to the baby, it is very common for the birth parents to disagree, often strongly.

One partner may feel that marriage is the only good answer, while the other may not feel prepared or willing to marry at that point in their lives. Upon learning of the pregnancy, one of them may want to consider abortion as an option, while the other may have a very strong moral stance against such a decision. I have also seen cases in which one of the partners feels strongly that adoption is wrong for one reason or another. This opinion is often due to a lack of correct information about adoption or to incorrect beliefs that have been developed. (See further discussion in Chapter 3).

Often the birth parents are somewhat supportive and open about the desires of the other person, but they may also be completely at odds over which decision is best for their baby and themselves. This may lead to emotionally trying disagreements, physical disputes, and even legal battles. Because laws vary in each state regarding birth parents' rights and adoption, there may be no clear answer about who should make the final decision. And because it involves permanent and eternal decisions, both parties may feel compelled to fight to the utmost extent to protect their interests.

Not only is such fighting painful and costly for the birth parents and their families but it can also be damaging to the child. This is why it is so valuable for birth parents (and their parents) to work with an outside, neutral party. (I will discuss both ecclesiastical leaders and various professionals who can fill the role of a neutral party.) A third party can help to mediate the decision and find solutions that will work for both birth parents.

When the birth parents are able to work together peacefully, everyone benefits. It is also better for the birth parents themselves, as it is painful enough to let go of a child without feeling the further repercussions of a legal or emotional battle as well. It is better for the adoptive parents, who can be at peace knowing their adoption is stable and both birth parents were involved in the decision. And it is better for the child, as that child can receive medical and psychosocial background information from the natural parents, as well as letters or personal information about both parents.

The birth father often wants to do the right thing. But birth fathers sometimes get a bad rap. True, when I hear the boyfriend described as a hopelessly bad guy, I can certainly understand. Some birth fathers really have done harm, and many avoid taking responsibility for the child they've helped to create. Still, I have seen the birth mother and her family make the birth father into a scapegoat—even when that birth father may show sincere interest in trying to resolve the problems he has helped to create. The fact is, there are many good birth fathers out there. Consider Shawn's story.

SHAWN'S STORY: A CONCERNED FATHER FEELS POWERLESS

Shawn seemed like everything you would ever want in a boyfriend for your daughter. He was studying hard in school and headed for big things in a career. A returned missionary, Shawn had been strong in the Church and spiritually active. He showed a strong drive to do the right thing in his life, to be honest, loyal, and hardworking. He was very attractive, clean cut, articulate, and pleasant to be around. And he was the father of a baby conceived out of wedlock.

Shawn stayed in contact with me throughout Bethany's pregnancy. He wished to be supportive of the baby's mother and to do right by his unborn daughter. Bethany insisted that she had no desire to see Shawn ever again. She expressed feelings of anger towards him, not because of the pregnancy but because they had broken off their relationship before they discovered the pregnancy and Shawn was already in a relationship with someone else when Bethany told him about their baby. She felt alone and scared at the struggles that lay ahead of her and did not want to sacrifice any more pride in seeing him again.

They were probably better off staying apart. She was working to make decisions that would benefit her and were likely in her best interest. But

Shawn also needed to be involved in the decisions that would have to be made for the sake of this baby. And fortunately for the baby, unlike so many other situations, this birth father was willing to go through the pain involved and, in doing so, to send a strong message to his daughter that *he* loved her as well. In this situation, our goals were to get them to work together congenially for the sake of this baby, while respecting the birth mother's desire to have little if any contact with the father or his family.

This proved difficult. "How can I be supportive of her if she won't even talk to me on the telephone?" he asked one day. "I want to do what is best and show her that I'm taking responsibility, but no matter what I do, I'm the bad guy here." In a sense he was the bad guy. He had left Bethany for someone else when she was pregnant, even though he didn't know it at the time. But now he was trying to show some responsibility, and she was less than cooperative. Shawn was frustrated, and I could understand why, just as I could understand Bethany's resentment. I've seen situations where the emotions run so high that each will blame the other for all their pain and struggles, and neither party will take responsibility for the problems that occur.

Clearly the birth father is in a precarious position once a pregnancy is discovered. Sometimes he is blamed for the fact that they were having sex—most often by the parents of the girl with whom he is involved. And it is often true that he has been the more sexually aggressive partner in the relationship. There are, however, many circumstances in which the young woman has been more experienced or more aggressive—though few people seem willing to believe that. I've met with girls who realize their role and are frustrated that their boyfriend is taking the fall when they know themselves to be just as responsible for having sex in the first place.

The birth father's involvement may vary due to differing legal rights from state to state. Some states give the birth father full rights and do not allow a child to be placed for adoption without his written consent. (Ironically, in many of those same states a mother can abort a baby without the consent or knowledge of the baby's father.) Other states mandate that a birth father show efforts of good intent or his rights may be forfeited. The birth father may sometimes seem to have too much power and other times too little, and these situations need to be managed by both birth parents.

Although it is not always the case, I have found many birth fathers who love their babies just as much as the birth mothers do, and many of the incredible people I have met in my experiences with adoption were birth fathers who intensely wanted to do what was best for their babies. Shawn was one of those people. But for her own reasons, Bethany was absolutely unwilling to change her opinion of his intentions. She did understand, however, that he cared for the baby as well, and she was willing to work with him, albeit separately, in placing their baby for adoption. Amidst much juggling, the adoption worked out despite the birth parents' initial differences, and both Bethany and Shawn were able to express love for their baby and take responsibility for her.

I have seen God work through very imperfect, immature, and mixed-up people, including birth fathers whom we might otherwise discount as irresponsible. We should not shortchange unwed parents. Just as they can surprise us sometimes by making bad choices beyond what we thought possible, they can also surprise us by making positive ones. When they feel loved themselves, and when they are invited to feel the transforming love of that unborn child, they can become wise enough to accept good guidance and make good choices.

The Grandparents of the Baby

Besides the unwed parents themselves, their own parents are the most powerful directing influence guiding the decisions that will be made. As with so much of parenting, this is an awesome responsibility, made more difficult by the fact that the parents must deal not just with their errant child but with their own deep disappointments. They wanted their child to find a mate but not this way; they wanted to have grandchildren but not like this. They wanted to believe that they were good parents—which they may well have been—and yet this situation suggests they have failed in their duties to teach or to protect their children. The birth grandparents may feel at a loss about what to do as much as the birth parents.

But just as the birth parents must learn to trust their own capacities to arrive at good decisions, so the baby's grandparents can look past their grief and focus instead on the well-being of their struggling child and arriving grandchild. As a parent myself, I know that my children's actions can send me into a tailspin, but I also know that as we rely upon our spouses, our Church leaders, and the Lord, we as parents can rise to the task and lead our

children away from danger, sin, or trouble and back to the principles, commandments, and behaviors that promote eternal happiness. Children may
disappoint their parents; parents may also disappoint their children. But children still look to their parents and generally follow their direction in these
issues, and parents—despite their own failings or those of their children—
still have a divine mantle to oversee the well-being of their offspring. When
they choose to parent in a Christlike way, they can find the strength and the
resources to deal with whatever situation their children may have created for
themselves.

Parenting is never easy because children rarely cause trouble at con-
venient times or when we are at our best. We are tempted to shout when we
shouldn't, or to slip into the mode of cleaning up messes in the short run
instead of training our children in ways that will serve them in the long run.
Because of the gravity of immorality and the consequences of unwed pregnancy, Latter-day Saint parents can be sorely tempted to feel bad about themselves, to be angry toward their child (or the boyfriend or girlfriend), or to
be overly protective. But as with the unwed parents themselves, I have found
that birth grandparents can make great decisions in spite of insecurities or
disappointments. They need to, for their children depend upon them for
direction. Jeni's story is a great example of parents who proved very supportive to her despite the struggles they were themselves having in dealing
with this unhappy situation.

Jeni and Her Parents' Story: Growing Together

I first learned of Jeni when her bishop telephoned me, seeking guidance
for a problem he was feeling unprepared to handle. "I need to know what to
do in the situation of an out-of-wedlock pregnancy," he said somewhat
haltingly.

"Have you had this issue come up in your ward before?"

"No, I haven't. I've been a bishop for only four months." He sounded
uncertain about this new challenge, and I felt for him as he talked about this
ward member who was struggling.

"Do her parents know of the pregnancy?" There was a long pause.

"Yes, we do. We just found out yesterday. The girl who is pregnant is my
daughter." This strong spiritual leader, who was carrying the concerns of so
many ward members on his shoulders, was now facing a devastating trial in

his own family. He broke down a bit, and I could tell he was talking through tears. "She's such a good girl. I just can't imagine the thought of her going through this when she is so young."

Later, Jeni and her parents sat in the waiting room without speaking much—in fact, looking embarrassed to be there. Jeni was a very cute, very young-looking girl. Her father, smoothed by the humility that comes from being a bishop, was a kind-looking man who seemed far too young to become a grandfather. Jeni's mother was neat in her appearance, but she looked like an absolute wreck.

Jeni was an incredible girl, and I grew very fond of her. I come to feel that way towards most of my clients—maybe because when people are in such a period of personal growth and change, they are very real and candid. When they come to the point of honesty where they can evaluate themselves and work to improve their situation, they are incredible. It's too bad we do not trust in our own goodness enough to allow others to see this part of us more often. I count myself fortunate to have been a witness to so many of these experiences in the process of therapy. Jeni was one of these people. As I worked with her throughout her pregnancy, I watched her transform.

But her transformation would not have been possible without the loving support of her parents, and they had to work to change some unhelpful attitudes themselves. What really mattered, they decided, was not what Jeni had done in getting pregnant but who she could become because of the trials she was facing and how she should care for the baby conceived.

They themselves had struggled through some things both individually and in their marriage, but their daughter needed them both right now. It was ultimately this fact that caused them to work hard to support Jeni. It was a slow process, but they worked at their own problems while working to address their daughter's. I admired them for being willing to improve themselves personally in order to better care for their family.

And not only did they grow and thrive but Jeni thrived as well. She placed her baby for adoption, completed the repentance process, and went on to college. The last time I saw her, she was with her husband and baby girl. She reported she was doing well, and her husband confirmed she was an exceptional woman. By working through their own problems, Jeni's parents were able to clear the way for her to make the hard decisions necessary for her own child, benefiting everyone involved.

Without doubt parents can be the most powerful influences in their children's lives. Jeni was fortunate because her parents worked diligently to be in a position where their guidance would most benefit her. Many parents simply take control of the situation of an unwed pregnancy, often to the detriment of those involved. This is illustrated in the story about Sheila (see page 35); even though Sheila placed her baby for adoption, the fact that her parents had not allowed it to be her choice had devastating consequences. Parents can and should be the best possible guides for these young people, but they can also be obstacles. This usually happens when they fall prey to the temptation to dominate the decision-making process—even if they do so out of loving concern.

The grandparents of the baby are most often the ones carrying the burden of support for the birth parents through loving understanding and gentle but firm guidance. Sometimes the best choice seems clear and obvious; however, parents should guide, not coerce, and their best influence is not in forcing a choice but in taking their child through the process of decision-making with the best information and guidance from qualified sources. An attempt to take control of a decision that is not theirs to control will only cause pain and frustration. One of the best ways parents serve as guides is by helping their child choose wisely which other sources of guidance should be trusted and to what extent. Parents can offer loving counsel while guiding their child to the bishop and to a professional counselor as well.

EXTENDED FAMILY

Like the parents of birth parents, the extended family is often very influential in providing guidance. And while the extended family can be a great source of strength for those struggling with an out-of-wedlock pregnancy, family members need to be aware of the degree to which they should become involved and the extent to which they should not interfere. I recall a family in which the birth mother's uncle expressed his opinions very strongly in pushing to adopt the child himself. It created such a rift between family members that the birth mother and her parents felt quite the opposite of support from the larger family. The uncle believed they should keep the baby in the family no matter what. This notion is very costly. While it may seem to be expressing a kind of responsibility or loyalty to one's bloodline, the fact is that it does not respect the agency of the mother and can lead to detrimental consequences for the child as well. Often, the very best support from extended family is *not* to act as though they are the ones making the decision. The birth parents and their parents need to be the ones to deal with the situation and decide what is best for the baby.

The decisions regarding what unwed parents should do are always difficult, and they are often compounded by different generations of family members having developed ideas about what to do that are dramatically different and strongly expressed. This can be bewildering for the birth parents, especially if opinions from extended family are not consistent with current counsel or practices. For example, one very enduring belief is that when pregnancy occurs outside marriage, marriage is the only way to resolve the situation, even though the Church has recently and repeatedly emphasized that marriage is the best option only when a lasting marriage is likely (see First Presidency letters dated 1 February 1994; 15 June 1998; 19 July 2002). Also, some people believe they know all about adoption; they may even have experienced it firsthand. But adoption is very different today from what it was thirty years ago, and it is likely that extended family members are basing their ideas about adoption on practices that are no longer current. Extended family members are not being helpful if they try to influence such important decisions based upon unreliable or outdated information.

Extended family members may be a great support to those in an out-of-wedlock pregnancy. Generally they are very loving and supportive and feel great concern for the loved one who is dealing with the pregnancy. And the birth parents themselves must realize that this pregnancy does have an effect upon their family members. Because of this, I will often invite the birth mother's parents and all siblings who are old enough to understand to talk together with me about the pregnancy and delivery before the baby's birth. That way, everyone will know what to expect when the baby is born. Children and teens of all ages are profoundly affected by the birth of a niece or nephew, and if they also must say good-bye to the baby, it can be a very difficult and emotional event for them as well.

This brings me to a point about families. Dealing with an out-of-wedlock pregnancy can be either good or bad for the family of the birth parents, depending on how it is handled. As with any type of adversity, this difficulty can weaken or strengthen a family. There may be a tendency to keep the pregnancy a secret, either out of embarrassment or out of concern to protect feelings. That is understandable, and certainly there needs to be some discretion regarding who should know, how much they should know, and when they should know it. Immediate family members, for example, will be more affected and may need to know more information sooner than extended family members. But let me suggest why it is best to be generally open and honest with family members both about the pregnancy and then about the adoption, if that is what is planned. If secrecy or embarrassment is involved in discussions about the situation, the pregnancy or adoption can become a shameful family secret that no one is able to talk about—and yet many know something about. When the issue is secret, there can be no answering of questions or discussion about concerns. Children in particular will draw their own conclusions about what is happening and why, and those conclusions are likely to be far worse than the truth.

It is better to pull together as a family and handle these issues together—repenting and seeking forgiveness, praying and asking for guidance on what direction to go, and then relying on the strength of the family while working towards the path directed by Heavenly Father. This process can teach each member of the family important gospel principles, not the least of which is that *as a family we can get through the difficult times and become stronger because of them.* Imagine how important this lesson is to each family member, particularly the one who is pregnant.

MADELEINE'S STORY: A FAMILY PULLS TOGETHER

I remember one experience when a birth mother, Madeleine, chose to share her final day with her baby with her brother and two sisters. Here was a family that really pulled together to help one another get through. The whole family had prepared for the birth of this baby, and after spending a day and night with her they were all very humbled and emotional, deep in thought. It was touching to see how close they were and how tenderly they handled each other's feelings.

The night before the placement, Madeleine's family joined together in her hospital room. Each family member took time, between taking turns to hold the baby, to write a letter to send with the baby. As they passed these letters to the adoptive parents the next day, the new parents held the letters from Madeleine's family as if each one contained something precious. They did contain something very precious—their feelings, advice, and love for this precious little girl. Each of Madeleine's siblings, from ages eleven to seventeen, had shared in this powerful family experience. And fortunately their experience would be of a loving family that didn't turn one member out when mistakes were made but instead gathered around her in loving support. Madeleine would remember the love shown by her family members and be able to draw strength from that loving support into the future, but her siblings would learn from the experience as well. Madeleine's family members shared these letters (see "Saying Good-bye: A Family's Letters to 'Cassandra,'" in Part 2).

It is so important to feel support from family members. When a young woman or man is trying to decide what to do following the discovery of an out-of-wedlock pregnancy, family members and friends who learn of the situation and want to influence the decisions to be made generally do have good intentions. Those can, however, sometimes translate into pressure—pressure that is painful and unproductive. Whether the girl is planning to place the baby for adoption and her family wants her to parent or she is planning to parent and they want her to place, the pressure often works against the hoped-for outcome. Coercion towards the best choice is itself a bad choice that will have consequences sooner or later.

That said, I do believe that family members—especially the parents of the unwed parents—have a duty to encourage (and even insist, depending on the situation) that their son or daughter look at the options carefully and come to an understanding of what following through with each option would be like. It is useful to counsel with the young prospective parent and be a sounding board, helping to direct the young person's thinking to healthy, realistic conclusions. It is helpful for parents to share with their daughter or son, again depending on the individual circumstances, their own feelings regarding the pregnancy, along with their understanding and support of their daughter's or son's need to make this decision. In this way the unwed parents can be guided towards the right path without being dragged by force.

It takes a great amount of trust to step out of a decision and allow a young person to have the control and carry the weight of the responsibility for the decision about whether to marry, to parent, or to place for adoption. And there will be fear. The person in whom the trust was placed may not do that which he or she was entrusted to do. The only way a family member or friend can find peace in these circumstances is to trust that Heavenly Father will guide those birth parents to do the right thing and can also guide others as they offer support. It is helpful to remember that the birth parent is a child of God, just as the baby is a child of God, and He loves them both. Heavenly Father does not sacrifice any hope for the birth parent's life so the baby can be saved. He also loves the grandparents, and eventually there can be peace for everyone involved.

SEEKING COUNSEL OUTSIDE THE HOME

Parents and extended family members often pull together to deal with an out-of-wedlock pregnancy because it is a "family problem," one that can be handled within the family unit. For many people, the idea of getting spiritual or psychological counseling for any reason is out of the question—whether the counsel is given by a bishop, a professional therapist, or even a trusted loved one. But in the situation of an out-of-wedlock pregnancy, for both practical and spiritual reasons, counseling can ultimately lead to better decisions being made. Still, there are some people unwilling to seek or receive counsel.

I think about the first time I tried to sew a dress for my daughter, using a pattern to do so. Growing up with a mother who was a talented seamstress and who sewed most of my clothes, I should have gleaned a bit of skill from her in this area. Unfortunately, I was uninterested in the process and, I'm told, a bit stubborn. In fact, my sewing teacher in high school said more times than I like to remember, "Monica, don't be difficult!" in her frustration of explaining to me why the pattern must *always* be followed. So it isn't surprising that my first attempt at making a dress went less than smoothly.

Although when I was working on the dress I imagined that I was more humble and teachable than I had been before, I came to a point where the pattern instructions showed how to sew together the sleeve of the dress. Unfortunately, I had retained a bit of that stubbornness. As I looked at the instructions, I deemed that my own way would be better, simpler, and far easier than the one the pattern suggested. And so, putting the pattern aside, I proceeded to sew the sleeve together as I imagined best. The results became for me a lesson in humility—the sleeve did not turn out.

It was backwards in its stitching and would never have worked as a sleeve at all. What had seemed perfectly nonsensical in the pattern now made a great deal of sense to me. I could see very plainly why those who had written the pattern (likely people who had made dresses before and knew much more about what to do) directed that the sleeve be sewn as they had. If I was not humbled enough by the haphazard sleeve lying on the table before me, I completed the process of finding humility as I picked out the stitches one by one.

I think that is how it is when seeking counsel in difficult times. Counseling is not mandatory, of course, but it is a tool or support for helping us along the process. Whether from a bishop, a professional therapist, or both, counseling can offer extra help in navigating the more difficult situations of an out-of-wedlock pregnancy and in emerging from the experience further ahead.

Some do not feel counseling is necessary. I agree. If I were to set out on a journey of a hundred miles by foot, it is likely that with enough determination I would make it eventually to my destination. Having a car to drive that hundred miles would not be necessary. It would, however, be extremely helpful and would make my trip more efficient and more likely successful. That is how it is with counseling. It is not the only way, but some tools prove so useful that we would be foolish not to use them to help us navigate situations in our lives.

There are a number of places to seek counseling outside of the home regarding how to deal with an out-of-wedlock pregnancy or adoption, and there are different reasons for seeking counsel. A lawyer might be consulted for legal counsel, the same as a medical doctor would be enlisted for help in understanding the medical aspects of pregnancy. So it is with seeking counsel for psychological and spiritual issues. There are those with the experience and knowledge to be useful guides along the path of adoption, and seeking counsel from those who are familiar with the path that many others have taken can make the journey much more successful.

Professional Counseling

Although I will emphasize the primary role of spiritual counseling from one's Church leaders, I would first like to address the role of professional counseling. Ideally, these two kinds of counseling can work hand in hand, just as counseling from other experts also contributes to working through the issues. Reminding us that it is wise to seek good counsel during difficult times, Brother Daniel K Judd quotes the Old Testament: "Where no counsel is, the people fall: but in the multitude of counsellors there is safety" (Proverbs 11:14). He continues:

> In addition to parents and the bishop, it is also important to seek the services of competent and faithful health care providers, including those who are trained to deal with psychological, emotional, and social issues. A well-trained therapist can help the birth parents as well as the extended family deal with the present issues, as well as help all of them understand the dynamics of the past that may have contributed to the present problems and make sure such a crisis isn't repeated. (Personal correspondence)

Elder Richard G. Scott has spoken clearly regarding the way in which spiritual and professional counseling can complement one another to benefit those struggling with abuse issues. Those who become pregnant outside of marriage frequently deal with similar issues, such as self-esteem (see Chapter 5). Elder Scott's advice can be applied to those in this situation:

> Your bishop can help you identify trustworthy friends to support you. He will help you regain self-confidence and self-esteem to begin the process of renewal. He can help you identify . . . professional treatment consistent with the teachings of the Savior. ("Healing the Tragic Scars of Abuse," *Ensign,* May 1992, 31)

Discovering an unwed pregnancy is a crisis, at least within a culture such as ours. And the very family members to whom we naturally turn can be among those most affected and least objective about what can or should be done. Professional counseling is not a substitute for family decision making or inspired counsel, but such counselors have dealt with many people and have seen, over time, very clear patterns in what can be expected with respect to any given course of action. Therapists draw from the combined experience of hundreds of others in similar situations, and they can objectively lay out facts based on their accumulated experience. Their professional detachment can also prove a great advantage. Because they are not directly affected by the actions and decisions of those involved, they can often see things that those who are closer to the problem cannot.

A professional counselor can help people in making important decisions, following through with those decisions, and changing behaviors that have contributed to their current situation. A counselor can provide realistic information and rational thinking that will be helpful regardless of the choice the young man and woman make about their baby. One of the ways I do this in my own work as a professional counselor is to assist my clients in carefully considering *all* of their options before making any decisions. After all, such decisions will affect their own lives and the lives of many other people, and they do not want to have regrets after the baby is born. I help them think through each of their options in detail (see Chapter 3) and point out considerations that have mattered very much to others but which they may not have taken into account. For example, over time I have seen the profound wisdom in the First Presidency's counsel that "unmarried parents should give prayerful consideration to the best interests of the child" (First Presidency Letter, 19 July 2002). Without any question, as a counselor I have witnessed the most happy outcomes resulting when the baby's needs are put first. And while it is not my role to teach them about following inspired counsel (since this is the bishop's stewardship), I can provide objective information about how each possible course of action is likely to affect that coming child. A counselor who is not emotionally involved with the decision can help the birth parents and their families see the situation more clearly.

If a decision has already been made by the birth parents, they can work with a counselor to increase their ability to succeed in the decision they have made. A counselor can help birth parents realistically address and prepare for whatever decision they have made, whether it is by giving premarital counseling to a couple choosing to marry, by finding emotional support and necessary resources for those choosing to single parent, or by doing preparation and follow-up support for those choosing to place the baby for adoption. And, as discussed in more detail in Chapter 5, professional counselors can also assist people after the fact in working through emotional and psychological issues that might have led those young people into the unhappy situation they are in.

Of course, many adoptions are arranged outside of LDS Family Services and without assistance from professional therapists. There are many types of adoptions, and some are handled with little or no attention to psychological issues. I have worked with girls placing their babies for adoption through different venues, and I have also seen many who did adoptions privately without counseling or support. Nonetheless, I encourage anyone who might be planning to place a baby, whether through an agency or privately through a lawyer, to find a trustworthy counselor to help with the process. Far too often I have seen a young girl place her baby without any preparation, without knowing what to expect before or afterwards, because there has been no counselor there to help her prepare. As a practical matter, an adoptive placement will be far stronger if the birth parents have received counseling and support both before and after the baby is born and placed. And the birth parents themselves can be stronger and more at peace in their choices if they have worked with a skilled and sensitive counselor throughout the process.

Not every counselor provides everything one might hope for, and it is certainly true that the counseling received will be only as good as the counselor who gives it. To someone who has sought counseling only to be disappointed in the outcome, I would make two recommendations. First, evaluate whether you were open and teachable as you sought the counsel. I have seen clients who had decided they did not want counseling long before I ever met them for the first session. Sometimes people seek counseling because they are being pressured by someone else to do so, and they will be unlikely to see much success. Give the counselor some time before you determine he or she cannot help you in your circumstances. Second, if you have been unsuccessful in therapy, don't decide that all therapy is unhelpful and refuse to try again. Remember that therapists themselves vary and can be helpful to different people in different ways.

Ecclesiastical Leaders

As a Latter-day Saint and as a professional counselor, I can join with others in affirming the central role of Church leaders in providing the spiritual counseling so necessary to those who are dealing with these issues. The work I do with my LDS clients would mean little if I did not consult with the Lord's inspired servants who have stewardship over these individuals.

Seeking spiritual guidance from one's bishop or other appropriate ecclesiastical leader is essential. To begin with, it involves another person to help deal with the crisis. Those dealing with the pregnancy can feel the love and support of someone who cares deeply about them and can receive help in establishing other resources to help the family. Counseling with the bishop will give those struggling the support they need to endure the pain they will face, guidance in the choices they will need to make, and a reminder of the

Atonement and the knowledge that sins can and will be forgiven and lives repaired. It also begins the process of repentance and finding peace which is so urgently important. Once the bishop is involved, it is far less likely that a rash decision, such as choosing an abortion, will be made.

Seeking spiritual counsel can be not only a great source of comfort and peace but a source of practical guidance as well. Ecclesiastical leaders who have been set apart as stewards have also been given information about how to guide and direct those in their care. These worthy servants of our Heavenly Father are tremendously helpful and too often remain untapped resources for those struggling with an out-of-wedlock pregnancy. A bishop is a loving guide, prepared and ready to help those in need.

Professional counselors and ecclesiastical leaders can be particularly powerful as they work together as part of the support system for the one who is struggling. My favorite experiences in working for LDS Family Services have been in the interaction I have had with the bishops and stake presidents of the clients I have seen. Such cooperation allows for work on a completely different level of strength. Clients are in a stronger position to bring about change when they are working alongside a loving bishop. Bishop Lind was such a bishop, and his story shows how Latter-day Saints can pull together for the benefit of both unwed parents and childless couples.

EDWARD LIND'S STORY: THE POWERFUL INFLUENCE OF A BISHOP

"That couple felt like Heavenly Father had forgotten them." As he had sat with the young couple, Bishop Lind felt pangs of sadness listening to their expressions of frustration in their many attempts to conceive a child.

He shared the experience with me briefly as we spoke over the telephone. He had spent countless hours with them, sharing repeatedly his faith in Heavenly Father's love for them and his belief that they would someday be blessed with the deepest desire of their hearts, that of becoming parents. He prayed for them; the ward prayed for them. Together, they shared in the pain as this young couple exhausted every resource for conceiving a child. Finally, as they came to the decision to begin the process of adoption, this good bishop shared in their hopes and their fears.

"When this couple was finally chosen to adopt a baby, the whole ward felt like they were new parents. The enthusiasm of those members for this couple was tremendous. That baby was practically royalty in our ward. In fact, he still is. They've adopted another baby since, and they can't walk down the halls on Sunday without being talked to by everyone in the ward. It was just such a miracle for our ward to witness, an example of the way the Lord works to answer prayers." There was a thoughtful pause on the other end of the line. "I guess I hadn't really thought much about that baby's biological parents until now."

He was calling not to tell about the adopted baby but rather to consult with me about a young member of his ward who was fifteen years old and pregnant. She and her parents felt it was best to place the baby for adoption. He shared with me the circumstances and was particularly moved by how many people, himself included, were affected by the life of this single unborn child.

I met with Whitney and Bishop Lind later that week. "I guess I've really messed things up," she said as she sat awkwardly in one of the chairs in the interview room. As Bishop Lind listened to her speak, he looked a bit overcome himself. Here was a young woman in his ward, a girl he had known since she was a baby, someone he had watched grow up over the past fifteen years into the talented, smart Mia Maid she was today. And she was pregnant.

Bishop Lind had not taken this information lightly. He was deeply weighed down by feelings of concern for this girl and her family. Her father was his second counselor, and he felt a great deal of respect for both him and her mother and a love for the family they were raising. He had learned they were only recently aware of her pregnancy, and he imagined the pain they must be experiencing themselves. He realized they had come to him for guidance, for some direction about where to go for help. He also knew they needed to obtain some peace from him, some hope that their lives might be back on track at some point in the future. They were relying on him for direction.

Bishop Lind had spoken with Whitney and her parents at some length, offering guidance and counsel. He related to me some of the feelings Whitney's parents had expressed. "I worry about how she will ever get through this," her father had said. "But the more I think about it, the more people I realize will be affected. I first thought of Whitney, and of course of her mother and me. Our lives will never be the same again. Then I thought of her older sister and her three younger brothers. What will this pregnancy do to them? And I don't know how we'll even tell my wife's and my parents and brothers and sisters. We have a large, close-knit family, and her pregnancy and the subsequent decisions she makes will affect them as well. Then, of course, there is the child to think about." At this he found he had difficulty speaking.

"This would be our first grandchild. For years Arleen has looked forward to having grandchildren."

Arleen had interjected. "I didn't want it to happen like this, though. I wanted to first share with Whitney a beautiful temple marriage to a wonderful, *worthy* young man. I wanted her to be able to finish high school, attend college, have a good life."

As Bishop Lind shared these experiences with me, the heaviness in his heart was evident. I had worked with him before, counseling other members in his ward who were struggling with other types of problems. And I knew him to be a loving leader of his ward. He was always gentle as he counseled those members, and I had a great deal of respect for his plain understanding of gospel principles. He loved all the members in his ward, but I knew he had a soft spot in his heart for the youth. Like so many bishops, he was faithfully fighting for the souls of those young people. So it was particularly painful for him as he worked with Whitney.

Sometimes we might unfairly put bishops on an untouchable pedestal where we feel they can do no wrong and feel no pain. I had a friend who once joked that "a bishop is just a good man with a bad calling"—a *hard* calling, I might have said. They are good men and not without tender feelings. I have seen what a strong sense of love and responsibility they have for those within their care. Bishop Lind spent many sleepless nights praying for Whitney and her family. He stayed involved in my work with Whitney to offer support and counsel along the way. And he, like so many other Church leaders, wanted her to make good decisions and be happy.

Whitney went on to make many positive decisions about her life. She ultimately chose a loving couple with whom to place her baby for adoption, continued her schooling, and became stronger in the gospel than she had ever been before. She eventually married in the temple and is now working as a volunteer for the LDS Family Services agency in her area. Largely because of the love and support of her bishop, she had the strength she needed to change the path she was on.

The Lord gives bishops discerning powers and entrusts to them a sacred stewardship over spiritual matters. When members are uncertain about themselves or their ability to go about things the right way, they can turn for guidance to God's inspired servants. Brother Judd refers to this key passage from the Doctrine and Covenants:

> And unto the *bishop of the church,* and unto such as God shall appoint and ordain to watch over the church and to be elders unto the church, are to have it given unto them to discern all those gifts lest there shall be any among you professing and yet be not of God. (D&C 46:27; emphasis added)

He continues:

> While it is important to include parents and others involved in such weighty decisions, it is the bishop (or branch president) who holds the keys of repentance and forgiveness that are vital to resolving the situation in the Lord's way. The bishop is the one to whom the Lord has given the responsibility to judge and will assist [someone dealing with an out-of-wedlock pregnancy] to be in a position where she can gain confidence in her own ability to communicate with the Lord. In my work as a bishop and as a stake president I have known many young women who have gained testimonies as they have struggled through similar situations. If they are faithful, the Lord consecrates their afflictions for their gain (see 2 Nephi 2:2). (Personal correspondence)

These powerful words support what I have repeatedly seen within my own experience in dealing with unwed mothers: young people and their families who involve and pay heed to their bishops, as Whitney and her family did with Bishop Lind, can more easily make choices that help them rebuild their lives successfully; those who do not consult their bishop or ignore his counsel give up their best opportunity for a spiritual resolution to these difficulties.

There is no shortage of people volunteering to guide unmarried parents. Ultimately, it is the influence of trustworthy guides that can make the difference between a good experience and a bad one. Obtaining the correct information and seeking spiritual counsel from those who are in authority to offer that counsel can allow for better decisions to be made. I would like to share one other powerful experience in which inspired ecclesiastical leaders were able to make a difference in many lives by affecting one young man and one young woman.

SHANNON'S STORY: STRENGTHENED THROUGH CHURCH LEADERS

Shannon had been in labor for fourteen hours with no signs yet of her baby being born. She was eight days overdue and had been in an aggressive psychological wrestling match with the baby's father for the past six months. It had been a very long pregnancy, and it was now proving to be a very long delivery. So it came as no surprise when hospital security contacted Shannon's family, alerting them that Shannon's ex-boyfriend was causing trouble in the lobby by attempting to get into the delivery room.

Troy was a very pushy guy. He and Shannon had been dating throughout their junior and senior years in high school before she became pregnant. There had been a great deal of conflict between them concerning the decisions to be made about the pregnancy.

Over the past months, Shannon and Troy had both struggled, feeling frustrated and confused as they worked to determine what choices should be made. Throughout the pregnancy, they had met with Shannon's bishop and, later, her stake president as well. Little did those leaders know at the time how crucial their rapport with this couple would become. Without their involvement, the outcome for Shannon's baby would have been different.

As Shannon and Troy carefully examined their options, they became more strongly divided. The more Troy pressured her to get married, the more her parents encouraged her to consider adoption. She considered both options thoroughly before ultimately choosing to place the baby for adoption. Troy grew more panicked and controlling as the pregnancy progressed, which ultimately led them to a falling-out and a dissolution of the relationship. But Troy did not give up pushing her.

Shannon felt her reasons were strong for choosing not to marry. She and Troy had seen many struggles in their relationship, including periods of serious conflict. They had little extended family support, largely because Shannon was LDS and Troy was Catholic and neither family was supportive of a union between the two. Shannon's parents wanted her to be able to marry in the temple someday, an opportunity she would likely never have if she married Troy. Although Shannon herself struggled with her own spirituality, she felt her baby should have the blessings of the sealing covenant. Fortunately, despite their religious differences, both parents consented to work with ecclesiastical leaders who had taken an active interest in their situation. I also had many opportunities to visit with these two great men, the three of us working as part of a team to help Shannon and Troy make a good decision for themselves and their child. Remarkably, Troy held a great deal of respect for both Church leaders and reportedly spoke openly and honestly with them. But the further the pregnancy progressed, the more urgently he fought to stay with Shannon.

Troy became increasingly aggressive and threatening, and by the time Shannon finally went into labor, she was afraid of what he might do. When Troy arrived at the hospital, Shannon and her family were concerned. As the situation intensified, Shannon's parents contacted their bishop and me for support, and we both went to the hospital right away.

The bishop's earlier involvement paved the way for him to play a crucial role at this moment, for the bishop was able to have a calming influence over Troy. Still, Troy was very determined to prevent Shannon from placing the baby for adoption.

The baby was born at 4:27 in the morning, a healthy baby boy, but this little boy's future, and the future of many others, hung in the balance. Troy was calmer but would not budge from his position. Time passed without progress. It was this way for quite a while when an incredible thing happened. Shannon's stake president felt an impression of concern for Shannon and, upon learning she was in the hospital, went to visit with her. He was there long enough to speak with Shannon and her family and learn of the situation before asking to speak with Troy for a few minutes alone.

Hope may sometimes feel lost, but it is also easily regained, and many of us who were there felt a spark of optimism as they closed the door behind them to talk. They were in that room for some time, maybe an hour, but it seemed like ten hours. Finally the door opened and President Eldon stepped out into the hallway.

"Sister Blume, Troy would like to visit with you for a few moments. Would you join us?" I followed this humble and effective servant of our Father in Heaven into the room. I could see they had both shed some tears over the prior sixty or so minutes. Troy told me he felt he understood why Shannon wanted to place the baby for adoption and wished to sign his own paperwork in support of that decision. After filling out pages of background information, he spent some time alone with the baby. As he said good-bye to the baby along with Shannon the following day, I marveled at what had occurred.

Shannon's bishop and stake president had devoted hours of precious time to her life and the life of her baby. And in Shannon's situation, they were precious hours indeed, hours that had changed the outcome of that baby's future. Because two priesthood leaders cared enough to stay involved in the life of a struggling member as well as her struggling nonmember boyfriend, the life of their child was forever changed.

And Shannon's life was forever changed as well. President Eldon may have never known how important it was that he followed the Spirit and intervened. He had the courage to take a stand about what was right and what was not right, and in doing so he affected many lives. I'm sure that the couple who have been sealed to that precious child have no idea how important that stake president's visit was to the life of their child.

Accepting counsel from those who have a greater understanding about the issues involved can enable us to navigate through adversity and find success as we endure. Spiritually, we've been given a pattern to follow as we face challenges in our lives. As we make decisions affecting the direction our lives take, we can be well guided by those who know the path better than we do. Elder Joseph B. Wirthlin of the Quorum of the Twelve Apostles said, "We weave into the fabric of our lives the pattern that we will present as our finished product. Our mortal lives are woven each day as we add our deeds into something intrinsically beautiful, following the Master Designer's plan. When we make wrong choices, we must retrace our steps through repentance and remove errant threads we have woven into our character . . . and replace them with the finer threads that our Maker intended for us to use" ("The Time to Prepare," *Ensign,* May 1998, 16).

As I learned when I sewed that dress so many years ago, the guidance I received from the pattern, when followed correctly, helped turn a fumbled job of stitchery into a beautiful little gown that three daughters have worn since. I may at times be stubborn and difficult to teach, but that was a lesson I have not had to learn again—the value of following trustworthy guides.

GOD AS GUIDE: ADOPTION AND REVELATION

As baptized members of the Church of Jesus Christ, all of us have the privilege of receiving inspiration through our heavenly guide, the Holy Ghost. With other believing members of His Church, I know that God reveals His will through powerful and personal inspiration. He is a perfectly trustworthy guide—especially in matters dealing with the welfare of our families and children. I have seen God guiding those I have worked with, and I am grateful for the restored gospel that gives us the faith and courage to seek His will and direction in difficult matters.

Being a close witness to so many Latter-day Saints working through vital family matters, I have learned some important lessons about the nature of revelation and inspiration. First, I am convinced that God can and will be a part of this process if He is invited into it. Of all the guides we have discussed, He is the most valuable, and His counsel should always be sought and heeded.

I have also learned that God does work in mysterious ways and through small and simple means to accomplish His purposes. Within my work in adoption, I have witnessed seeming coincidences that I do not feel were coincidences at all, and I have seen how many seemingly small matters within the process of adoption have proved to be ways by which God is working through various people and events to accomplish His purposes. Adoptive couples who may have been waiting for years, for example, suddenly feel inspired to telephone on the very day that a birth mother has selected them to receive her baby. This has taught me to allow for God in the process and to expect His help in matters both large and small.

I have learned that revelation is as personal as it is powerful. Many of my clients and their family members have shared with me some of the ways God has made known His guidance to them through dreams or other incidents that they interpret as being manifestations of God's will. I have no doubt that God does communicate through many different means. I have learned not to dismiss the personal inspiration available to individuals.

But at the same time, I have also observed that my clients—or sometimes their family members—will receive what they believe to be inspiration from God that appears to be unhealthy, inappropriate, or inconsistent with other divine guidance given through the prophets. While I do not question the right to personal revelation, Church leaders have counseled us to exercise caution in following any path that diverges from gospel principles or from inspired prophetic counsel. It is highly uncommon for the Lord to set up general rules and then inspire us to become an exception to them. Our modern prophets have given pointed instruction regarding adoption being the best alternative if marriage is not a good option for unwed parents. When birth grandparents tell me they have received revelation that their daughter, facing devastating and harmful roadblocks, is to single parent, it is natural for me to wonder why they would receive revelation that contradicts the prophet's counsel. I therefore strongly encourage birth parents and their family members to work with their bishops as they seek to know what God would have them do in their individual circumstances.

We have been taught that we have the right to revelation regarding our own lives and stewardships, but we need to use caution in obtaining guidance for someone else's life. Still, for some reason—possibly because others do not trust the young unwed parents to make sound decisions—it often occurs that the birth grandparents or even extended family members will apparently receive revelation for what a birth mother is to do with her baby. This puts the birth mother in a difficult situation, taking away her opportunity to receive revelation regarding herself and her child. In one instance, a client I was working with had already chosen a family to place her baby with when her mother said she had received revelation that her daughter was to parent the child. This put my client into a great state of confusion. She felt she had followed the Spirit in choosing the family for her baby. Was she wrong?

Brother Judd reminded me of counsel from the Prophet Joseph Smith regarding personal revelation. The Prophet stated, "We never inquire at the hand of God for special revelation only in case of there being no previous revelation to suit the case." Brother Judd adds:

> While circumstances may differ, the counsel of the Lord through his servants has been clearly stated. Caution should be taken concerning any counsel given by individuals, family members, or anyone else which is contrary to the counsel given by those we accept as prophets, seers, and revelators. "For his [the prophet's] word ye shall receive, as if from mine own mouth, in all patience and faith. For by

doing these things the gates of hell shall not prevail against you; yea, and the Lord God will disperse the powers of darkness from before you, and cause the heavens to shake for your good, and his name's glory" (D&C 21:5–6). (Personal correspondence)

Spirituality requires humility, and our personal revelations can best be trusted if we are humble enough to see if the inspiration we receive is consistent with principles of the gospel, with the counsel given by prophets, and with the inspired direction of our own bishop. In my orienteering analogy, we learn that our path is best determined by checking as many trustworthy reference points as we can. In spiritual matters of great consequence, it is worthwhile to check ourselves by comparing our inspiration with the guidance offered by all of our spiritual guides—the Holy Ghost, our bishop, the prophet, the scriptures, and so forth. If the counsel we receive from family members or if our own feelings tend to contradict those of our spiritual guides, we should be very wary about proceeding.

Sometimes intense emotion can be mistaken for inspiration, and to protect ourselves from making faulty decisions, we ought to be sure any inspiration we follow makes sense to those less emotionally attached to the situation. Again, this points to the great importance of involving Church leaders in the process. I have seen bishops bring spiritual grounding to pregnancy and adoption issues, clearly showing how God works through these leaders.

The Holy Ghost can be our lifelong companion and divine guide. As we grow in our spirituality, we become better at heeding the promptings of this member of the Godhead—at knowing how to receive inspiration and understanding the revelation God gives to us. Spiritually mature members carefully interpret something as revelation only after comparing it with prophetic instruction and the guidance of the local ecclesiastical leaders who preside over them.

In the many experiences of adoption I have witnessed, I have never seen one that wasn't a deeply spiritual experience. I have not shared many of these experiences, as they are truly sacred. But spirituality is a part of adoption, and it is this spirituality that reinforces the correctness of the experience for those involved.

The stories of those involved with adoption are often amazing and usually very spiritual and sacred. Those whose lives have been touched by an adoption, whether as the birth parents or the adoptive parents or their family members, will often see clearly their Heavenly Father's guiding hand in their situation. I have never believed adoption to be a random thing.

Although it seems impossibly difficult, I can understand the desire of a young woman to place her child for adoption because she has received the spiritual confirmation that it is right. It is so incredibly painful to do so, however, that I wonder how those without that spiritual confirmation and peace are able to follow through with the decision to say good-bye to their child.

I have seen birth parents who were Church members choose adoption solely so that their child would receive the blessings of the sealing covenant. In young members and old members alike, faith has been shown amidst great pain. And I believe in my very soul that adoption is sanctioned of God. The aspect of spirituality is so important along the path of adoption. As the young men and young women with whom I have worked have grown stronger throughout the process of discovering a pregnancy and placing a child for adoption, I have always felt it was because of the spiritual lessons they learned. In working with adoptive couples who are wrestling with their own desires and trying to follow the Lord's guidance, this process only makes sense to me when I examine it through spiritual eyes.

For me, as for many others, adoption is deeply connected to the eternal plan of happiness. It has extraordinary implications when examined in light of the Savior's Atonement. The counsel we have received about adoption through our prophets is divine and dear to my heart, as I know it is to the hearts of many others. It is a humbling process to witness and experience.

I have come almost to take for granted the combination of events that occur when a child is conceived who is ultimately placed for adoption. All of the events fall into place to allow the birth mother the opportunity to make the decision she feels directed to make, for the adoptive parents to follow the paths they are guided to follow, and for the baby to have the opportunities he or she is entitled to have. I do not believe there are coincidences in adoption. I have seen too many adoptions to believe they occur through happenstance rather than being directed by God. Birth parents struggling with an out-of-wedlock pregnancy can find peace and resolution by handing over their own will to the Lord and trusting in His guidance towards building eternal families. Birth parents must trust their Heavenly Father to guide them towards the best decisions for themselves and their baby.

When something occurs that hobbles us as we journey along the path towards eternal families, the most important thing is that we find our way back on track. Although it is necessary that we make decisions ourselves that immediately affect our lives, there are guides along the way who can direct us towards the best route. And while finding all those who can help is a key part of the work that must be done, it is ultimately necessary for us to yield to God's will, to make the Divine Guide our central guide. Aligning ourselves with His will can allow for growth and peace throughout all of the decisions that need to be made along the way.

Chapter Three

WHICH ROAD TO CHOOSE

JANUARY 9—

I'm ready to make some serious decisions about what will be best for my baby. I know it won't be an easy process, but I need to know for certain that the decisions I make for her will be the right ones.

I've certainly heard a lot of opinions about what I should do. It seems that everywhere I go, people ask me if I'm planning to keep the baby or give her up for adoption. Total strangers ask me while I'm standing in line at the grocery store! I usually just say I don't know yet. That's the truth.

I know my parents are hoping I'll place the baby for adoption. I'm not sure if they really think it would be best for the baby or if it would just mean less embarrassment for them. They don't talk about it much, even now. They suggested I shouldn't come home for Thanksgiving, to avoid people asking questions. So I'm spending the holiday with my cat.

I need to figure out what I'm going to do. It's time to make some decisions.

What are the choices unwed parents can make regarding their situation? Every path before them will be difficult in some way or another; any road chosen will have eternal consequences, and all of them lead to further sacrifices and trials.

In addition to the many guides who can counsel and direct those who are facing these situations, our religion provides a secure framework within which to make these choices. As Latter-day Saints we have already made certain fundamental choices: we choose to work towards eternal marriage; we choose to seek children; we choose to create eternal families. Circumstances or choices we make can delay or prevent our achieving those goals, but keeping our eyes fixed upon the good choices we have already made gives clarity to our present situation. We may not always have the simplest trek ahead of us; it is sometimes not possible to reach these destinations directly. But with the gospel's eternal perspective and our belief in the sealing powers of the temple, even murky cases grow more clear.

So it is worth it to scan the horizon, to get our bearings from an eternal perspective. The question is not so much *Which road to choose?* as it is *Which of my present choices will best lead towards building eternal families?* This is why even when unwed parents seem to have little choice in what to do, and when they come to me having already decided upon their path, I still encourage them to consider other possible choices. That way, when the road they choose inevitably turns uphill at points, they will not be left wondering if they have chosen correctly.

Good choices are usually not sudden choices. As we have discussed, there is sometimes a tendency to make a life-changing choice very suddenly in these situations (see Chapter 2). To be fair, it is true that the time to make these choices is sometimes quite limited. But even in a short period of time, it is still possible to rely on the best resources for choosing, to consult the best guides for finding the right journey forward, and to consider clearly and carefully the consequences of any given choice.

I make no apologies for the fact that I am a proponent of adoption; it is a better choice than many realize, and I hope to dispel misinformation about adoption and to give clarity regarding that particular choice. Adoption is not, of course, the only right choice for unwed parents. But as with the other alternatives, information about adoption should be laid out accurately so that it becomes a real choice to those involved.

The options for unwed parents can be summarized very quickly. Some choose the tragic path of abortion. This is an unpleasant reality, and I discuss it here not as a choice to *be* made but as a choice that *is* made, all too often— even by Latter-day Saints. Many others will choose single parenting. This is a very difficult road for both mother and child, yet it is by far the most common choice. The better choices include marrying and creating a family, or placing the baby for adoption. These last two choices are often the hardest to choose between, because Latter-day Saints support not just marriage but the blessings of temple marriage, and adoption can be the most direct path to those blessings, depending on the situation. The correct choice is ultimately a personal decision for those involved. But as with the pregnancy itself, the lives of many will be affected regardless of which road is taken.

None of these paths is easy; every choice has very real personal costs and eternal consequences. That is why it is so important to have a spiritual orientation to these decisions, through prayer, study, and consultation with trustworthy guides (as discussed in Chapter 2). As my clients come in to see me, I show them that they are at a crossroads. I want them to look all the way down each of the roads open to them so they can decide if that is where they would like to go.

Young people dealing with an out-of-wedlock pregnancy may feel that they already know their chosen road, but looking at their options will help them be more successful even if they stick to their original choice. For instance, if unwed parents are planning to marry, it is helpful for them to explore the alternatives to this choice. That way, when they inevitably come to difficult moments in their marriage, they can look back and say, "We looked at all of our options, we studied it out, prayed about it, and we *knew* that marriage was the best decision." This realization helps them work through the problems that will arise better than if they were to say, "Maybe we should have done something different. I wish we had considered the other choices." A couple who actively makes the decision to marry after exploring the other possible choices will be stronger as they make the decision work.

Still, the decision-making process can be agonizing. Some may see every path as an unhappy one and their choice as only the lesser of evils. Others may feel as if their hands are tied, that their circumstances dictate a single unhappy road. Both perspectives are in error. There are many choices involved, especially the choice to see one's situation more as an opportunity than as a crisis. At these crossroads, if the right road is chosen, the choice will not just return the birth parents from a detour but it can lead them upward and forward.

ABORTION: THE WRONG ROAD

Latter-day Saints believe abortion is wrong, so why even bring it up? I address the issue because it is a choice that is considered, even by Latter-day Saints. I wish I could say that the Saints are free from this sin, but we are not.

When I work with pregnant girls who complain about the birth father leaving once he has learned of the pregnancy, I ask them if they, too, ever wish they could step away from the whole situation. After all, it is a natural instinct to wish to escape an unpleasant reality. The reason a birth father leaves the pregnant mother and her child is also the reason a birth mother might consider abortion. Both rationalize that it will free them from devastating pain, including having to tell their parents or family members, feeling embarrassed or ashamed, and experiencing the pain of giving up so many of their best hopes for the immediate future.

Many are ready to help young people rationalize abortion. For example, I have heard people outside the Church claim that abortion is better emotionally because abortion leaves no loose ends, no child "out there" to worry about. But within our faith, we believe children are sacred, even if they come into the world under less than ideal circumstances. Once we focus on the child and plan for his or her welfare, then better options come into focus.

Brother Daniel K Judd shares a personal experience from his time as a bishop that helps to confirm the inspired nature of our Church's stance on abortion:

> "Members of The Church of Jesus Christ of Latter-day Saints must not submit to, perform, encourage, pay for, or arrange for an abortion" ("Abortion," *True to the Faith: A Gospel Reference* [Salt Lake City: The Church of Jesus Christ of Latter-day Saints, 2004], 4).
>
> These words, sanctioned by the First Presidency, clearly state the Church's position against intentionally ending the life of an unborn child. The Lord's servants have also indicated that there may be exceptions to this policy, "such as when a pregnancy is the result of incest or rape, when the life or health of the mother is judged by a competent medical authority to be in serious jeopardy, or when the fetus is known by competent medical authority to have severe defects that will not allow the baby to survive beyond birth" ("Abortion," 4). While the Church recognizes that there are some legitimate circumstances in which abortion is justified, in most cases it is considered a grievous sin.
>
> Years ago as a young bishop, I counseled with a member of my ward who had been advised by her physician that she should have an

abortion. At forty-four years of age this sister was in poor health, had six children, and was in a rickety marriage that was in the process of ending. Her physician believed that carrying the child for nine months and giving birth was much more than her body, mental state, or marriage could bear. The doctor also said that in addition to the pregnancy putting the mother's health in serious peril, he had reason to believe the baby would not be born healthy.

I could sense that we were on sacred ground as we discussed what she should do. Was this a situation where even though the Lord had stated "Thou shalt not . . . kill, *nor do anything like unto it* " (D&C 59:6, italics added), abortion was indeed justified?

In addition to the counsel given above concerning when abortion may be warranted, the First Presidency has also stated: "These circumstances [rape, incest, health issues, etc.] do not automatically justify an abortion. Those who face such circumstances should consider an abortion only after consulting with their local Church leaders and receiving a confirmation through earnest prayer" ("Abortion," 4).

Our stake president wisely counseled me that the husband should be invited to be a part of the deliberation and that all of us should join in fasting and prayer concerning the decision. At the end of our fast, all of us (including the stake president) met in my office to discuss the matter. After the husband and wife shared their thoughts and feelings, believing they should go ahead with the abortion, the stake president gently stated, "While I can understand and can accept your decision, I must tell you that I think you should keep your baby." The president then asked this couple to spend more time studying, praying, and counseling together about their decision. The couple was sobered by his counsel and agreed that they would not make the final decision until they had taken some more time.

During the next several months I witnessed a miracle. The sister and her husband decided against the abortion, and almost immediately her health began to improve. Even the health problems she was experiencing before the pregnancy began to clear up. Miraculously, the marriage began to strengthen as well. The baby was born healthy and not many years later became the terror of the ward nursery as well as a source of great joy to his parents and a symbol of God's love for them and all who knew them. (Personal correspondence)

How can we understand the fact that even faithful Latter-day Saints will consider abortion? Latter-day Saints know well that modern prophets have said abortion is only an option in certain extreme cases (rape, incest, or endangerment to the mother's life). Simply conceiving a child out of wedlock obviously does not fit the criteria for those exceptions, especially if mother and child are healthy; however, I have seen believing Latter-day Saints rationalize that their daughter does in fact meet these criteria. For example, some rationalize that their daughter was not old enough or mature enough to give consent, and therefore it was as though she were forced. Or they rationalize that having this baby would indeed endanger their daughter's life. "She is too immature physically and emotionally to handle the burden of carrying a child to term," they reason to themselves. People facing these situations often feel desperate, and despite the clarity of prophetic counsel, they sometimes believe abortion to be the lesser of evils. Even in those situations when abortion seems justified, we might ask, as did Elder Russell M. Nelson, "Why destroy a life that could bring such joy to others?" ("Reverence for Life," *Ensign,* May 1985, 11).

How I wish Shauna's family had considered that question! Hers is a story that illustrates the tragic consequences of failing to use prudence in consulting Church leaders before considering abortion.

Shauna's Story: Rationalizing Abortion

The first impression I got from Shauna was how very immature she seemed. And as I think of her now, I recognize that of course she was immature—she was fifteen years old at the time. Her mother, Helen, explained why they'd come. She was nervous and distressed, clearly seeking affirmation from me that her actions with Shauna were correct. I could see in her eyes, as I have recognized in the eyes of many parents, the loss of her dreams for the life of her daughter. She was still somewhat in a state of shock. However, rather than moving through that stage of loss towards resolution, this family would be going through a much deeper loss, I soon learned, because of the tragic way Shauna and her parents handled the pregnancy.

Apparently Shauna had been raped when leaving work, Helen told me, but because she never saw her attacker she had not said anything until she discovered her pregnancy. Devastated, her parents promptly scheduled an appointment with the family doctor. Because they were active Church members, I wondered why they didn't also schedule an appointment with their bishop. Oddly, Shauna showed no emotion as her mother recounted the story to me.

The doctor got them right in to his office and reported the "good news" that it was not too late for an abortion. Of course an abortion was difficult for these Latter-day Saints to agree to, but Shauna had been raped, and so this must be the best thing. The doctor immediately administered a shot of medication that would begin the process of aborting Shauna's unborn child. This had happened less than an hour before they came to see me.

The pain must have shown on my face as Helen described how the abortion would work. Within a couple of weeks Shauna would begin to experience cramping and bleeding. She would report to the physician's office weekly to receive more of the drug if necessary. It would be a simple process, taking possibly as long as six to eight weeks, for the unborn baby to slowly die inside her. "It's better this way," Helen insisted. "If Shauna had carried this child to term, she would have missed out on one whole season with her basketball team. And we didn't want her to have to face that kind of pain."

Helen was in clean-up mode. I have often seen this with parents of pregnant girls. They want to quickly restore things to how they were before this troubling problem—perhaps for themselves as much as for their daughter. They feel they must take charge and make the tough decisions in order to get their child back on track. Unfortunately, their haste can lead to poor judgment.

When I spoke privately with Shauna, I began to wonder if her story was true. She clearly showed less concern about having been sexually violated and more concern about her mother. "Is there anything you can do to get my mom to quit telling me what to do all the time?" she asked.

Shauna's life was not quite what her parents believed it to be. She told me about experimenting with alcohol and drugs and reported having had many sexual partners since she was thirteen. She eventually admitted she had lied about being sexually assaulted. The reason her parents had used to justify the abortion proved not to exist; this abortion would only deepen Shauna's problems.

It was strange for someone to come to my office for counseling in adjusting to having had an abortion. This was, after all, LDS Family Services, and our sponsoring church does not accept or condone abortion except in very limited circumstances—a position I fully support. I continued meeting with Shauna partly because there was a small chance the baby could survive the procedure but also because Shauna's lifestyle would likely lead her to become pregnant again. Given her parents' approach this time, Shauna would likely see abortion as the most immediate and pain-free solution another time. But even if abortion were not a matter that modern prophets have told us is wrong, it would still be anything but the easy solution. Abortion appears to solve some problems, but it creates others that are far worse.

It took several weeks before the doctor determined the baby was dead, and I shuddered to think of what it must have felt like for Shauna to carry a child, waiting for it to die rather than to live. And Shauna continued to have problems that were not aborted with her child. It turned out she was very insecure and sought out physical relationships with boys. She exchanged her feelings of self-worth for a brief period of apparent affirmation from young men and then paid for it in the end when the "relationship" was over.

Among other problems, Shauna's immaturity was certainly a factor contributing to her current situation. Shauna's parents were not about to leave a life-changing decision in the hands of such a young person. I have heard many parents say they could not allow a *child* to make a decision of this magnitude when the consequences for that choice would largely fall in their own laps, anyway. And yet, if Shauna's parents had treated their daughter as responsible not just for her past actions but for her present situation, then Shauna would more likely have been honest with them and abortion would likely never have become an issue. While it is important that birth parents receive good guidance towards the best decision, it is still vital that the birth parents be treated as the ones responsible for making the decisions regarding the child they have created (see Chapter 2). Taking control of their child's decision may spare them trouble in the short run, but it will hurt them in the long run. Allowing their daughter to make the decision about the baby she has conceived gives her a chance to grow into the adulthood that she has already rushed into through sexual activity.

I have seen how a young and quite immature girl dealing with a pregnancy can do remarkable things when she needs to, and someone who has previously been nothing but self-serving can make the most unselfish decisions in regard to her unborn child. A girl who feels she has made only poor choices can have the sweet experience of learning again to trust in herself and in her ability to make good decisions. She can begin to view herself as having done something great and incredible in her life, something completely unselfish even amidst tremendous pain. She can experience the love that a mother has for a child. Through personal revelation, she can feel the extent to which her Heavenly Father loves her and cares about her life. She can receive the peace available regarding this unborn child and her own life as well—that is, if she is given the opportunity.

Shauna was not given the opportunity to grow through the pain of pregnancy or from the love she might have felt for her unborn child. She missed out on the chance to take responsibility for her actions and on the opportunity to realize the serious consequences of the immoral choices she had been making. She was kept from these opportunities by her parents' "protection." I've seen young women and young men change everything about their lives because of one tiny child, but Shauna went down a different road.

I had one final conversation with Shauna's mother a couple of months after the abortion. She asked how I felt Shauna was doing, and I was painfully honest. Helen cried as she listened to me confirm what she had already guessed to be true about Shauna's promiscuous lifestyle. I could see the realization in her face of the hastiness of seeking an abortion and realizing that this decision that she initially thought would save them pain would end up causing greater pain for years to come. I talked with her about the missed opportunities for Shauna and for their family, but I also suggested that Shauna had qualities neither she nor her parents were recognizing. I believed it was still within Shauna to do good in her own life.

Did I have hope that Shauna and her family would change? If I have come to believe anything in my years as a therapist, it is that people can change. I don't know if Shauna ended up making the changes she needed to, but I certainly believe she had it in her to do so.

To their credit, most clients with whom I have worked have not seriously considered abortion, and most who have thought about it do not consider it for long. Is it normal to consider abortion when faced with an unplanned pregnancy? I think it is normal for people to go through every option possible and rule out those that do not fit within their moral code. It is normal to want to avoid shame and embarrassment for ourselves and for our loved ones, but choosing abortion is choosing to resist not just pain but growth. The great lie of abortion is that the pain is removed along with the baby's life. As Helen and Shauna's story shows, they merely exchanged one kind of pain for another, less redemptive kind.

SINGLE PARENTING: THE BUMPY ROAD

An LDS unwed mother who does not believe in abortion has three options: to marry, to single parent, or to place her child for adoption. None of these choices is simple, nor is any one of them the only right choice. However, Church members can rely for direction upon "The Family: A Proclamation to the World," which articulates LDS family values (*Ensign,* November 1995, 102), and upon the specific counsel about children born out of wedlock that has been provided in letters from the First Presidency to priesthood and auxiliary leaders (see, for example, letters dated 15 June 1998; 19 July 2002; "Policies and Announcements," *Ensign,* April 1999, 80).

The Proclamation on the Family states that parents "have a sacred duty to rear their children in love and righteousness." While some may interpret this to mean that the mother or couple must parent that child at any cost, the First Presidency has emphasized the critical factor of a child being raised with the blessings of the temple sealing (Letter, 19 July 2002). In today's world we can understand better than ever the protection that temple blessings offer to families and children. For a young girl to raise a child without those blessings, without the strength of priesthood and fatherhood, is to put the child at risk from the day it is born. Nevertheless, it is a sad fact that most single pregnant women will choose to raise their child by themselves. Why?

Many choose single parenting out of a sense of obligation. Latter-day Saints believe that parents "have a solemn responsibility to love and care for each other and their children" and that mothers and fathers "will be held accountable before God for the discharge of these obligations" ("Proclamation," 102). From a gospel perspective, we are to take responsibility for our actions and are obligated to care for our children. But if marriage is not possible, is single parenting the only or best way to fulfill one's parental obligation? The First Presidency has been pointedly clear on this matter, instructing us that "birth parents who do not marry should not be counseled to keep the infant as a condition of repentance or out of a sense of obligation to care for one's own" (Letter, July 2002). As a mother of six children, I know that parenting can be a bumpy road even with a strong temple marriage and a husband who honors and exercises his priesthood. How much more difficult the road is for those who decide to travel it without companionship and without the fortification provided by a temple marriage! I have seen firsthand how disadvantaged those young women are who try to travel it alone. That was the case with Jamie.

JAMIE'S STORY: "I CAN RAISE MY BABY ALONE"

"I wish everyone would just leave me alone. I know what I'm doing, and I'm going to prove to everyone that I can raise this baby by myself." This is what Jamie told me early in counseling. Still, I invited her to make a list of pros and cons about single parenting. (Most of the cons were written down only after I recommended that she consider them.)

Single Parenting

Pros:

> I will get to keep the baby
> I will know how my baby is being raised
> Having a baby will help me get my own life back on track
> It's mine
> Because I can take care of it
> I love it already
> I love babies & always wanted to be a mother

Cons:

> I might have trouble finishing school
> I'm too young to be a parent
> My baby won't have a father
> I could be dependent on parents for longer

When I asked Jamie which would be her number one reason for choosing to parent, she said that she was parenting because it was her baby and she wanted to keep it. And despite the "con" list, she firmly believed her baby would help her to get her life together, finish school, and find the independence she so badly desired. It seemed that her choice to single parent was not an active choice as much as it was the only choice for her. She simply could not allow herself to consider anything else. For Jamie, the choice to single parent was pretty much made when she decided to become sexually active.

She attended counseling at the encouragement of her mother but felt it would be of little use to her. She stopped showing up for counseling sessions when she was about eight months pregnant. At the time of our last appointment, she still had a host of problems. She was struggling in her relationship with the baby's father and barely attending high school. I suspected she was drinking; although she never spoke openly about it, she referred to the "partying" she would have to give up once the baby was born.

Nearly a year later, I happened to be in her area and called to see if I could visit. Jamie's mother answered and encouraged me to stop by. She was a very kind, hard-working member of the Church. I knew that she wanted what was best for her daughter and grandson. And I could hear in her somewhat apologetic tone that Jamie was having a difficult time adjusting, but she said to me as we walked back to Jamie's room, "She's really a good mother."

Jamie was expecting me, which made her room seem all the more shocking. Jamie was in an old pair of sweat pants and a tee shirt on which she wiped the baby's nose several times during our visit. She was sitting on her bed while her now eight-month-old baby son scooted around on the floor. She was watching a TV she had set up next to the crib, the crib having taken the place of her bookshelf, stereo, and beanbag chair. Her room was packed with an unnatural combination of scattered teen paraphernalia and the tools of motherhood. Apart from the tissues strewn around the floor and the most recent messes of curiosity created by her little son, her bedroom was not terribly dirty, just crowded.

Now as I have said before, I am a mother. There can be days when I am still in my pajamas by mid-afternoon, amidst more messes of curiosity than I can keep up with from my children. Being a mom brings a lesson in empathy towards other mothers. So it wasn't so much the surroundings that made me feel so sad as it was hearing about Jamie's life.

Jamie didn't talk much, as she was watching a popular talk show on TV. Her mother told me that Jamie was taking some time off from school before she went back for her GED. Jamie didn't have a job and mostly stayed home with the baby. Her mother said that the only time they really got to spend much time with the baby was when Jamie went out on the weekends with her friends. "Not enough time for me to get away, either," Jamie chimed in. Because Jamie felt her parents were being unfair by not babysitting more, she had decided not to allow them to spend much time with her son when she was home. She didn't have a car, although it didn't look like she would have gone anywhere if she had. She had no solid future plans for either herself or her baby.

Jamie's prospects were bleak but not atypical. Statistics paint a most unhappy picture for young women who single parent. It turns out that less than one-third of unmarried teen mothers complete high school, and more than 80 percent end up living below the poverty level. Moreover, only 1.5 percent of unwed teen mothers have a college degree by age thirty, and studies note that differences in economic status and emotional well-being of mothers in the United States correlate directly with whether or not they are married (Rebecca A. Maynard, "Kids Having Kids: A Robin Hood Foundation Special Report on the Costs of Adolescent Childbearing," 13 June 1996; available online). Suicide rates among teen mothers are nearly seven times higher than those of teens who are not parents ("Teen Pregnancy and Parenting: Myths and Realities," *Children's Services Practice Notes* 1, no. 1 [Winter 1995]).

And, of course, the children of single parents are strongly affected. Children of single teenage mothers are more likely to drop out of school, to become pregnant out of wedlock if they are girls or to be involved in delinquent behavior if they are boys, to divorce or separate later in life, and to depend on welfare (Maynard, "Kids Having Kids"). These shocking statistics regarding single parenting support counsel from the prophet that those involved in an out-of-wedlock pregnancy ought to consider marriage and adoption above single parenting.

Despite the information we have about the welfare of mothers and babies in single-parent homes, almost every birth mother I have ever seen who is choosing to single parent believes she will be one of the very few who beat the odds. Hope springs eternal, and when faced with the choices of single parenting or placing a child for adoption, many young women will take whatever risks are necessary to keep their baby. But it is important to remember that becoming a parent does not lead to a young person suddenly acting responsibly.

Someone who is considering parenting a child needs to have the necessary skills and abilities to manage everyday life *before* he or she takes on the responsibility of another life. Choosing to parent a child with the hope that doing so will help clean up one's own life is like playing roulette with the child's well being as the stakes. That is what Jamie was doing. Certainly it is true that a child can be the occasion for bringing change into one's life. In unhealthy marriages spouses might believe that getting pregnant will warm cool relations between them, for example. But if there is not a substantial foundation, the occasion of the coming child cannot alone redeem a bad marriage. Similarly, a troubled teen cannot expect that raising a child will repair her own damaged life. It is far more likely that her problems will bring troubles into the life of the child.

Even single parents whose motives are purely altruistic, who choose to give up possible personal opportunities to raise their child alone, may not realize that, ironically, everything they sacrifice to give their child more will likely end up giving their child less. I have met many young women and young men who were willing to make almost any sacrifice for the sake of their child, and I applaud their motives; however, when the decision is made to single parent, those sacrifices radiate out to the life of the child as well. The baby will also give up something.

Family members and friends may contribute pressure to choose single parenting by promising to support or assist the birth mother. Although this offer may be made out of love and altruism, it can lead to most unhappy consequences, as Lindsey's story illustrates.

Lindsey's Story: Choosing the Grandchild over the Child

Lindsey was one of those young mothers who wanted to do the right thing for the child she was carrying. Lindsey was twenty-two, bright, and incredibly insecure. She remains a valued daughter of our Heavenly Father, and her story is one I tell with some sadness. Years after her pregnancy, she felt a desire to share her experience with others to help them make better decisions for their baby than she had for hers.

Lindsey was an only child. Her mother and stepfather had tried unsuccessfully for years to have other children, but her mother had not been able to carry a child to term. When Lindsey announced that she was pregnant and planning to place the child for adoption, they felt indignant at having to lose another baby. They were angry with Lindsey not only for having sex without being married but also for apparently not wanting a baby when they had sought one for so long.

Still, Lindsey's parents knew she was very immature and incapable of properly caring for this child. So, at first, they agreed that placing the baby for adoption was the right choice. As the pregnancy progressed, however, her parents began pressuring Lindsey to parent the child. They expressed how much they would love and support the baby—with Lindsey, of course—and they became almost desperate that she keep the baby.

The parents of the unwed mother are such a powerful influence upon her that they can prove to be either helpful and supportive guides or dominating and detrimental influences. Lindsey's parents were at first helpful, but as they began thinking more of their grandchild than of their daughter, her well-being was set aside in painful ways.

At first it did not seem so. Indeed, Lindsey found that her parents were giving her some much appreciated consideration. As Lindsey was deciding what to do, she found herself receiving from her parents the attention she had sought from them for years. Although for some time she waffled back and forth between adoption and single parenting, her parents clearly influenced her final decision to keep the baby.

For a while, things looked better than ever. Over the final months of her pregnancy, Lindsey and her parents talked of the beautiful nursery her parents had prepared for the baby, of the names both Lindsey's parents liked, and of how wonderful it would be for Lindsey to live with them for several years as she got her feet on the ground and prepared herself to care for the baby alone. I was happy for their enthusiasm but a little worried about how Lindsey could achieve maturity and independence when her own parenting would be tied so closely to that of her own parents. After the baby was born, Lindsey and her parents stopped coming in for counseling and left with high hopes of raising this baby together.

Four years later Lindsey came back into the office for the birth parents' support group. She had agreed to be a member of a panel of mothers who were single parents. Through this panel discussion, girls who were considering single parenting could hear what it was like from those who had made that choice and were living with it. Lindsey was open and candid, talking of the many difficulties in parenting a child alone. She spoke of her child's desire to know why he did not have a father like the other kids in preschool and of the difficulty in introducing him to men she was dating. She told of the amount of time she spent caring for her child while trying to work and attend classes at the local community college. She talked of how many guys had sprinted in the opposite direction after learning she had a child and of her diminishing hopes of marrying in the temple and having a family with a worthy husband. She spoke candidly of the many unexpected problems she had encountered after taking the baby home. Most fervently, she spoke of the difficulty of trying to be a mother and a daughter at the same time in the same house with little control.

"I still live with my mother and stepdad, and it will be a while before I will be able to afford to get a place for me and my son." She handed around a picture of Andy as she talked, a smiling, mischievous-looking preschooler with curly brown hair. "My relationship with my mom went from bad to really, really bad. My parents disagree with every decision I make for Andy. They let him do anything he wants, but when he acts up because of it, it's my fault. The most difficult thing about raising my child under my parents' roof is that to him, I am always the bad guy and my parents can do nothing wrong. It really began to hit home to me that I was messing with a little kid's life when he started calling my mother 'Mom.'"

Lindsey had been crying throughout her part on the panel, and she made many hard-hitting points to the young girls in the room, but her final comment still strikes me in a powerful way. She looked around at the girls in the support group—many who had placed their babies for adoption and many who were still undecided. The looks of rebellion, fear, disbelief, and pain on their faces were familiar to her; she had spent many weeks in group sessions herself during her own decision-making process. She looked hard at the girls and said, "For every day you have cried because you miss your baby, I have cried for my son. I have cried for the things he will never have and for my lack of control to give them to him. He wants a father more than anything else in this world, and there's very little I can do about it."

Unfortunately, Lindsey's chances of marrying and being able to provide that wished-for father are slim. Fewer than half of unmarried mothers will marry within ten years after the child's birth (Maynard, "Kids Having Kids"). Girls like Lindsey are actually far more likely, statistically, of having another child out of wedlock than of marrying (D. W. Nelson and K. A. Moore, *The Right Start: State Trends: Conditions of Babies and Their Families across the Nation, 1990–1998,* Child Trends KIDS COUNT Special Report, Annie E. Casey Foundation, 2001; available online).

Over time Lindsey discovered that her early eagerness to please her parents gave way to regret for the sake of her child. Like her, many others who have chosen single parenting have seen the price their children have paid for that decision. Having witnessed the consequences of single parenting over the years, I strongly believe this is the least desirable of the three serious choices available to Latter-day Saints. Unfortunately, it is still the choice most commonly made.

To Marry or Not to Marry?

If single parenting is the most common choice made, despite its drawbacks, then marriage is often seen by many as the only choice that can or should be made. The doctrines we espouse as Latter-day Saints and the honor we give to marriage and family in general all seem to suggest that if a pregnancy occurs outside of marriage, then the best and quickest solution is to have the birth parents marry and begin working towards a temple sealing.

Ideally, that is the best course to take. Still, it is important that Latter-day Saints not mistakenly believe it is the only course of action. Indeed, we are fortunate to have very direct instruction on this matter from living prophets.

"The Family: A Proclamation to the World" says that "marriage between a man and a woman is ordained of God and that the family is central to the Creator's plan" (102). Some Latter-day Saints may interpret this statement to mean that an unwed mother can only do the right thing by marrying. Yet the First Presidency says that "when the probability of a successful marriage is unlikely, unwed parents should be encouraged to place the child for adoption" (Letter, 15 June 1998).

Latter-day Saints believe that parents "have a sacred duty to rear their children in love and righteousness" ("Proclamation," 102). Some may interpret this to mean that a couple must parent that child at any cost, but the First Presidency has emphasized the essential element of a temple-worthy family, and "unwed parents are not able to provide the stable, nurturing environment so essential for the baby's well-being" (Letter, 19 July 2002).

We believe that parents "have a solemn responsibility to love and care for each other and their children" and that mothers and fathers "will be held accountable before God for the discharge of these obligations" ("Proclamation," 102). From a gospel perspective, we take responsibility for our actions and are obligated to care for our children. But is marrying always the responsible thing to do? If a marriage is unlikely to succeed, have parents fulfilled their obligation to care for their child by marrying, especially if there is a better alternative available for the baby?

Marriage is ordained of God, and Latter-day Saints in this situation should consider it carefully. There are couples who do manage to overcome a bad beginning, reach the temple, and go on to raise strong families. But not many. Statistics show that approximately 70 percent of teens who marry will divorce, and such marriages are under further distress when pregnancy is involved ("Would This Teen Marriage Survive?"; online at divorcesupport.about.com). Marriage should be considered seriously not simply for the moment but for the future. Are the unwed parents giving "prayerful consideration to the best interests of the child" (First Presidency Letter, 19 July 2002) by marrying now if a divorce is likely or if a temple marriage is unlikely?

On the other hand, couples who have the faith that they can meet the prophet's requirements regarding the creation of a "stable, nurturing environment" (First Presidency Letter, 19 July 2002) and who see eye to eye on the central importance of the temple sealing should not be afraid of making this commitment. As with the other choices, they should go into it with their eyes open, knowing the specific kinds of sacrifices and difficulties that will present themselves. Perry and Caitlin were one couple who made the decision to marry and made it work.

PERRY AND CAITLIN'S STORY: MAKING MARRIAGE WORK

Perry and Caitlin sat in my office, all of us laughing at the funny face made by their three-year-old daughter. She was a darling child, just like their other two children who accompanied them to our counseling sessions. Each session with me included at least a couple of crazy moments because of the large number of people crowded into my tiny office. Perry always sat on the recliner, and Caitlin teased him that he did this so he couldn't chase the kids around during the appointment as easily.

This was our last session of marital counseling. Perry and Caitlin had started their family before getting married, and after six years of marriage they had come to see me on the recommendation of their bishop. At that point, their marriage was in a precarious state, and they wanted to save it. Their willingness to work was one of their great strengths, as was the strong support they received from their bishop.

And the two of them had made great progress together. We all knew their relationship would get sticky again, as relationships do from time to time, but they had learned and grown and would be able to work out problems as they arose. It hadn't always been this way. I thought back to earlier sessions with this couple, sessions in which the sound of crying was far more common than the sound of laughter. Perry and Caitlin had fought bitterly, often during the sessions. A primary issue in their disputes was learning how to treat each other with kindness and respect. These basic components of a relationship are usually worked out before marriage, and they found themselves having to learn to know and get along with each other at the same time that they were already raising children. It was not impossible, but it was very difficult.

They had struggled financially, were still struggling financially, and had moved around quite a bit following jobs and potential careers. They were both away from the children a great deal of the time, and they were seeing some negative behaviors from the children as a result. They had decided to sacrifice financially for Caitlin to be home with the children during the day, and Perry was in a promising position as a restaurant manager which they hoped would allow for this.

They struggled spiritually. Perry drank on and off throughout their marriage, continuing habits he had begun in high school. Caitlin hadn't been strong spiritually herself, feeling unworthy to seek Heavenly Father's guidance after becoming pregnant. She had struggled to take the children to church with only faltering support from Perry. She eventually stopped going, but with the encouragement of her parents and the Relief Society president, she started attending again after the birth of their third child.

They both told me marriage was hard, harder than they had expected it to be. Still, they expressed love for each other and for their children and gratitude for all the people who had helped them make it through the difficult times. They had plans to continue to make it through those times, even to make it eternally.

When a couple involved in an out-of-wedlock pregnancy is considering marriage, it is important to go beyond the idea of both people being *willing* to marry and explore the concept of their being *able* to build a stable marriage and family. Sometimes marriage may seem like the only way to atone for an unwed pregnancy. It may feel that marriage will make the situation right again. But marriage is not set up as a way to atone for past mistakes, and a marriage based primarily upon that premise is not on solid ground.

President Gordon B. Hinckley has said: "Marriage is the more honorable thing. This means facing up to responsibility. It means giving the child a name, with parents who together can nurture, protect, and love" ("Save the Children," *Ensign,* Nov. 1994, 53). When a couple is mature enough to make the commitment to marry and care for the baby, and when they have eternal goals and love for each other and for their family, then marriage can be the best option. A couple who is stable financially and emotionally and who can care for all of the needs of a child should consider marriage. The couple needs to feel a deep sense of love and commitment for each other and their child and be prepared and willing to make the sacrifices they *will* need to make.

Many factors affect the successfulness of marriage, and Perry and Caitlin realized this completely only after they married. For instance, both of them were members of the Church, and their parents were active in the Church. Perry, however, was inactive at the time he was dating Caitlin, and she struggled with inactivity after they married. Differences in religion or spirituality are factors in divorce, and they affected both Perry and Caitlin. They disagreed about how their marriage and family should be run. Another factor that affected Perry and Caitlin's marriage was their young age and the fact that they were expecting a baby when they married. As said above, more than two-thirds of couples who marry when they are teens will divorce ("Would This Teen Marriage Survive?"). Such breakups occur for obvious reasons, primarily that a very young couple is unprepared emotionally and practically to handle the responsibility of a marriage, and they are under far greater stress when a baby is involved. There is also the strong likelihood that additional children will soon contribute to the stress on the young family.

Perry and Caitlin found that even with strong family support they were often struggling financially and felt exhausted from fighting the battle. Financial instability has long been known to be among the leading factors contributing to divorce for couples of all ages, and it is a predictable source of tension in marriage. When young people go from only having to think of themselves to never getting to think of themselves, they are sure to face bumps in the road. It is normal to gradually move out of an adolescent role and into an adult role, but it is difficult for young people to manage when they are thrust into the responsibilities placed upon them with a spouse and child. For well-adjusted and mature young people, marriage is hard work; it is all the more so for those without such advantages.

Perry and Caitlin were working hard to make it through the tough times. They had been successful so far because both of them were committed to making it through. I do not know if they are still doing well, but I know there are many couples like them who make it. It is possible to build a strong marriage with rough beginnings. Some do succeed against the odds; however, it is important to remember that all believe they will be in that small proportion of those who make it—and that is not the case.

"How did you decide to marry when you found out you were pregnant?" I had asked Caitlin and Perry early in the counseling.

"We never really thought of anything else," said Caitlin. She added, "My mom wanted us to consider placing the baby for adoption, but it wasn't something I could even consider. I was determined to keep the baby, whether I married Perry or not."

Perry nodded. "I never thought much about adoption because Caitlin never thought about it. I guess I felt that I owed it to Caitlin to get married. We were young, maybe too young, to realize the magnitude of the decision we were making. We probably should have considered adoption."

Now Caitlin was nodding. "I love our son more than anything in the world, but I have to admit that after we had him, I started thinking about what our lives would have been like, what his life would have been like, had we placed him for adoption."

If a couple has prayerfully considered their options and come to feel marriage is the best choice, there are some things they can do to strengthen the likelihood of success. For instance, they should counsel with their ecclesiastical leaders and their parents prior to marriage, listening to the concerns noted and working to strengthen areas of weakness in their relationship. They should seek premarital counseling by a qualified professional and actively work to strengthen their relationship before they marry. They need to be thinking alike in terms of spiritual commitment and desired goals. And they need to have a deep sense of long-term commitment, not just *trying out* marriage or parenting to see if it works for them.

Perry and Caitlin left my office, chasing their children down the hall. I was fond of them and hoped that their situation would continue to improve. I wanted them to succeed, prayed for them to succeed. Their lives mattered, and they were good people trying to do the best they could with the circumstances they were in. I wanted them to be happy because the lives of those three young children depended on it. I smiled as they turned the corner.

CHOOSING ADOPTION

I am an advocate of adoption. I advocate it because I have seen it transform the lives of so many people. I have seen the lives of hundreds of adoptive couples and birth parents blessed by it. But I am not the only one who believes in adoption.

There are hundreds of thousands of people whose lives are positively changed by adoption. Our prophets and other Church leaders have been inspired to encourage adoption and have been doing so for years. Not only have the Brethren sent repeated and forthright letters to ecclesiastical leaders encouraging the consideration of adoption, but there is rarely a general conference in which adoption is not mentioned. Even beyond advocating adoption, the Church has established LDS Family Services to support and guide those in the position of considering adoption and to facilitate adoption in a way that ensures the child can be sealed in the temple to a loving family. This is why the Church has been so active in advocating adoption: "Placing the infant for adoption enables unwed parents to do what is best for the child and enhances the prospect for the blessings of the gospel in the lives of all concerned" (First Presidency Letter, 15 June 1998).

Adoption is truly a blessing and an opportunity. But adoption is not the right choice if it is forced upon someone, or if those involved do not think through the consequences of this option as thoroughly as they might any other. Adoption is often a better choice than people realize, but it is not an easy choice, and even if it is the right one, the birth mother must be educated and encouraged about adoption so that she can decide for herself that adoption is the best decision both for her child's sake and for her own.

AMANDA'S STORY: CHOOSING ADOPTION

Amanda's experience in arriving at the choice to place her child for adoption is indicative of many others'. When she first discovered her pregnancy, Amanda was confused about what she should do. Although she knew she wanted what was best for the baby, she did not know in the beginning what that would be. She began working towards a decision by following the counsel from the Brethren.

To begin with, she knew that she would not be considering an abortion. True, at weak moments she let herself wish for a miscarriage as an easy way out, but Amanda could never seriously think of voluntarily ending the pregnancy. She knew that was wrong. From the first flutters of life that she felt within her womb, Amanda knew she had to do the right thing for her baby.

Just what that was, however, was not clear. Single parenting, marriage, and adoption were all viable options in Amanda's situation. What should she do? Fortunately for Amanda, she turned to her bishop for counsel. He helped her to understand priorities in these matters as outlined by the First Presidency of the Church—specifically, that the first step is to consider the likelihood of "establish[ing] an eternal family relationship." When a temple-bound marriage is not likely, the counsel from the First Presidency is to "place the child for adoption" (Letter, 15 June 1998). Church leaders rarely suggest single parenting, and after Amanda thought through what it would mean for her baby and herself if she were to parent alone, she could see why such a choice was not recommended. When I became involved in counseling Amanda, I invited her to consider carefully the consequences of each option: single parenting, marriage, and adoption. She wrote out the pros and cons of each choice to evaluate these choices objectively:

Single Parenting

Pros:

>   I would get to keep the baby

Cons:

- ✓ The baby would be raised in daycare
- ✓ The baby would have fewer opportunities spiritually and financially

>   I would struggle financially, with school, and in dating

- ✓ My future husband might not love/accept the baby as his own
- ✓ The baby will not have a father

>   The birth father would always have a say in what I do

Marriage

Pros:

- ✓ The baby will be raised by two parents

>   I wouldn't have to deal with this alone

- ✓ It is a suggestion by the Brethren

Cons:

>   I don't love the birth father and I am not ready to be married

>   The baby's father is from a very different culture and religion

- ✓ We would likely never be sealed in the temple
- ✓ We would struggle financially
- ✓ We would have little or no family support

Adoption

Pros:

- ✓ The baby would be raised by two parents with a strong marriage
- ✓ The baby would have more opportunities spiritually and financially
- ✓ The baby would have the blessings of the sealing covenant
- ✓ The baby would have a father and a stay-at-home mother
- ✓ It has been recommended by the Brethren

  I could finish school and be more stable financially

  I could marry someone in the temple

Cons:

  I would have little control over how my baby was raised

  I would have been pregnant for nothing

  I would have to say good-bye to my baby

The check marks by some of these are where I asked Amanda to look over the points she had made about each choice and mark those that had more to do with what was best for the baby than with her own desires. She checked most of the points listed as cons under "Single Parenting," half the cons listed under "Marriage," and most of the pros listed under "Adoption." There were not nearly the advantages for the baby under the marriage option as there were under the adoption choice. Amanda knew that ultimately she wanted to do what was best for the baby, even if it meant sacrificing some of her own desires.

Amanda, like so many other young women and young men, placed her baby for adoption because she wanted her baby to have a life she couldn't give her alone. She placed her so that she could be sealed to two parents, a mother and a father, who were emotionally and physically prepared to care for all the child's needs. She wanted her baby to grow up in an environment where the baby's mother and father lived together in a strong, happy marriage, and where the baby would be raised in the gospel in a stable, healthy environment.

Amanda could have taken care of her baby. But she had the maturity to look beyond the diapers and formula to recognize other needs her baby would have. Beyond all of the other reasons why adoption would be a good thing, she chose it because she wanted to give her baby the best chance possible to return to her Heavenly Father.

Adoption can be a wonderful thing. But why don't more people consider this option when faced with an out-of-wedlock pregnancy? There are a number of reasons. Sometimes decisions not to consider adoption are based on personal biases, unfounded fears, or incorrect or outdated information.

For example, the notion that a baby being placed for adoption is whisked away at the birth, without ever being seen or held by the birth mother, is an outdated scenario, but it remains a persistent fear. Some birth mothers worry they will place the baby for adoption without knowing anything about the baby's life. They may worry they will have no control over the decisions made for the baby's placement or be denied information about the baby afterwards. Although many years ago adoptive placements were kept strictly within the control of professionals, there is now much more openness and opportunity for birth mothers and their families to interact. Information about degrees of openness is more clearly outlined in Chapter 4.

Some birth parents do not look at all their options because they are afraid they might actually choose adoption. For some people the idea of adoption sounds perfectly impossible, and for girls finding themselves in an out-of-wedlock pregnancy, the thought can be terrifying. Without knowing much about adoption, besides maybe the isolated experience of a friend who was adopted, they will rapidly develop reasons why it is not something they should consider. Few teenagers can imagine reasons compelling enough to simply hand a cute little baby over to someone else and walk away.

Often a girl may discover a pregnancy, and before doing anything else, she determines that she will keep the baby, no matter what sacrifices are involved. And if she looks at the options before her, she might decide that the best course of action is one she cannot get herself to do—place her baby for adoption. I have frequently seen birth parents make a serious mistake in believing one decision is best but choosing another because they do not feel personally strong enough to do what is right.

Others struggle in considering adoption because they believe it would mean some kind of permanent unhappiness. But placing a baby for adoption does not mean the birth mother will sacrifice everything. The very things she is giving to her child through adoption she makes more possible for herself. It is never just the life of the unborn child that Heavenly Father cares about; He also wants what is best for the young birth parents involved.

Let me qualify this by reiterating what has been said by the Brethren. When choosing, "the best interests of the child should be the paramount consideration" (First Presidency Letter, 15 June 1998). I believe it is not only helpful but necessary to put the best interests of the child ahead of every other consideration. But I also do not believe that Heavenly Father would sacrifice the happiness and salvation of the birth parents for the sake of the child. He loves them both. The Brethren have not recommended that adoption be considered simply because they want what's best for the baby. They have suggested that adoption be considered because they want both the birth parents and the baby to find their way back to their Father in Heaven.

Another impediment to considering adoption is the incorrect idea that an uncooperative birth father can prevent the birth mother from placing her child. Different states have different laws, but many states now employ a birth father registry. Birth fathers who have an interest in decisions made about the child must register their paternity through the judicial system. If he does this, then he shows a level of interest and responsibility and can therefore have a say in the decision made for the child. If he does not do this, his rights will be forfeited if the birth mother chooses to place the baby for adoption. In cases of adoption, working with a reliable adoption agency will help ensure that sound legal counsel is given. When placing privately, it is helpful to seek counsel from an attorney familiar with adoption.

In most cases, it is best to involve both parties in making a decision about a pregnancy. Contrary to what some may believe, the vast majority of birth fathers care about their child, just as the birth mothers do. In situations of abandonment or abuse, however, state laws allow for the parent who is shouldering the greater responsibility to have more of a say in the outcome. If a birth mother feels she has no choice about placing her baby because she does not believe the birth father will sign the forms making it possible, she may unnecessarily eliminate an option that would have been very positive for herself and the baby.

I have also seen many birth fathers who initially stood adamantly against adoption but came to feel it was best and ultimately signed the forms making it possible. It is a process for them, just as it is for the birth mothers. They likely have incorrect information or beliefs about adoption, and as those false beliefs are dispelled, they can come to recognize the great benefits for their child and themselves in considering adoption. It is best for a birth mother or birth father in this situation to seek counsel from the caseworker and/or a lawyer to address the legal issues.

Another fallacy that prevents some from considering the adoption choice is the notion that babies who are placed for adoption somehow end up compromised emotionally or psychologically. In the past there has been the idea that those placed for adoption feel unwanted, abandoned, or unloved. This is simply not the case. There is resounding evidence to show that children who are adopted actually fare better in most cases and overwhelmingly better than those raised by single parents.

I have been amazed by people who felt it was morally better to abort a baby than to place a baby for adoption. There are those who feel that aborting a child is a more responsible and kinder decision for that child than allowing him to be raised by anyone other than his biological parents. This feeling may go back, in part, to the belief that children who are placed for adoption will almost certainly struggle with psychological and emotional problems. It plays on the idea that a child can never feel as loved by or as attached to parents who did not give birth to him. It also assumes that no one can love a child more or even as much as the biological parents of that child. And yet, adoptive parents who have come to realize what a divine gift a child can be, through their years of struggling to bring a child into their home, have a tremendous capacity to love an adopted child. I have prayed often that I would appreciate and treasure my own biological children as much as the adoptive parents and birth parents whom I know have treasured babies placed for adoption.

Jerry Harris, a marriage and family therapist who has spent many years working in the field of adoption, shared his findings on these issues:

To many birth parents and adoptive parents alike the well-being of the prospective adoptive child is an important question. The general public often has a negative view of the mental health of adopted children. This is often because of two factors: (1) Some early studies found negative outcomes when investigating the social and mental health of the adopted child, and (2) The popular press often picks up on the adopted status of anyone reported in a negative light (e.g. criminal behavior, eccentric activities, etc.).

There was a time when the term "adopted child syndrome" was used in the media. While this term was not often used in the clinical community, its occasional use in the popular press assisted in creating a negative image of adoption.

Questions were raised about the well-being of adopted children. How will the adopted child fare? Is that child better off than if he had been raised by a single mother? Is adoption, after everything is evaluated, ultimately good for the child?

There is abundant research to indicate that adopted children do as well or even better than their non-adopted siblings or the general population in any area of competence in which they have been compared.

Despite the fact that adoption has been used as a scapegoat, studies have concluded that adoptees do not have more problems than their non-adopted siblings with whom they are raised (Peter L. Benson, Anu R. Sharma, L.P. and Eugene C. Roehlkepartain, "Growing Up Adopted," *Search Institute,* June 1994 http://www.search-institute.org/archives/gua.htm). A large survey conducted in 1993 by the Search Institute included 881 adopted adolescents, 1,262 parents and 78 non-adopted siblings. The authors of this study realized some overwhelmingly positive findings, some of which were as follows:

• Adopted adolescents are as likely to report positive self-esteem as their non-adopted siblings and more likely than a comparable national sample. The vast majority said they seldom or never wish they lived with their birth parents.

• Adopted adolescents are far less likely than adolescents in general to experience parental divorce or separation (90% of adoptive marriages were still intact), and adoptive families are marked by high

educational attainment and family income above the national average. Also, adopted adolescents are as likely as their non-adopted siblings, and as likely as or more likely than their non-adopted peers, to
report positive child-parent relationships, warmth, and positive communication.

   • The study found that the issue of adoption is not predictive of
mental health of adopted children. Families who promote an acceptance of the child's differences promote healthy development.

   These findings strongly indicate that adopted children and their
families are doing an excellent job at overcoming the obstacles theo-
rized by some researchers.

   I believe it is fair to say that most adopted children demonstrate
successful adjustment at a rate comparable to children in general.
The following summary by Dr. Jerome Smith in his book *The
Realities of Adoption* (Lanham, Madison Books, 1997) reflects my
thoughts on adoption: "A number of variables, previously thought to
bear on outcome and therefore major issues in agency adoption practice, proved to have no factual basis.[. . .] The principal factors [of
success] seem to be parental attitudes toward the child—their unconditional acceptance of him and the degree to which they have worked
through feelings of entitlement."

   The evidence is highly weighted for us to believe that adoption is
much better for the child than single parenting, and adoptive children overwhelmingly turn out well-adjusted and successful.
Therefore the birth parent asking herself if adoption is a viable
option for her to consider regarding what is best for her prospective
child is given every indication that adoption is a good option.
Adoptive parents wondering if adoption of an infant is going to be
a successful endeavor are also given every encouragement to proceed.

As Jerry Harris states, there is resounding evidence that being adopted
can be a positive, rather than a negative factor in a child's development of
family attachment and personal identity.

Once misconceptions and other pieces of misinformation are dispelled
and factual information is obtained about the choice of adoption, the decision must become one of much thought and sincere prayer. Those who are

considering adoption but do not know where to turn should talk with their ecclesiastical leaders or contact any LDS Family Services office for direction. Other reliable, trustworthy adoption agencies or advocates may be available to them as well.

Less informed people criticize adoption as being a selfish choice, an easy way out. It is certainly not an easy way out, and to gather the courage to place that child in another mother's arms is a selfless act, not a selfish one.

Adoption is a very difficult choice to make, especially at first. One of my clients wisely described her two choices, single parenting versus adoption, this way: "With single parenting, it is easier at first and it gets harder and more painful as time goes by; with adoption, it is harder at first and then gets less painful." For Josie, it was her vision of how things might be for her child in the future that helped her decide, finally, to place her child for adoption.

JOSIE'S STORY: "I WANTED MY BOY TO HAVE CHICKENS"

"I wanted my boy to have chickens," Josie said as she shared her story in a support group for birth parents. She was resting her hands on her protruding belly, and she spoke softly to the many listening girls. Josie knew that many of those girls were still trying to decide what choice to make about their unborn babies, and she also knew that many had already decided to single parent, as she herself had decided at one point.

"When I found out I was pregnant, I was scared and disappointed in myself. I knew I had been making the wrong choices and that I needed to get my life back on track. But I didn't make changes right away. I just tried to keep my head above water." Josie was like many young girls I see dealing with an out-of-wedlock pregnancy. Although they have made some wrong choices, many have a sense that they are still loved by their Heavenly Father and should go back to the things they know to be true.

"I knew from the beginning that I wanted to keep my baby. My baby was not *unwanted,* just unplanned." Josie loved her baby; she had from the beginning. And as she shared her story with the girls around her, she rubbed her stomach and smiled when she felt movement from inside. Her gentle manner could not hide her strong will and sense of independence, and I could see clearly her desire to do right by her child.

"So I made plans to be a single mom. My son's father didn't want to be in our lives, but I knew we could make it anyway. I got an apartment and moved in when I was about three months along. I quit college and found a job that could support me and my unborn son. And we could have made it."

"Then why are you planning to place your baby for adoption—I mean, if you don't have to?" The question came from Kari, a younger girl in the group session who felt that placing for adoption was only for those who didn't have any other choice. Josie's reasons were very personal to her, but she shared them in the hope of helping the other girls.

"I was standing on the back patio of my apartment one day, where I could see into the backyard of a house around the block. I was watching the children in the family. There were four of them, along with a mom to stay home with them and a dad to care and provide for them. The children were running around together in the backyard, chasing chickens! They were laughing together and tripping over each other and tripping over the chickens. Tears filled my eyes as all I could think was, 'I want my boy to have chickens.'" Tears filled her eyes again. She so wanted for her son to have the kind of life she believed he deserved.

Josie went on to share her adoption decision. It hadn't been easy to think about, but it would have been impossible for her had she not had such a compelling love for her child. If Josie had done what *she* wanted to do, she would have been buying baby clothes. She had been willing to sacrifice her own hopes and dreams for the sake of this precious child. But when she realized she would be sacrificing *his* opportunities, she had to rethink her decision. When she thought about what she wanted for her son, instead of what she wanted for herself, the decision became clear to her. She needed to place her baby for adoption with a family who was prepared to give him those things he would so very much need—things like a temple sealing, a mother with the time and resources to devote to his upbringing, a full-time father, and, of course, chickens to chase in the backyard.

Josie's experience was not unlike that of so many young women and young men who are intently working to make the best decision for their baby and for themselves. After discovering a pregnancy and dealing with the losses associated with that discovery, it is very painful to imagine losing the child as well. Coming to the decision of placing the child for adoption involves seeking a true and realistic understanding of what is involved for the birth parents and for the child. It often involves much time, thought, and prayer to determine what is best.

There are many ways for those involved in a decision about adoption to come to the right choice for them. Loving and supportive family members can give strength and guidance. Working with an unbiased counselor who supports the birth parents' ability to arrive at a good decision can also be helpful, and the counsel of a loving bishop is essential for spiritual guidance in discovering Heavenly Father's desires for that child. But it is never an easy decision. It is a decision that can only be made by a loving parent after much studying, pondering, and praying. And it is a decision that should be respected as one made out of love for the child. President Gordon B. Hinckley has stated, "Experience has shown that adoption, difficult though this may be for the young mother, may afford a greater opportunity for the child to live a life of happiness" (*Ensign,* Nov. 1994, 53).

When birth parents are seeking the right path for themselves and their unborn child, those choices can best be made by becoming educated about the outcome of all of the options, being prayerful and humble in seeking the best choice, and being actively intent on finding out what is best for those involved, both in the present and in the long run, especially for the child. If the child's needs are placed first, birth parents will find themselves making the best decisions all along the path of adoption.

Chapter Four

THE PATH OF ADOPTION

MARCH 29—

This pregnancy is quickly coming to an end. I have never felt so huge in my life, but I will miss feeling this sweet little girl kick me awake in the mornings. It might sound hard to believe, but I'm not sure I'm ready for it to be over. I am really going to miss having her with me.

The adoptive family I chose for her are wonderful, they really are. I met them last week, and I felt like I had known them forever. Ellen is getting her degree in child development, and Rick is a general contractor. They sent me pictures of her nursery, all decorated and waiting for her to be born. She's going to be a very fortunate little girl.

I just can't think too long about what it will be like to actually place her in their arms. That will be the most difficult day of my whole life.

Making the decision to pursue adoption is only the beginning. Many other decisions follow. And the time between making the choice to place the baby for adoption and then actually doing so is a path of both practical matters and matters of the heart. It is a time to rely upon God, upon family members and loved ones, and upon professional and ecclesiastical help. This is a time when the paths of birth parents and adoptive couples come together, joining their experience of adoption. And while they are together only briefly, both the birth parents and the adoptive parents are forever affected by their counterparts and by the child they love.

After adoption is chosen, one must consider how much confidentiality is desired. Birth parents and adoptive couples each go through a selection process to find the right match—birth parents choosing the adoptive parents who will raise their baby, and adoptive parents deciding what type of baby they desire to adopt. After these choices are made, birth parents and adoptive parents will most likely meet face-to-face before the baby is born as a way to prepare everyone for the upcoming placement of the child. Along with these decisions and the logistical preparations, there are important emotional preparations to be made.

Perhaps the most intense point in the journey of adoption is the actual placement of the baby. Months of preparation for an adoption lead to the day of the baby's birth, and the subsequent placement will finally, yet all too soon, arrive. After the placement of the baby comes the painful and difficult period of adjustment when the birth parents and their families have to know for certain that the decisions they have made were the right ones. During that time, they may question everything they know personally and spiritually, but if they are able, they come out of that period with new insight, understanding, and peace.

WHICH TYPE OF ADOPTION TO CHOOSE?

When I ask clients what type of adoption they prefer, I am referring to the degree of openness or confidentiality desired by both parties. Adoptions are generally on more of a scale of openness rather than being simply "open" or "closed."

There are benefits of openness and also reasons for confidentiality. The important thing is that those involved—birth parents and adoptive parents— each decide how much openness they desire with the other party. Both parties need to feel comfortable with the level of interaction they will maintain, for their own sakes as well as for the sake of their family members and for the benefit of their child.

This is an aspect of adoption about which people have very strong and differing opinions. There is not simply one correct approach to be chosen. A combination of openness and confidentiality may very well be the most healthy way to go.

When I began my work in adoption, the agency was doing strictly confidential adoptions. This meant that the birth parent not only did not know the names and locations of his or her baby's adoptive parents but also did not communicate with them either before or after the birth of the baby. The couple was often chosen by the caseworker and not by the birth parents, and the birth family relied on a small amount of information given by the caseworker. The adoptive parents had very little information given them about the birth parents of their baby, and they never had any face-to-face contact with them.

Adoptions are handled very differently today because, generally, more openness has shown to be a benefit not only for the birth parents and the adoptive parents but for the adopted child as well. Certainly as adoptive placements have moved towards more interaction and openness, concerns have arisen. For instance, how would more openness in adoption affect the birth parents and the adoptive parents? More importantly, how would more openness affect the child being adopted? What we know now is that although confidentiality may be important in some areas of adoption, there are some real advantages with openness as well.

THE CASE FOR OPENNESS

1. Increased contact before and after the adoptive placement can help the birth mother and birth father feel more at peace with their decision to place their baby for adoption. Birth parents who receive letters and pictures from their child's future parents before the birth of their baby can feel more secure in their decision to place when the time comes. It is often helpful for a birth mother or birth father to develop a relationship with the prospective adoptive parents prior to placement. It can allow her to picture her baby within their family and develop feelings of trust that she will not be forgotten either by the adoptive parents or her child. Correspondence through letters and pictures after the placement allows for the birth parent to see that all of the reasons for placing that child are indeed being fulfilled, meaning that the baby is happy, secure, and loved. This allows for the birth mother or birth father to move on with life in a healthy and happy manner, knowing the baby is taken care of in a healthy and happy manner as well. Openness in the experience allows for birth parents to feel more in control and less easily panicked about the situation. This can build self-esteem and help them see that they can choose the direction of their lives, replacing bad choices with good ones.

2. Openness can help the adoptive parents feel and be more secure in the placement. Through their contact with the birth parents, adoptive parents can come to love and trust the birth parents. They can better understand why the birth parents are placing and feel assured that they do not desire to threaten the adoption later on. These feelings of greater comfort and security can help the adoptive parents move forward as the parents of the child, without worrying every day that they will become attached and then lose him. They can also feel more peaceful in the placement knowing that the birth mother or father is happy and moving on with life goals. Rather than feeling sadness at breaking a young mother's heart by "taking away" her baby, they can recognize themselves as having played an intrinsic part of an eternally binding experience that is positive for all of the parties involved.

3. Openness can help the child who has been adopted have a more stable life. Because contact between the birth parents and the adoptive parents can help the placement to be more stable, the child can consequently have a more stable and secure life. His parents can be more comfortable with the idea of adoption and can then raise the child to feel more secure with himself as an adopted child. But more importantly, the child can grow up learning more about his birth parents. Not only can the child who was adopted know from his parents what his birth parents were like and how they felt, but he will have letters from them telling him exactly why he was placed for adoption. He may also have pictures of his birth parents and the advantage of more extensive medical background information about his birth parents and their families.

These are only some of the benefits to the increased openness now possible in adoptive placements, but there are some cautionary points as well.

The Case for More Confidentiality

1. Too much contact can inhibit the birth parent's ability to move forward in her or his own life. Placing a baby for adoption is a major life event and can often be a turning point for a young person's life. For a time the birth parent desires and needs contact with the child's adoptive parents and family for reassurance and support, as well as to ease the pain she or he is experiencing after saying good-bye to the baby. There comes a point, however, when the birth mother or father needs to be able to move forward without still holding on to the baby. Whether she does not want to let go of contact with the child or feels unable to do so without feeling she has abandoned the baby, having limits on openness allows for, or encourages, moving forward when the time is right.

2. Too much contact can inhibit the adoptive parents' ability to move forward as the parents of the child. Maintaining a great deal of correspondence with the birth parents may be extremely beneficial and rewarding to the adoptive parents, but it can be exhausting as well. Having limits on openness can allow them to move forward and focus on their child, living a life as parents rather than forever as adoptive parents. If the adoptive parents are feeling guilty because they have not shared every detail of the child's life, contact may be an unhealthy hindrance to their own ability to be good parents.

3. Too much contact can take away the opportunity for the child to decide how involved he wants to be with his birth family. In considering what is best where openness is concerned, it is important to remember the child in this equation and not just the birth parents and the adoptive parents. Part of the reason the child was placed for adoption was so he could have a happy, "normal" life. Growing up with two mothers and two fathers actively involved can cause more harm than good. One adult adoptee said to me as the openness in adoption began rapidly increasing, "Remember the child's feelings in all of this. When my birth mother found me when I was twenty-eight, it was a lot to deal with. I'm glad I had the chance to meet her, but I wonder what that would be like for someone who was much younger or less prepared to deal with it. Just remember to do all possible to allow the children being adopted some control in their own lives."

Although there are strong benefits to openness, there are benefits to some degree of confidentiality as well. The level of openness desired is something to be closely evaluated and carefully studied out by both the birth parents and the adoptive parents. It is possible to find a good balance with the contact desired as well as the boundaries necessary for everyone to move forward in a healthy, happy manner. Establishing a schedule of correspondence in the beginning may help to clearly define the desired level of contact. Everyone's expectations should be clear to the others.

Just as deciding on the desired level of openness is an important step in the process of preparing for the adoption, so is determining which adoptive parents are right for a child.

CHOOSING A FAMILY, CHOOSING A CHILD

One birth mother shared with me her feelings after choosing to place her baby for adoption. She looked perfectly worn out by the process of coming to that decision. She put it this way: "I thought after I made the choice to place the baby for adoption, I would be through making the really hard decisions."

Choosing a family is yet another big decision, especially when the birth mother has just recently made one of the biggest decisions in her young life and thought she would have less to think about so intensely once it was made. But the path of adoption is one with ongoing decisions that cannot be taken lightly. Take Courtney's experience as an example. Courtney was trying to find the perfect family for her baby.

COURTNEY AND ERIC'S STORY: SELECTING A FAMILY

"I just don't know how I can choose a family for my baby." Courtney sits with her face in her hands, resting her elbows on a stack of profiles of prospective adoptive parents. She has read through them already, taken them home, read through them again and again. Her family has looked at them also, as has the birth father, Eric, who is sitting next to her. Surprisingly, she is not having trouble finding one she likes; she is having trouble narrowing it down from the three she likes best.

"They all seem like such great people. I like the first family because they are so active. They like skiing, camping, and water sports. I can picture my baby in a home like that, having so many great experiences. I like the second family because they are both educated and financially very strong. They seem more mature and are very stable in their marriage, after being married twelve years with no kids. But then I look at the third family, and they're so much like my own goofy family! They are just everyday people, not super wealthy or really unique, but they spend a lot of time playing games with their extended families, they love to read like I do, and the adoptive mom teaches piano lessons just like my mom did all the years I was growing up. I thought I would have a problem finding a family I liked, not finding too many families I liked." She was frustrated but positive as she shared her struggles with me.

"That's because you were so sure you would never find a family you felt was good enough for your baby," Eric teased. He good-naturedly bumped her shoulder with his. "I think they're all great. I'm behind you with whichever family you feel is the right one."

"See what I have to deal with?" She smiled. "Everyone is so supportive, and no one will just tell me which one to choose!"

"Courtney, you know we love you, but you and Eric need to be the ones to make this decision." She knew I was teasing her, but she also knew I was right. This part was hard, but it was good for her.

Courtney had not always been at this point. After taking a very long time to make a decision about placing her baby for adoption, she felt sure she wouldn't be able to know a family well enough through their profile alone to select them to raise her child. And she was considerably nervous about looking at families at all.

"It just feels so permanent," she had told me during one of our sessions, "as though I'm actually going to come to the point of placing my baby into their arms. That really scares me."

Choosing a family is a tremendous leap of faith. Even though a great deal of information is available about prospective adoptive couples, it is still difficult for a young mother to choose which one is the best family for her baby. She might want a family mirroring her own, like Courtney had been considering. She may have had a bumpy childhood and therefore wants a family very different from her own. Often she has a list of characteristics that she has in mind, only to change them after she begins reading the profiles. Whatever her expectations about the family she will choose, the decision is never simple.

In many cases, a birth mother chooses a family through some sort of connection, either through an attorney, a physician, or someone the birth parent's family member knows. If she is going through an adoption agency, they will likely provide her with several families from which to choose. Her experience in selecting a family can be very different depending on the type of adoption she chooses, but in any situation she will work to find the best family, one that can meet her needs and expectations for herself and her child.

Many birth mothers I work with are approached by people who want to be considered as parents for her baby. They may act respectfully or be extremely pushy, and her reaction to them can be different based on how she feels about being approached. When word spreads that a pregnant young woman is considering adoption, potential parents come out of the woodwork. Although many people may feel it important to make their availability known as a prospective adoptive couple, it is also important to respect the birth mother's feelings and desires in the process of choosing a family. It is sometimes only the connection she feels to the adoptive parents that gives her the strength she needs to follow through with an adoptive placement.

It is also important that the birth parents find a couple who is compatible in their desires for contact and openness. When the birth parents and the adoptive parents have differing ideas about what constitutes openness in a placement but do not discover those differences until after the baby is placed, feelings of disappointment and frustration are inevitable. Being clear about expectations in the beginning can prevent a great deal of heartache later on.

Of course, choosing a family for one's baby is not a simple decision arrived at by weighing all the good and bad qualities and selecting the most practical fit. It is an intensely personal and spiritual decision. For most birth parents, the decision is based on the idea that there is a *right* family for that baby, one that will be the very best family for that particular child. For prospective adoptive parents, applying to be chosen is an equally arduous task.

DENNIS AND KAREN'S STORY: PREPARING THE PROFILE

Dennis and Karen had been filling out paperwork for what seemed like ages now, writing and describing every detail about themselves and their lives. The process had felt somewhat invasive, and Karen had thought more than once about the many parents who do not need to be *approved* by someone as good parents before they can finally have a baby. Still, she knew it would be worth it.

She thought for a minute about her close friends Jeff and Jana, friends she and Dennis had come to love through their shared struggles with infertility. She thought of how she had seen Jana go through this same process in their pursuit of adoption. She remembered Jana's concern that everything be just right in their profile. And she thought of the precious daughter that had been placed with Jeff and Jana only a few months earlier. Watching them with their daughter was the turning point for her and Dennis, seeing how much they loved that baby *and* their daughter's birth mother. They had felt more strongly than ever after their friends' placement that they should also pursue adoption. And now here they were, almost finished with their home study. (This file contains information about the couple. It is generally required in order to pursue an adoption of any kind.)

Karen had been prepared for this process by Jana. It seemed a small task to write her own profile, as she thought of the choice that lay before the birth mothers who would be reading her information in selecting parents for their babies. But now as she described herself and Dennis, she hoped she would be able to show a clear picture of what their family was like.

"Make sure you describe me as extremely buff and strikingly handsome," Dennis added after talking about what they wanted to share.

"Do you think she would recognize you when she meets you if I do that?" Humor lightened the burden they shared and broke the all-too-present silence in a home where there weren't any children making noise. "I'll say you are somewhat attractive whenever you aren't wearing those awful green shorts you have on right now!"

I had no concerns for either Karen or Dennis, and during the approval process I was not searching for some reason to eliminate their opportunity to adopt. I knew already that they were good, faithful people who were doing all they could to be wonderful parents when the time came. I also knew they were human and wanted to present them as such in their home study.

"Somewhere out there is a birth mother who is looking for the qualities you possess. If we present you as an immaculately perfect couple, then we will not only be lying to the birth mother but will also be taking from you an opportunity to find just the right fit with a birth mother and a child." It might be surprising to some, but many birth mothers look for parents who are not perfect. I still laugh when I think of one young birth mother who described the couple she was looking for: "I want a mother who is very nice, and I want the father to be educated but not too smart!" What she meant was that she wanted him to have a good education to support the family, but she didn't want someone who was a real intellectual. The couple she chose had a caseworker who trusted in the system enough to present the prospective parents as they really were, rather than as they wanted to appear.

Next came the discussion about the child's race. Dennis and Karen realized that they differed on which races they were open to and had to work out which to mark on their preference checklist. Such a decision does not reflect bigotry. There are simply additional responsibilities involved in adopting a child transracially, and they had to think through whether they were prepared for that or not. They also had to decide whether they would be open to an at-risk placement, where the child's legal status might still be pending. They had to choose whether they wanted to be considered for twins or a sibling group.

But the truly difficult point in the process came when they had to make decisions about what qualities to accept or reject in the child they were hoping to adopt. As the list of questions began, they found they had to discuss each one at length. There were questions about medical conditions in the birth mother, the birth father, and the child. They had to choose whether they would accept a child presented to them with a club foot, a cleft lip, even hay fever.

The issue of genetics leads to two mistakes I sometimes see adoptive couples make in their decision to adopt a child. The first is the idea that any baby conceived out of wedlock is compromised genetically more than one conceived by a married couple. Although we might like to believe that couples who are married have no familial genetic defects and only babies who are conceived out of wedlock might suffer this plight, this is simply not the case. I find myself disturbed by this notion, particularly when I see couples taking an elitest approach to choosing a child. They might say they are not open to a child whose biological parents or grandparents have an ailment such as diabetes, allergies, or near-sightedness. Certainly none of us wants our child to suffer from these problems. Still, if that same couple evaluated their own biological background information, they would likely find some of the same concerns. Adoptive parents who are too restrictive with respect to the traits that are acceptable to them may limit their opportunities unnecessarily.

Equally problematic is the choice to adopt indiscriminately, believing that any and all possible problems with the child will be overcome. I have seen in adoptive couples the desire to adopt any child without considering the baby's biological and emotional background information. A couple who feels they would like to adopt a child should be certain they and their family members are prepared for any known problems. Such a situation is most likely to occur in the placement of an older child or a child with special needs, but in any circumstance it is important to understand and be prepared for concerns that exist. A couple may feel that if they love the child enough, they can overcome any biological or psychological problems the child might have. In choosing to adopt, prospective parents should carefully consider and evaluate *all* of the known information before adopting in order to have a more stable and successful placement.

After what seemed like months of working on their profile, Dennis and Karen finally finished it. They had searched their feelings on many issues and learned much about each other in the process. And along the way, they had become all the more unified as propsective parents.

MEETING FACE-TO-FACE

Adoption was once a very private affair in which birth parents and adoptive couples were kept secret from one another. It has proven healthier for everyone involved to have more open communication in the process—within the reasonable boundaries noted earlier. Birth parents and adoptive couples generally meet each other face-to-face well before the birth of the child. This is one of the most important events in the journey of adoption, and although these meetings are naturally full of anxiety for both parties, I have seen them become overwhelmingly positive experiences.

CARRIANNE, KEVIN, AND NAN'S STORY: MEETING FACE-TO-FACE

Nervous didn't begin to describe how Carrianne felt as she waited in the small office at the end of the hall. As she smoothed her shirt, she spoke anxiously with her mother and father. Carrianne thought of how much she had liked this couple from the first moment of reading their profile and how after several weeks she had finally chosen them to be *the ones*. And so she was both excited and scared at the prospect of finally meeting face-to-face. What would they be like in person? Would they look like they had in their pictures? Would the meeting be awkward, or casual, or something in between? Mostly, would they like her?

Walking down the hallway, Nan and Kevin were having many of the same thoughts. What would she say to them? What would she look like? Would she ask questions they didn't know how to answer? And how would it be to finally meet the biological mother of their first child? Nan thought how excited she had been to learn about this baby and to come to know Carrianne through the letters they had exchanged. She knew she would like Carrianne—she already did—for her thoughtful attitude and the spirituality she had sensed in the letters. But she still felt worried, worried that maybe

Carrianne would not like them after the meeting. Or worse, maybe they would become attached and then something would change and she wouldn't place the baby with them after all.

As they entered the office, Carrianne and her parents stood to greet them, and Nan couldn't help but give Carrianne a hug. Within minutes, both Nan and Carrianne had tears rolling down their faces, followed in suit by Kevin and then Carrianne's mother. As they all sat down, there was a moment of silence while everyone gathered their feelings, and then Carrianne began to talk. "What are you going to name her?"

That is a normal question to ask an expectant mother, not traditionally tied to intense feelings of emotion; however, the young girl with the impossibly large belly asked the question of the woman who was clearly not pregnant.

"We've always planned to name our first baby Claire, Claire Elizabeth, after Kevin's mother and my grandmother." Nan watched Carrianne carefully as she spoke, looking for a hint as to her feelings about the name they had chosen.

But Carrianne was simply polite, saying that she thought it was a very pretty name. "Have you already decided how you're going to tell her she is adopted?" She was again listening intently for Nan's response.

Kevin looked at Nan before sharing his thoughts. "Well, we just plan to always talk about it. We want this baby to grow up knowing that she is loved by both her adoptive parents and her birth parents, enough to be placed for adoption so she could have everything she needed in her life."

"We want her to grow up knowing everything she can about you. What do you want us to tell her?" Nan squeezed Kevin's hand tighter as she asked.

"Tell her I love her. Tell her I will always love her. Tell her she was placed so she could grow up with a mother *and* a father, something that was very important to me. Tell her I never placed her because I didn't want her. Help her to know that her Heavenly Father loves her and chose you to be her parents. And teach her to listen to her parents more than I listened to my own, because they know what they're talking about." Her mother smiled as she placed her arm around the shoulders of her daughter. "And don't let her ever forget me. Because I will never forget her."

This was the first time for this birth mother and adoptive couple to sit face-to-face and share their hopes and dreams for the same unborn baby girl.

The birth mother had been through a refiner's fire, repenting of mistakes she had made and making the most difficult and most unselfish decisions of her young life. The couple had also been through a refiner's fire, growing individually and as a couple through seven years of trying unsuccessfully to conceive a child.

This was not the way any of them had felt their lives would be played out, and they had experienced pain they would not have wished on anyone. But I don't think either would have exchanged the pain for all they had learned. They had each, in their own sphere, grown. The adoptive couple would never take for granted the blessing of being parents, and neither would the young birth mother when she was someday blessed to raise a family of her own.

During the course of the meeting they found they had many things in common. They learned that Carrianne's love for animals of all kinds was shared by Nan, when Kevin shared how she was always rescuing some disadvantaged animal of one sort or another. They discovered that when Nan and Kevin felt they should put in their papers for adoption, Carrianne was just discovering she was pregnant. They realized that through a series of experiences, different but alike, they had come together to provide a life for a baby entirely dependent on the decisions made by those who loved her.

They felt a kinship at the end of the meeting, a closeness described by all present as one of extended family members who hadn't seen one another for a time. And as they embraced in parting, they each whispered feelings of appreciation and gratitude and expressed that they would be in one another's prayers as they separately anticipated the birth of their baby girl.

The next time they would meet would be shortly after the baby's birth. Until that time, they would correspond to support one another as they all awaited the coming baby.

Preparing for the Big Day

It is important for a birth mother to be emotionally prepared for the placement of her child, both to give her the strength she will need to follow through when the time comes and also to allow her to move forward in a healthy and peaceful manner afterwards. It is as important for her own well-being as it is for the well-being of the baby and the adoptive couple that she be able to follow through with her decision to place her baby for adoption if she feels it is the best thing to do.

Adoption is a remarkable thing. Even though the experiences and details vary, the feelings experienced are often the same. And those who have been through it in any capacity—the heartbreak, the sadness, the happiness, the hope, the love, and the humility—all attest to the sacred nature of the experience. It is important to respect all those who are involved in the process, their opinions and their feelings. And because there are so many others who are intimately involved, there is a need to go into the experience well prepared. Nicole's story shows how important preparation is to having a positive hospital experience.

Nicole's Story: Emotionally Unprepared

Nicole had been planning to place her baby for adoption from the beginning. From the first moment she learned she was pregnant, she knew that adoption was going to be best for herself and for her child. And she was not a girl who was easily swayed when she believed something to be best. She was strong from the first time I met her.

Nicole was a small girl with short, blonde hair. Despite being raised in a strong Latter-day Saint family, she had been dating Kim, who was not a member of the Church, for more than two years and had become sexually involved. But she felt now, because of his rebellious and sometimes controlling personality and behaviors, that she did not want him to have a lifelong influence over her or their child.

When she learned she was pregnant shortly before moving to Utah to attend Brigham Young University, she chose, through her bishop's and parents' counsel, to move to Utah anyway until after she had completed the repentance process and could attend BYU. Because Nicole felt so strongly, as did her parents and bishop, that adoption was best, this plan was set into motion. So it was that Nicole found herself in Utah carrying a baby she felt belonged to another set of parents.

She was very open in counseling and actively involved in group sessions, sharing her feelings that it was better for this baby to be raised by a mother and father who were married and well-prepared to care for and raise a child. "I know that I could provide for this baby. My parents would help me and of course we would love her and provide for her. But I know that Kim would be fighting me all the time, about everything I did, where she was concerned. And more than that, I'm afraid Kim's mother would try to take control or even push him to take the baby away from me. I just don't think it is best for her to grow up in a divorce-like situation."

The months went by. As Nicole proceeded to choose a family and meet them, she continued to feel that placing her baby would be a matter of logic and sensibility and that she wouldn't have an emotionally difficult time following through when the baby was born. Although she didn't feel a strong connection to the adoptive parents at the face-to-face meeting, she had faith that Heavenly Father would lead her to the "right" family. It wasn't until she held the tiny infant in her arms for the first time that she realized how incredibly difficult saying good-bye to her would be.

Nicole was blindsided by her strong feelings of love and attachment for her baby. Her feelings of intense love were valid, of course, and only to be expected in her situation. But because she had always planned to place the baby for adoption, she hadn't expected to feel so attached. She cried for two days in the hospital as her sense of practicality about the well-being of her child collided with the emotions of motherly love that flooded over her. Despite hours of counseling with her parents, who found themselves also painfully wanting to take this granddaughter home, and with her bishop, who tried to remain an unbiased counselor in the midst of the pain he was witnessing, Nicole decided to return to her home state and parent her baby.

I asked Nicole about her reasons for pursuing adoption for her baby in the first place. She recounted the reasons we had discussed so many times in the prior months. I asked Nicole if those reasons had changed now, if the logic on which she had based her decision to place was now irrelevant. She said no, there was still logic in those reasons.

"I just don't feel I could ever part with her. I know the problems will be problems I will have to face with my decision to keep her. I guess it just sounds better to me than having to give her up."

When Nicole was released after her two days in the hospital, I said good-bye to her parents and to her as they headed back home with the baby. I encouraged them to contact the local LDS Family Services representative for counseling as they pursued their new plan, and I shared with them my desire to be helpful if there was anything they needed in the future. I also asked

Nicole to keep in touch with me to let me know how she and her baby were doing so I could offer encouragement.

As Nicole left, I felt sad. I was sad not primarily for the adoptive couple who had prepared to become parents that day, although that was indeed sad, but they would be chosen again and have another chance. My real sadness was for Nicole for a number of reasons.

Nicole had now had two strong experiences in which she knew a certain choice was best but did not feel personally strong enough to do it. The first experience was the conception of her baby, something she chose to do even though she knew and believed she would be safer and happier if she remained morally pure. The second was choosing to parent her baby when she felt a strong conviction that it would be better for herself and her baby if she chose adoption. She would likely continue to see herself as someone who had strong convictions but was not strong enough to follow through with those convictions and do what she believed was the right thing. That is why it is so important to prepare for the day of placement, not only for the well-being of the child but also for the well-being of the birth mother and birth father.

Nicole's story did not end this way, however. As I have said, Nicole was a strong person, and she ultimately did something much more difficult than saying good-bye to her baby after two days. She said good-bye after two weeks.

Nicole called me on a Sunday morning from her home state. She said she felt she needed to place her baby for adoption and would be leaving right away to drive straight through to my office. The family she had previously chosen was no longer available, so she asked me to prepare new family profiles so she could review them and place her baby daughter with a family that evening. She told me she would explain everything when she arrived but that she and her parents felt that this needed to be done for the sake of her baby.

After twelve hours of driving, Nicole and her parents arrived at a nearly empty LDS Family Services office on that Sunday afternoon, carrying a beautiful two-week-old baby girl. Nicole shared with me her experiences over the past two weeks. Upon arriving home, she and her parents had spent some honeymoon time with this new baby. They were from a small town, and many came to visit and express their willingness to help in any way they could. These visitors included the baby's father, Kim, and his mother. They quickly wanted to spend more and more time with the baby, including taking the baby to spend days at their home without Nicole. Discussions were emotional and heated between Nicole and Kim, often involving Kim's mother and Nicole's parents. Fairly immediately, Nicole and her parents began to see that the life of this precious baby daughter was becoming exactly what they had so much wanted to avoid. When Nicole planned to return to Utah for a week to collect her belongings, Kim's mother intensified her pursuit to keep the baby, and Nicole felt she was losing control in the life of her daughter.

These were very powerful experiences for Nicole. She shared with me her feelings about what she was learning.

"I realized two very important things about myself. First, I realized that I love this baby and care about her so much that I want her to be happy no matter what pain is involved for me. Second, I remembered that I didn't have to do this alone. If I *wasn't* strong enough to do what I believed was right, I could rely on Heavenly Father to buoy me up. And I know now that I *can* follow through with what I believe is right, to place my baby for adoption. I had a long talk with Kim about why I felt adoption was best."

Nicole chose a family, and that family received a call that day to meet the mother of their new baby. During the face-to-face meeting, there was a strong feeling of connection between Nicole and the adoptive parents, and she and her parents repeatedly shared their feelings of correctness about her decision. At the end of the meeting, Nicole and her parents kissed the precious baby for the last time and placed her in the arms of her adoptive parents.

The ride home was a very difficult one, and the weeks following were painful not just for Nicole but for her parents and siblings and others who had cared for and loved her baby. But Nicole went on to be happy. I still have the picture she sent me some time ago of her with her husband and daughter.

Preparing for the birth and placement of a child is not a simple or clear-cut task. There is no formula that will ensure preparation. While it is not possible to know exactly how everyone will feel after the birth of the baby, an awareness of emotions that will likely be felt can be helpful. It is possible and important to prepare emotionally for those very difficult days. The following points can help.

1. Have correct and necessary information. Birth parents placing a child for adoption need to anticipate all reasonable options and explore them thoroughly. Although Nicole strongly believed that she would choose adoption, it was helpful in the end for her to have considered what the other options would be like if they had been chosen. She could see where the life of her child was heading when she chose to parent because she had thought about the possibility beforehand. She had explored the possibility of single parenting enough to know where she might struggle, so when she began to struggle, she recognized the problems she and her baby would face if she continued down that road. Exploring other options helps the birth mother know before she is overwhelmed with emotions that she does not want to choose those options. It's easier to think clearly and logically without the emotions that are present after the birth of the baby.

It is important to think through possibilities of what could go wrong in the hospital in case such a situation arises. "What will I do if I don't feel strong enough to follow through with my desire to place?" or "How will I handle it if my family members seem to be in great pain about my decision to place the baby? Will that change my reasons for placing?" Preparation can help prevent these situations from causing doubt or uncertainty about the decision. Nicole was unprepared for the feelings she was experiencing because she never expected to feel them.

2. Have support in place. The birth mother should have someone unbiased to talk with openly when needed. Most likely she will have fears, problems, second thoughts, and so forth after the birth of the baby. All of this is normal and does not mean the decision is wrong. But it is helpful to be able to talk through such feelings with someone who can be supportive and understanding. If a birth mother knows she has made the right decision before her baby is born, she will be able to work through her feelings again afterwards. She does not need pressure or strong influence during the time just after the baby is born, only clear, supportive, realistic counsel. Nicole had spent hours talking through her feelings with me. Although I functioned as a sounding board for her to bounce off her feelings, it was important that I not tell her what she should do. Ultimately, she continued to talk openly *because* she could talk to me during that difficult time without worrying about what I would think.

Along those same lines, the birth mother needs to protect herself at vulnerable times from those who will try to sway her from her resolve. When the baby is born is not the time for worrying about what everyone else thinks. That is a time for the birth mother to be protected from conflicting voices she has had to deal with throughout her pregnancy. One example might be a nurse who feels the birth mother should not spend time with the baby as she had planned and therefore keeps the baby away. Or it might be friends who make insensitive comments, such as, "He's so cute. I don't know how you can even think of walking away from him." Although it is important that she know how she feels in the face of differing opinions, the emotionally tender time when the baby is born is not when she needs to flood herself with them. An advocate, such as her counselor, her parent, or the hospital social worker can help protect her from these situations.

3. Be emotionally prepared. It is important to deal with any concerns you may have *beforehand*. If a concern exists for the birth mother or one of her support people, that concern should be addressed before the birth so it doesn't cloud the situation when the baby arrives. Nicole was an example of this situation. She did not think it would be a problem, and she did not feel an attachment to the adoptive couple she had chosen. She did not address it earlier because she felt she would never waver in her decision to place her baby for adoption and that it wouldn't be a problem for her. But as soon as she began to waver, her lack of attachment toward the couple became a huge issue. Her feelings of detachment toward the couple could have been resolved before placement, either through a second face-to-face meeting or by some other means. If *any* concerns are unresolved for those making this decision, the time to address them is before the placement.

The birth mother needs to have a sense of control in the situation before the birth of the baby. Young mothers may begin to question their decision if they feel they are losing control over what will happen before they relinquish their control. Birth parents know that by placing their baby for adoption, they are relinquishing the control they have over the circumstances of that child. For the placement decision to be a healthy one for them, they themselves need to be the ones to give up that control rather than have it taken from them. A mother can better face the hospital knowing that the experience will move at her pace, at her comfort level. I remember one difficult example of taking away control when a young birth mother asked that her baby be circumcised. Any other mother in that hospital would have been able to make this request, but because the doctor had heard she would eventually be placing, he refused. The mother had signed nothing; she was no different from any other mother in the hospital. And yet a well-meaning, albeit misguided, physician felt he was doing the adoptive parents a favor by refusing to honor the birth mother's rights and judgment. In fact, the birth mother had discussed the option of circumcision with her adoptive couple prior to the birth and found they were in agreement. This birth mother was nearly unable to follow through with the placement because of how she had been treated. It is important that the birth mother have control when appropriate so she can feel all right about giving it up later when she is ready to place her baby for adoption.

Also, if the birth mother's parents or others supporting her in the hospital have not been prepared, when the pressure is on they may be the ones to crumble. A birth mother should not need to take care of her family members while she is in the hospital to give birth. She needs to be able to deal with her own feelings in the safety of strong support from those around her. Specifically, if she finds herself asking, "Am I going to be okay after this is all over?" she needs her parents to be able to respond, "You are strong. You can do this," with conviction because they themselves are prepared. In Nicole's situation, her parents were prayerfully supportive, sharing not only their concerns about her but also their belief in *her* ability to make a good decision and to do the best thing for herself and her baby. Nicole knew that her parents would support her in whatever decision she made because they trusted her. When she later changed her mind and decided to place her baby for adoption, her parents again supported her.

Finally, it is vital to have a sense of spiritual peace about the decision. Recognizing and being able to rely on a spiritual confirmation about the decision can sometimes be the only thing that gives the birth mother or birth father enough strength to get through the placement and the following days. Knowing she will not be alone to deal with the pain afterwards, as well as knowing that her decision is one she has made through prayer, can offer great strength following the birth of the baby. For Nicole, the spiritual confirmation she had received about placing her baby for adoption was the only thing that did not fit for her after she took the baby home. Her sense that her Heavenly Father had guided her to the decision to place her baby for adoption gave her the strength to follow through with it in the end.

Preparing for the birth of a baby and the placement of that baby for adoption can be essential to following through with the decision, having a positive experience, and moving peacefully forward afterward.

The steps of preparation are valuable in the outcome of each family's story: it's worth doing right. The birth mother has to be prepared by having a plan of how everything will go after the birth of the baby, and then she has to be prepared for everything about the plan to change.

When everyone is as prepared as possible, the experience will go more smoothly all around.

Good-bye and Hello: The Placement

Perhaps no part of the adoption journey better illustrates how many people are deeply affected by the love of a child than when one loving mother places her baby in the arms of another mother. The placement of the child often moves me to tears for both birth parents and adoptive parents. This part is not just an important point in the journey; it is the pinnacle of the experience and one I hope to portray with proper accuracy and respect.

For this reason, I have chosen to tell about the presentation of Amanda's baby to her new family in a dramatic way, representing this same important experience from the point of view of six different parties, each of whom played their role as Amanda's daughter became part of a new family. I believe these vignettes accurately represent how all concerned play their role and how the love of this child can be transforming for birth parents, adoptive parents, and everyone who surrounds and assists them.

The Adoptive Parents

Ellen and Rick sit waiting at their home. The two months since they met Amanda have passed slowly as they all awaited her due date. Now that the baby is here, it seems each minute is an hour long. At 5:00 P.M. they will meet their daughter for the very first time. They have been shopping today, in part to complete last-minute details of preparation for the baby's arrival, in part to make the time go by faster.

Ellen has waited until this week to buy the car seat and set up the crib. When they painted the nursery last week, she couldn't help but feel scared that something would change and they wouldn't have this young daughter, finally, in their family. She was afraid they would have to walk by the nursery each night without a baby to fill it, afraid to feel the familiar pain of wanting a baby so badly and being unable to control her arrival.

Rick is feeling anticipation and excitement for this baby he has never seen, but he worries about his wife. What if Amanda changes her mind at the last minute and decides to keep the baby? Could Ellen handle any more heartbreak? She has maintained her gentle, tender attitude throughout their years of marriage, and Rick feels secure in how strong they have become as a couple, especially as they have worked to bring children into their lives. They are quiet as they load up the empty car seat and head towards the hospital.

They have waited for this day their whole lives.

The Nurses

"Room 212 needs pain meds." The nurses are changing shifts and passing along the necessary patient information. It's a busy day; the Women's Center is filled almost to capacity. There are four nurses covering twenty patients, and it seems that everybody needs something at once. Dr. Lewis is upset over a problem with the ultrasound machine, the patient in room 218 has had reactions to three different medications already this morning, the patient in room 211 is entertaining some rather rowdy-looking guests, and the girl in room 215 is an adoption case.

During staff meeting that morning, the nurse supervisor went through the situation of each patient and shared what she knew about the adoption in room 215. She said that twenty-one-year-old Amanda Andrews had had her baby two days ago. She was fine the first day, tearful off and on throughout yesterday, and today everyone was crying in her room. The supervisor told them the family of the girl was nice and seemed supportive but reported that the girl's mother seemed to be struggling today. Amanda's nurse, Rhonda, asked the supervisor, "Will the baby's father be here?"

"Yes," the supervisor replied, "but the mother won't be seeing him."

Rhonda mentally noted where she would have the birth father wait his turn to spend some time with the baby. She could work this out with the caseworker, who, she learned, would be in around 4:00 P.M. The actual adoption was planned for 5:00 P.M., just before the mother's discharge from the hospital.

It is close to 4:00 now, and Rhonda reviews the details of the paperwork the hospital will need. Her supervisor tells her to call the hospital social worker if she needs anything else, but she can see the caseworker arriving and knows she can relax. The caseworker will help handle all the different people who will soon be arriving for the adoption.

The Caseworker

I speak briefly with Amanda's nurse, Rhonda, when I get to the hospital. "I'm going to talk with Amanda," I tell her, "and then I'll check with you about the timing of things." I feel a responsibility as Amanda's caseworker to help this day go as smoothly as possible, and that means coordinating with everyone who is coming.

This morning I had called Amanda first thing. She was still feeling strong yesterday but was more emotional today. I wanted to find out how her night went and how she was doing today. "How do you want everything to go today?" I asked. We had already made plans for this important day, but I wanted Amanda to feel comfortable about everything. Even though many people had plans to complete the adoption today, if she felt she wasn't ready, we could and would postpone everything. I have learned that this is something the birth mother has to control, just as it must be her decision whether to place her baby for adoption at all.

After Amanda confirmed that she and I were still meeting at 4:00 P.M., I contacted the adoptive couple's caseworker. The anxious couple would want to know how Amanda was doing. I then phoned the hospital's social worker to let him know everything was in order and to confirm that he had arranged for a notary public for the adoption papers. For the next two hours I arranged my own day, finding a babysitter for the children and piling everything else on my husband so that I could be available to help Amanda, her family, and everyone else involved through this most important event. I had to remind my husband to be grateful that this wasn't Christmas Day, like the year before, when I had been gone to handle an adoptive placement.

On my way to the hospital I picked up the adoption papers that the office secretary at LDS Family Services had prepared, and I then swung by the McDonald's drive-through for a quick meal. I've learned that these are hours-long affairs, and I would need my strength, even if it was from a Big Mac.

As planned, I'm at the hospital a good hour before the others will arrive. Things are in order at the nurses' station, so I go to have a long, quiet chat with Amanda. I walk straight to the sink and wash my hands, knowing Amanda will want to show me her precious baby. Over the last few months we've built up a rapport, and I'm glad to be there with her to coo over the baby and to review with her once again the day's plans.

"Talk to me, Amanda. Do you feel prepared for today?" She's crying, as she will be off and on through the next few hours. This isn't the time for me to delve into issues with her. We have done some of this during the pregnancy, and there will be time later when she will need to talk again. Today, however, she just needs to get through the day.

"I'm ready. My dad and the bishop gave me a blessing yesterday. I know I'm going to be okay."

She's being brave. Her parents are there, and I check to see how they are holding up. Their strength will be most important today. "Have you taken time to write some letters?" I ask them. When the grandparents of the baby are able to convey their love in writing, it will help them in the present and the baby in the future.

"We wrote them last night," Amanda's mom tells me. "It was very hard." She shows me the pink and yellow afghan she finished crocheting just this morning to send along with the baby. They point out the cute little outfit the baby is clothed in and show me a picture with them all that Amanda's nurse has just taken.

I suggest to Amanda that we let the nurse come in and work through all the hospital discharge papers so that they are out of the way, and Rhonda comes in to handle this. On her way in she tells me that the birth father and his family have come and are waiting in the room that we have already arranged. "I'll be back in a few minutes, Amanda. I'm going to see how Ian is doing."

The Birth Father

I met Ian's mother yesterday when she came to spend time with the baby. Ian would get a chance to say good-bye again, but yesterday was his time to be alone with his daughter. I mention to Ian that the adoptive couple will be here any time, and then he'll have a chance to visit with them again. In Amanda's situation, since she and Ian parted ways several months before, they have decided it would not be good for them to cross paths during this already emotional day. So while Amanda visits one more time with the adoptive couple, Ian will say good-bye to the baby, and when Amanda is saying good-bye to her baby, Ian will speak again with the adoptive couple.

"I brought a letter," Ian says. He will give his letter for the baby to the adoptive couple, along with some gifts he and his mother have gathered—including a storybook he had grown up with that he hopes his daughter could also enjoy as she grows up. I sit down with Ian to review the paperwork, and since we've read over everything before, he signs the papers without saying anything at all.

Ian sits quietly, looking ahead through tear-filled eyes. His last minutes with his baby are nearing, and he is painfully aware that his own dear mother sits heartbroken beside him. He has been trying to add a few more words in his letter to send with his daughter, attempting somehow to explain a magnitude of love he has never before experienced. He wants to tell her of the love he feels, to tell her of the profound effect she has had on his life, to share his dreams for his daughter and his desire for the life he is choosing to give her through another father and mother. He wants to somehow be certain that his daughter knows why he chose to place her for adoption.

When it is finally his time with the baby, he holds her in his gentle, awkward manner and talks to her quietly. He watches her eyes open and close and thinks of the missed opportunities he has not taken. He tells her not of all he wants her to be but rather all he wants to become for her. He looks into her face and sees who he could be, and he vows to get there, to prove to her that her daddy did something good in his life. He desperately hopes she will want to meet him someday, that she will have the desire to know him. And he promises to himself that if that day ever comes, he will be someone she can be proud of.

As he hands her to his own mother to hold, he kisses her on the hand and tells her she is loved.

The Birth Mother's Parents

Carol and Dale have imagined holding their grandchildren, Carol especially, but maybe not so soon. As she holds the baby's tiny foot in her hand, she thinks about the past two days as well as the day to come. She ponders how much this infant looks like Amanda had looked when she was born, with the same crook in her nose and dimple in her right cheek. Carol never imagined she would be sitting in the hospital saying good-bye to her first grandchild.

Carol has never cried so much at any other time in her life. She feels as much pain within herself as she can imagine feeling, and she tenderly smooths the baby's hair through her tears. Who would ever have imagined that love could be felt so strongly for a child she has known for only two days?

She hands the baby carefully to her husband and walks over to her daughter. Amanda has been quiet today. She is now intently working on a letter she is writing to the baby, and she looks up to give her mother a weak smile.

"We're going to be okay, right, Mom?" she asks in a shaky voice. Carol simply hugs her daughter tight.

Dale watches as his wife and daughter embrace. He loves them both very much and worries about Amanda's question himself. He tries to hold fast to the counsel they have received as they went through Amanda's pregnancy, counsel to consider the needs of the child first. He thinks of the incredible experiences they have seen as a family—how they have come together to support Amanda when she felt so alone, how they have individually received a confirmation of peace about the baby and the adoptive couple who will receive her. He thinks of the blessing he gave earlier to Amanda, sharing promises with her from her Father in Heaven who also loves her, telling her that she will find happiness in the days to come.

Dale looks up as Amanda's three younger siblings enter the room. They have brought a basket of gifts for the baby, which they now carefully arrange to present to the adoptive parents. Dale has seen Amanda's sisters and brother come to love their older sister more deeply and to forgive her for the errors she had made. They have each grown through the realization that there are some things worth the sacrifice.

He knows this is right. He knows that Amanda has been directed by God to choose this family as the parents for this baby. But he also wonders if he can find the strength he needs to walk away. He wants to hold this baby forever, protect her from all the dangers of the world as he had wanted to protect his own children. He feels impossibly torn between doing what he earlier felt was right and changing his mind about everything.

They *could* take care of this baby. They are not wealthy, but they certainly have enough to share with this precious child. They could all make sacrifices, and she would be well loved. As he indulges in thoughts he knows are unfair to think, he glances again at his wife and daughter.

They are struggling, needing support and strength right now. They need to feel things are going to be okay. He feels a sense of responsibility to provide that stability. As he walks over to Amanda's hospital bed to comfort them, he again feels a desire to protect his daughter, the daughter who had once been so weak and lost but now seems to be the strongest person he has ever met.

The Birth Mother

The baby is beautiful. Amanda gazes at her sleeping quietly in her arms, thinking that she will kiss this infant girl for the last time in only one hour. She will be named Ella Grace, her first name after a grandmother and her second after a great-grandmother. Her name was carefully chosen by Rick and Ellen, the two parents that the baby will meet for the first time later today.

The caseworker comes in, and they chat for a while without the distraction of all of Amanda's siblings and family members. As comfortable as Amanda is with her caseworker, she knows that the sight of her means the moment will soon be here, and she has to cherish every last minute with her daughter.

Amanda holds her gently, changes her outfit yet again, and places the baby in her grandfather's arms for more pictures. Between pictures, she kisses her daughter repeatedly, as do her family members, whispering to the child how much she is loved.

Nurses come and go, carefully watching Amanda for signs of a breakdown and watching themselves more carefully so as not to contribute to her pain. Somebody enters and asks about the birth certificate. How should they complete it? Witnesses stand by as her caseworker reads over the paperwork Amanda now signs that forever terminates her parental rights. She has read these papers before, but they feel painfully cruel as she hears them read out loud in front of witnesses and a notary public.

Amanda has decided on the outfit in which her daughter should meet her adoptive family. She is tired, exhausted, eyes swollen from tears she shed throughout the night as she held her sleeping daughter and told her over and over how much she loves her. She has stayed awake all night, not wanting to miss a minute of the impossibly short time she has chosen to keep her before she says good-bye. She looks around her at the many people who care about her, all gathered to be with this precious new infant and to show their support for Amanda's decision. She can see in their eyes the pain she feels in her own heart, and not for the first time she is aware of the pain her immorality has caused to those she cares so much about. She no longer feels ashamed, however, when she thinks of this pregnancy. She has begun to trust in herself again over the past weeks, in her ability to make good decisions and in her knowledge that her Heavenly Father loves her and cares about her life.

Her father is holding his first grandchild in his arms and talking to the baby quietly. She sees tears swell again in his eyes. This decision seemed so easy at first, so practical. It was the counsel of the Brethren, the guidance of her bishop, the way to make this situation "right" again. It all made perfect sense—she was too young, her boyfriend was entirely unprepared to support a family, she wouldn't finish school. Every other moment the whole thing feels impossible to Amanda. She watches as her father tells his tiny granddaughter that she is loved beyond imagination, kisses her on her perfect cheek, and whispers, "You will always have a grandpa out there who loves you. Remember that." He places the baby gently in his wife's arms and goes to hold his daughter's hand. She is glad for his firm grip.

Her mother holds the baby silently as tears run down her own cheeks. Amanda can see she is trying to be strong, trying to hold herself together for the sake of her daughter. Amanda thinks of the family awaiting the arrival of this baby in their home. She imagines their excitement and remembers her mother saying she felt they were like family from the moment they met them two months ago. Amanda herself loves them also, but she can't help feeling envious that they will be with this child every day and she will not. Her mother smiles as she runs her finger across the curls of blonde hair on the baby's head; Amanda wore the same curls as a child. The baby is beautiful, and Amanda watches her mother wipe one of her own tears from the baby's cheek. She kisses her forehead and places the baby in her daughter's arms. She kisses her daughter on the forehead as well.

The family members and friends in the room stand, preparing to leave this young mother for some final minutes alone with her child. As they leave the room, they each kiss the baby she holds, some telling the baby quiet advice or whispering "I love you's" as they caress her tiny hand or foot. Many of them hug Amanda as they leave the room, and soon she and the baby are alone.

She smiles as the baby opens her eyes, and she sits down to speak to her.

She tells her again how wonderful her life is going to be, how loving her parents are. She tells her to use her long fingers to play the piano, like she did. She feeds her a bottle and ponders on how dependent the baby is on her, feeling a bit overwhelmed. She ponders how dependent she herself has been on the Spirit to guide her decisions. She says another prayer, asking her Father in Heaven to protect and love this tiny baby girl.

A myriad of thoughts fill her head as she remembers things she wanted to finish or send along with this baby. She wraps her in the blanket her mother helped her make, whispers, "I'll always love you! Please don't ever forget me," and carries her baby out of the room.

Her family follows her as she enters the room where the adoptive parents are waiting. As she holds the baby, her eyes again well up with tears, and the new parents stand and wipe tears from their own eyes as well. "She is beautiful," one mother says to the other as she sees her for the first time. Her husband has his arm around his wife, and tears run down his cheeks. The young mother walks to them, kisses the baby, hands her to her new mother, and kisses her again. The young father walks into the room, whispers "I love you" to the baby, and also kisses his daughter good-bye. He shakes hands with the baby's new father, who pulls him into a hug as they both thank each other. The other family members try to smile and say good-bye. Her father hugs the adoptive parents and asks them to take care of her. None of them wants to leave the room, and yet they want to be anyplace else but here.

The Adoptive Grandparents

The living room in the home of Ellen's parents is abuzz with excitement. All of the family is here, waiting for the arrival of this precious new member of the family. Ellen's mom is thoughtful and excited while she prepares the dinner they will have to celebrate when Ellen and Rick finally arrive with the baby. How long they have waited for this child!

Ellen's parents had watched with concern over the past several years, seeing Ellen's siblings' families grow while Ellen and Rick remained alone. They hadn't spoken of it much, but Ellen's mother had seen her wince through more than a few announcements of pregnancy.

This sadness had turned to hope when they quietly shared with family members that they were going to pursue adoption. Everyone had been involved. They all shared in the process of getting their file ready, and they all waited together for news of a baby. Ellen's parents knew they were not the only ones praying fervently for the blessing of a child to be bestowed upon this couple so ready to be parents.

After what seems like hours, there is finally the reflection of headlights in the driveway. The room becomes louder, until finally the door opens. And then the room fills with something of a hushed reverence, as Ellen gently lifts the blanket and brings a beautiful baby girl into view. Her eyes are red from crying, matching those of her husband. As they hold her close, Rick announces through new tears of his own, "Everyone, we'd like you to meet our new daughter."

* * *

There is a beautiful song by Michael McLean in which a birth mother lovingly relates how her child comes "from God's arms, to my arms, to yours." Clearly, many lives intersect within the adoption experience, especially at the center point in the adoption journey—the delivery of the baby to this world and into the life of her adoptive parents. Although I have tried to represent this experience so that others can understand, I also know that nothing I can say about the presentation of a baby from one set of loving parents to another will properly convey the depth of the experience. While the experience, in fairness, is most intensely that of the birth parents and the adoptive parents, much of it radiates to others. There are a myriad of people whose lives are deeply touched by the placement of a precious child. And whether or not they are entitled to share in the intensity of the feelings matters little. They are there, they share what occurs, and they are changed by the experience.

GETTING THROUGH THE EARLY MONTHS

I have emphasized the joy of adoption and how positive the journey of adoption can be for birth parents, adoptive parents, and many others. But I have also tried not to overly romanticize adoption. It is difficult to make the adoption decision, and it is difficult to carry it through. That is true for both birth parents and adoptive parents.

In the early months following the placement of the child, adoptive parents must create a whole new kind of life. Not only will they, like all parents, learn to manage all of the traditional responsibilities of raising a newborn, but they will also fill some additional responsibilities—such as taking extra pictures of their child and frequently writing letters to the birth parents. In this way the birth parents can be assured that the child is safe and being cared for lovingly.

The birth parents will also face a whole new kind of life, managing from day to day as they deal with having said good-bye to a child. The time after the final kisses is an emotionally painful time, just as the placement itself always is. But in watching this process and coming to trust it, I have seen that even the painful parts are important in the overall experience. In fact, sometimes they are the most important.

This time is particularly difficult for the birth mother—possibly the most excruciating months of a young, unwed mother's life. While the experience is different for each young woman who goes through it, it is important to keep the experience in perspective. Of course this is much easier for me to say than it is for the birth parents and their families to hear. I can only assure those who struggle during this exquisitely painful period that time itself has a powerful effect on the intensity of the pain. There are many things that can be helpful to the birth mother (and the birth father, if he is involved) and her family during the early months after the baby is placed for adoption.

The birth mother needs to know from the beginning that she will have emotional support to get through the difficult months following the placement. Whether such support will come from her parents, family members, bishop, friends, or all of them, she needs to know she is not alone. When you've carried a baby with you everywhere for the past nine months and suddenly are parted from that baby, loneliness is naturally going to be a concern. This is a time for the family to continue to pull together to support one another, because family members will all be in pain.

It is important during this time for the birth mother to have someone to process feelings with and share concerns. That is one reason why working with a counselor throughout the pregnancy can be so helpful, because counseling will be particularly important after the baby has been placed for adoption. If a birth mother receives counseling before the baby is born, she will likely already have developed a relationship of trust with that professional. She needs to know that if she has a concern about the adoption, she will have help in addressing it. For example, if she finds that after the placement she wants more correspondence with the adoptive family than she originally thought, she knows she has someone who will help her communicate that wish to the adoptive parents in a healthy and positive manner.

Along those same lines, it is important for her to know that her baby's adoptive parents will not forget about her now that they have the baby. Letters about how the baby is doing and pictures of the baby are so important during those early months. They reinforce for her that she did what was best for her baby and that the pain she is facing is not in vain. They also reinforce for her that the baby is safe and happy—common concerns that any parent knows are easy to have where children are concerned.

One tremendous advantage to working through an adoption agency such as LDS Family Services is that through them a birth mother can meet with others who have been through this experience previously. Attending group sessions helps a birth mother be better prepared emotionally both before and after the placement of her child for adoption. After the placement, hearing from other girls in group sessions will buoy her up and remind her once again that she will be okay, that she won't be in so much pain forever, that it *does* get better. Attending group sessions, when she feels ready, can be one way for her to realize she is not alone.

During the months after the baby has been placed, it is particularly important that the birth mother stay close to her Heavenly Father through prayer. Faith that she could follow through with her decision was important during the pregnancy, and faith that she will be happy again is important afterwards. She also needs support from her ecclesiastical leaders and ward members in feeling that she is loved by God just as much as anyone else and that she will be accepted by others. Journal writing can be an important part of this process, not only for her spiritual development but also for her own healing process. This is a time of great learning and personal growth, and she may find it useful to look back on her writing at other points in her life.

Finally, when she feels ready, she should begin moving forward with her life. It is useful to grieve for only so long before the grief itself can become personally detrimental. That is not to say that the grieving stops, only that at some point it must be handled while moving forward. For a young girl who planned to go to college and pursue her goals, beginning on the path to those goals will help her reestablish her life from this point forward.

During the early months after Amanda placed her baby with Ellen and

Rick, she was in a great deal of pain. But she soon began returning to the areas in her life that were positive for her: church, school, and work. She was open about the experiences she had been through and had a solid support system already in place before her baby was born. She simply decided to pray her way through it. Even in the most intense times of pain for Amanda, did she ever regret her decision?

Amanda told me: "Knowing that what I did was the right thing for my baby was sometimes the only thing that kept me moving forward. When I questioned everything else, I never questioned that. She is where she needs to be. I know that. And I am also where I need to be. We're both going to be happy now."

It's true that adoption is a journey. From the first moment after learning there is an out-of-wedlock pregnancy to placing a baby in someone else's arms, it is an experience filled with strong emotions, varying opinions, and difficult choices. Though the intensity of the journey starts to level off after the placement of the child, the birth parents' journeys are only just beginning. Hopefully, the journey of adoption will have provided the birth parents with some wisdom about life, redemption, and the great plan of happiness, as well as a renewed understanding of who they are, where they are going, and how many people want them to succeed. To prepare for the best possible future following unwed parenthood, there remains one crucial portion of the adoption journey: understanding what conditions led them off the path. When these issues are addressed, they can feel confident about moving ahead with both feet solidly on the right path.

Chapter Five

MOVING FORWARD
WITH HOPE

OCTOBER 9—

I can't believe Gracie is almost five months old. It seems like I was just in the hospital holding her, and now I hardly recognize her as the same baby when I look at her pictures.

I'm finally starting to notice life going on around me again. For a while I just wanted to crawl under my blanket and never think again. But I find that I am happy more days than not, and that is an improvement. I wasn't sure if I ever would be.

I have a new friend that's been a great support to me. He's a really strong member of the Church, and he thinks Gracie's photos are adorable, too. He's never been judgmental of me—not even for a minute—about the mistakes I have made.

I'm graduating—finally!—from college next weekend. I don't know what I'm going to do now. I've thought a little about graduate school . . .

The crisis is over. The decisions about what is best for the baby have all been made. The blankets and quilts have been wrapped and sent along to the adoptive parents as keepsakes for the child. The intensity of the feelings of loss and sadness is beginning to soften. It can be a time for moving forward and for feeling renewed hope.

After a baby has been placed for adoption, I do not immediately terminate counseling with a client. The young birth parents (and sometimes their parents) are again at a crossroads. They can choose between continuing on with the same behaviors they had before the baby was conceived, or they can move forward with the experiences they have had—evaluating what happened in the past in order to make better choices in the future. I do not mean to suggest they spend years in psychotherapy working through issues. But by carefully examining what happened and what was learned, those involved in an out-of-wedlock pregnancy (or any other type of adversity) can further increase their ability to apply that new information to their own lives.

WHAT WENT WRONG? THE ISSUE OF SELF-ESTEEM

When an out-of-wedlock pregnancy is discovered, at first there is only time to address immediate problems. But after the baby is born there is an opportunity to evaluate more closely what went wrong, to see how the young woman or man came to find themselves wandering off the path. They can explore what factors led to an unwed pregnancy and change unhealthy characteristics that contributed to weakening their moral values. For a time they were focused on the pregnancy and child. But the very factors that contributed to their decision to become sexually involved in the first place can now hinder their ability to move forward. Placing a baby for adoption, powerful as it may be, is not enough to change some fundamental patterns of behavior that may still be present.

Various factors could have contributed to the pregnancy, but one predominant factor is very common—and it is one that can and should be changed to prevent other problems in the future. That factor is self-esteem.

Even when we as parents, leaders, or counselors dealing with troubled youth feel as though we have no control, self-esteem is definitely something we can influence. The issue of self-esteem plays a significant role in the breakdown of moral strongholds, but it is something that *can* be improved.

Following are two examples of clients I have seen whose struggles with self-esteem have not only contributed to their becoming sexually involved but also to the decisions they made afterwards.

SONALI'S STORY: NO SELF-ESTEEM, NO FUTURE

"Tell me about the baby's father," I asked Sonali, who was four months pregnant.

"Well, he's twenty-six, really into computers, lives about an hour away from here." She described him with a bit of defensiveness, and I could tell that she had already been grilled about who he is, where he came from, and why she is pregnant with his baby. "He's really smart," she added. I certainly agreed with her on this point. This was a birth father who was calculated in his selection of Sonali and carefully manipulative in his approach. Still, she was defending his image not because she cared about him. She didn't really even know him. She was defending her own image, her idea that she had more personal value because this young man was interested in her.

My story here is about Sonali, so I will not dwell now on what the birth father of her baby was like. But I came to know much about him over the course of her pregnancy. In short, he was a predator, looking for someone with precisely Sonali's diminished sense of self-worth and level of vulnerability.

Sonali went on to tell me about how she met him. It was a story I had heard before and will hear again. "We met on the Internet in a chat room." She blushes, and it's obvious that by her family's standards, Internet chat rooms are not an appropriate place to look for guys. "We had so much in common, and we could talk online for hours." He was very patient. She was extremely sensitive to attention from anyone male.

She had never dated anyone before. She was so insecure that she hardly spoke to boys at school, so you can imagine the surprise from her parents when she told them she was pregnant. Never a boyfriend, not even a date, and now she was pregnant. And Sonali still had no idea what had hit her. I would venture to say that she was willing to go through whatever consequences she might face just for that short time of feeling attractive and valued by a man.

She had characteristics similar to those of too many other girls who become sexually active before marriage. She had also been sexually abused as a child, which complicated her situation. But not all girls who get pregnant out of wedlock have been abused as children. And not all girls who are sexually active are victims.

Sonali is an example of just how much damage can occur when you feel you have little personal value. When I first met Sonali, she was a fairly plain eighteen-year-old girl. She always sat with her head down and spoke quietly. She wore no makeup, had a discouraging problem with acne, and her hair simply hung limply around her face. She put more thought into her clothing, which was immodest (I have found this to be a fairly consistent theme) and accentuated her imperfect figure. She wasn't so much timid as she was insecure.

I worked with Sonali for a very long time, not only throughout her pregnancy but for some years afterwards. She was a fascinating person. It is said that if you place a low value on yourself, the world will not increase it, and this was certainly the case with Sonali. I knew, and she knew, that the young man by whom she had become pregnant had no feelings of tenderness for her. She was learning quickly, in fact, that he would hardly even talk with her anymore, either by telephone or online. I find it ironic and quite sad that the very thing some girls do to keep the attention of men can ultimately drive them away.

So Sonali was left alone to deal with a pregnancy. She had sold her birthright for a mess of pottage, and what she thought was improving her self-esteem only damaged it further. She had almost no strength left to pull herself out of her situation. It is therefore not surprising that she could not consider placing her baby for adoption.

When you feel you have nothing, it's very difficult to think of giving up something good you will have in the future on the belief that it will lead to something better. I have found that girls who have something to look forward to in their futures consider adoption far more than those who have no goals and live day to day. If you feel unloved and ignored, having your own cute baby to love you can be very appealing. Let me reiterate this point: A girl (or boy) who feels some sense of hopefulness for the future will be far more able to imagine a more hopeful future for her baby.

Sonali saw this baby as a way out. Her mother and stepfather had been "nagging" at her to get a job or go to college, neither of which she wanted to do.

"I've always just wanted to get married," she told me repeatedly when I talked with her about what she would do with her life if she could do anything at all. When pressed for other goals or desires, I learned that she didn't see herself as an achiever, and my asking her what kind of education or career she might like was entirely foreign to her. She couldn't begin to imagine it. So, seeing herself with no future, there was no way she was going to be able to put her baby's needs before her own. The only time she suggested any sort of hope for herself, she spoke of dancing and maybe teaching dance someday—someday far away, because she saw no possibility of pursuing that dream now.

So Sonali worked towards parenting her baby, much to the increasing panic of her mother. Sonali's mother already had strong feelings for the baby Sonali was carrying, and she was afraid for the kind of life this baby would lead. Her mother worried because Sonali had no resources with which to raise the baby and was severely unprepared emotionally to take on the care of another person. She was immature and considerably unmotivated, and she looked forward to just holding the baby all day long. I believed her mother's concerns were valid, and I also worried about what single parenting would do to Sonali's sense of self-esteem and her future opportunities to meet a good young man and have the kind of life she desired but disbelieved would ever happen. Most of all, there was the concern about Sonali's patterns with men and the possibility that she might put the safety of her child at risk by dating less than desirable men.

But it was not my choice to make, nor was it the choice of Sonali's mother. And because the baby's father had removed himself from the situation completely, Sonali, who seemed to have no ability to think about any decisions at all, was left by default to parent her baby.

I found myself feeling that our counseling sessions were useless. As she worked towards her decision to parent this child, I encouraged her to prepare realistically for the demands of being a mother—a single mother at that. We talked of the needs of babies and children, of ways that she would physically provide for the child and someday even become independent of her mother's support. But Sonali seemed to make little progress in her thinking. We had a weak relationship, possibly because I was reminding Sonali of a reality she had no inclination or desire to face. Her low feelings of self-worth were crippling her ability to progress.

For Sonali to change the direction her life was going, she would need to come to believe that she could change it. Before continuing with Sonali, let me share another example of how self-esteem can affect a young girl's decision to become sexually active. This is a story about McCall and Tom.

McCall and Tom's Story: Pulling Each Other Down

The best way I can describe Tom's personality is by a comment he made once in a group session about McCall. He was talking about what they should do about her pregnancy, and he inadvertently shared just how shallow his thinking was. He said, "I guess we might get married. How bad could it be, really? I mean, look at her!" He gestured towards her in a trophy-girlfriend kind of way, pleased at himself for combining what he thought was a compliment to her with an opportunity to point out his own ability for attracting beautiful women.

Unlike Sonali, McCall seemed to have everything to feel confident about. A very pretty girl, she was a varsity cheerleader, smart, well-dressed, and socially flawless. She talked openly in group sessions and showed remarkable insight into her situation. Her boyfriend, Tom, was an attractive football player at her high school.

I will never forget McCall's mother when she spoke of Tom, because she always said his name with an emphasis that sounded like she was spitting out something unpleasant when she said it. McCall's mother felt she had reasons to dislike Tom, not the least of which was that her daughter with the bright future was now pregnant and very confused. And whenever she was around her daughter, there was Tom, "all over her." McCall's mother said she felt nauseated whenever she saw her daughter with him.

McCall's mother, and sometimes McCall, talked of how she had been a straight-A student before becoming involved with Tom. Once she started dating him, her grades slipped, and so did her relationship with her mother (who was a single parent herself). McCall had been dating Tom for almost a year, and her mom reported that she had become a completely different person. She seemed to be at his beck and call, bending her will to whatever he wanted. He was not mean, just critical of her intelligence, her family, her figure. Her self-esteem dwindled as she began to buy into Tom's belief that she was lucky to be with him.

McCall was like many other girls. She had low self-esteem to begin with which led her to a narcissistic guy. When she started dating Tom, his flattery felt good to her. She relied upon the emotional stroking Tom provided, and when she had to choose between keeping that artificial validation or staying morally clean, she chose to continue in the relationship and became pregnant in the process. Tom was invested in this relationship because he, too, struggled with his own feelings of self-worth. He compensated by diminishing her self-esteem to buoy up his own. Tom was not a bad person, just struggling himself in ways that damaged those around him. Clearly, they were not good for each other's well-being and had fooled themselves into thinking they needed each other.

McCall was perfectly confused. She was not blind to Tom's problems. In group sessions she expressed very clearly the way he brought her down. And though she cared a great deal for him and felt he also cared about her, she didn't know if she loved him. This is not a good foundation upon which to build a marriage. In fact, their problems would likely only deepen with time. Despite that, McCall believed marriage was still an option because she was comfortable with Tom and he continued to provide the superficial flattery to which she'd grown accustomed. She also considered herself one of the lucky ones compared to the other girls in the group. Unlike the others, the father of her baby was staying around trying to support her in the pregnancy (certainly to her mother's chagrin), and he seemed to be a fairly okay guy as well. He didn't do drugs or smoke, he was a member of the Church, and he treated her decently. But the relationship was still damaging to her, in ways neither she nor Tom could see.

McCall ended up making some good choices and some bad ones. She placed her baby for adoption and matured a great deal in the process. When I saw her last she was doing well and she looked happy. But she was still maintaining her relationship with Tom. When she told me her relationship hadn't changed much, she immediately followed with "I know . . ." She did know; she just needed to get to a point personally where she could expect more for herself.

Many young people who are in strong families and seem to have a stable foundation personally may still have trouble breaking out of a relationship like this one. It is a recurrent pattern: struggles with self-esteem lead to unhealthy relationships that become all the more difficult to escape from when the relationship becomes sexual. And this is not exclusive to young women. Young men can also be drawn into unhealthy relationships through low self-esteem. Sometimes young men I have seen have tried to be rescuers in their relationships. It is a boost to one's self-esteem to feel like a savior; however, the boost is short-lived if the relationship itself cannot be saved.

* * *

Although self-esteem issues are often a major factor contributing to teen pregnancy, not everyone who is pregnant out of wedlock is struggling with self-esteem. Other factors are involved (many of which are connected to self-esteem), such as immodesty, rebellion, abuse, and dating relationships that maintain a level of comfort and intimacy too early or too often.

Sex is a powerful tool, used for both good and evil, and cannot be dabbled with carelessly. Sometimes even the best people may find themselves in really bad situations. Immorality can be a temptation to the strongest people and should therefore be avoided with the utmost urgency. That is why I don't feel there must always be some identifiable pathology in the emotional makeup of those who break the law of chastity. People make bad decisions, sometimes devastating decisions. And although the consequences are severe and long-lasting, these people still have all of the opportunities of the Atonement. God can work miracles with people who turn their lives over to Him, even when they have struggled grievously in the past.

This point is especially important for the parents of unwed parents to remember. In evaluating what went wrong, it is very natural for the parents of the pregnant teenagers to blame themselves for what their child has done. Although I think there is merit in evaluating our circumstances and working to change and improve, I also think we have many examples of good parents who have disobedient children. Think of Lehi, Mosiah, Adam and Eve, even Heavenly Father. After all, within our belief system we *do* rely on the principle of agency. So I do not find it helpful for the parents of those pregnant out of wedlock to beat themselves up about the choices of their children. As parents, we like to feel a sense of security in the belief that if we do everything right, at least to the best of our ability, then our children will not make bad choices—especially with the law of chastity. To be sure, doing those things we are counseled to do strengthens our families. And growing up under these good influences will both prevent much harm and also allow children to more readily get themselves out of bad situations. But when parents take all the blame, their child may not see any need for changing the behaviors that led them to fornication. That hampers them in taking the necessary steps to change.

When young people are given the chance to understand the underlying causes for their misbehavior, they often show a remarkable ability to improve. That is what happened with Sonali. She came to believe that she could change, and she did.

One day, late in Sonali's pregnancy, she phoned me at home.

"Monica?" she asked.

"Yes, Sonali. Is everything okay?"

"Yes. Everything is really okay. I've decided to place my baby for adoption." Few telephone calls have been more of a surprise to me, before or since this call.

While I had watched Sonali's sense of self-worth deteriorate during the early months of her pregnancy, I heard in her now a new sense of determination, a sense of belief in herself and in her ability to have an impact in the world.

"I want to start looking at families right away. I want to find a family with an older brother or sister who has been waiting a long time for a baby. I want to meet them and tell them how much I love my baby, so she will know." To my surprise, Sonali had been thinking about this for some time, and she had laid out a clear plan for herself and her baby, which she continued to explain.

"I'm applying to go back to school. I'm going to study dance." I am embarrassed to say that I had begun to believe the value Sonali once placed upon herself. I was wrong.

Sonali transformed into a beautiful young woman. With each new accomplishment she made towards her goals, she believed in herself a little bit more. As she placed her baby, she found herself surrounded by those who admired her for her unselfishness and strength—strength, if you can believe it. She felt this strength because she never faltered in her decision to place that baby for adoption; she was experiencing firsthand her own ability to follow through with the most difficult thing she had ever done. She was coming to realize that if she could do this, then she could do anything. Through these actions, she was replacing low self-esteem with a healthier sense of self-worth.

CREATING HEALTHIER PATTERNS

Knowing what went wrong is only the first step in changing. To move forward, young people need to create healthier patterns for themselves so that they do not end up in bad relationships or compromising situations again.

People ask the question time and again, "Why do I always end up in the same bad relationships?" This is not as simple a question as it sounds. After all, if any of us knows we are doing something that is unhealthy (and we can all think of some behavior we do that is unhealthy), then why don't we just stop? I suggest that the answer is that we are not uncomfortable enough to change, or we don't believe we are strong enough to stop, or we just don't know how to change. Healthier behavior in the future depends upon believing that change is possible. Brooke's story shows how change can occur.

Brooke found herself in my office with a second out-of-wedlock pregnancy, conceived with a boyfriend very much like the father of her first baby. Brooke was a darling girl, intelligent and articulate. And because of her first experience she was painfully aware of what she would now be facing and the decisions she would need to make. Although I was not her counselor during the first pregnancy, I could see patterns that were perpetuating her relationship problems. And so could she.

BROOKE'S STORY: WHY DIDN'T SHE LEARN THE FIRST TIME?

Two years ago, while living with her parents in another state, Brooke had become pregnant, prayed for months for guidance from her Father in Heaven, and ultimately placed her baby for adoption with a family she had chosen. It was a painful process, beyond any description she could have given to someone on the outside, but one she had been able to navigate through personal strength and vast support from others. But clearly the pain she experienced did not inoculate her against future problems.

"I know that my family is wondering why I didn't learn my lesson when I became pregnant the first time. I sometimes wonder that myself. But when I think of all I did learn about myself and my Heavenly Father, I know that making mistakes later does not negate my earlier growth. The fact of the matter is that if I had not learned how much God loves me and my baby through my first pregnancy, I might not be able to handle facing Him again with a second. Getting pregnant was my fault. But at least I know I can go to my Heavenly Father despite the decisions I have made."

Brooke expressed feelings of disappointment in herself, as well as tremendous grief at the pain she knew she was causing to those around her. She wrestled for months with the knowledge of the pain she and her family would endure if she chose to place a second child for adoption. She was haunted by these feelings of responsibility for the effect her decision would have on the lives of others. She knew there would be pain because she had seen it during the placement of her first child.

She also knew, however, that she needed to do what she felt the Lord wanted her to do. She had come to believe through her first experience that she did not have the same knowledge her Heavenly Father had about her life and the lives of her two children. She had grown to trust her Father in Heaven to guide her, but she still had strong reasons to question her own judgment.

Although Brooke eventually regained hope in her own life and in her situation, we decided early in her second pregnancy that she needed to address some other issues after the crisis of this pregnancy had passed, and that is what brought us to this point in her therapy. We needed to evaluate why Brooke dated guys who were not good for her.

Brooke had found herself in an abusive and controlling relationship for the second time in two years, and she knew changes needed to be made. I began to understand why she kept getting involved in these situations when I learned more about her background.

I knew from interacting with her parents and bishop in another state that her parents were strong, upstanding people, respected both in the Church and their community. Her parents were certainly rigid in their parenting and family lifestyle, but they were trying to do what was right and best for their two children. Possibly the biggest suggestion of trouble in their family had been Brooke's pregnancies, and recently they had been seeing problems with their younger daughter as well.

We spent a great deal of time evaluating Brooke's situation, and we came to realize that there were two definite contributors to her repeated problems with men: her attraction to the wrong types of men and her ability to attract the wrong types of men. We began first to figure out what types of guys she was attracted to, and Brooke set out on a study to determine specifically what she looked for in guys. She spent a week profiling the men she felt drawn to, and by the time she returned, we had a fairly clear picture of who she might see as attractive.

"During the week I realized that I really look at guys who show some sign of rebelliousness, such as a pierced ear or tattoo." I believed it also might feel less intimidating to her to date someone who had made a few mistakes himself.

"I like tall guys with muscles and very modern, trendy clothing—the ones who look like they have a lot of money. And I have noticed that all the guys I find attractive end up being fairly crude in their language. I hate it when guys talk like that, and it always seems like I get stuck with the ones who use the worst language." Brooke was very open, and I felt she intently wanted to understand where she was going wrong.

"The guys I would have dated have been the ones who were very forward and would have come on to me quickly." She smiled when she said "would have dated" since we had made a deal that she wasn't going to date anyone while she was figuring this out. I liked Brooke's maturity in assessing her situation and her good humor about changing it. "There's just something about these guys that is so much more masculine than a nice, clean-cut returned missionary who invites me to a fireside after three weeks of beating around the bush."

This assessment certainly gave us a pretty good image of what sort of guy Brooke was drawn to and also a fairly plain understanding of why she hadn't found much success in her love life. I then asked Brooke what type of guy she wanted to marry. I wanted her to take into consideration what would make him a good husband and father, someone who would share her desires for a temple marriage and eternal family. She wrote me a list, which was clearly something she had thought of before in her twenty-two years. Her list looked something like this:

1. *Must be attractive.* (Her actual words were "totally hot.")

   –taller than me

   –well-dressed (she had expensive taste)

   –confident in his manner

2. *Must have a good job or be going to school.*

   She pointed out that this would suggest he was motivated and would do something with his life. She also commented that the guys she dated were usually "between" good jobs or good schools.

3. *Must be an active, strong member of the Church.*

   This was a new one for her. Although she knew she wanted someone who was a member of the Church, she had generally dated guys who had been inactive but were now "working their way back."

4. *Must be respectful.*

   Brooke decided that in order to stay worthy herself, knowing morality was an area of weakness for her, she would have to find someone who was not just respectful of her desires to remain morally clean but who also had his own moral goals. She felt that if she was the only one trying to be good, she might eventually fail again.

5. *Must be honest.*

This was huge for Brooke, having learned in both her serious past relationships that her boyfriends had been unfaithful to her. She questioned whether any guy was truly honest when it came to relationships.

6. *Must be loyal.*

She shared with me that being loyal meant when she was with her guy and other people, or when he was somewhere without her, he would speak highly of her and not put her down. This would suggest he was secure enough in his own self-image that he didn't need to put her down to raise himself up.

7. *Must like children.*

Having kissed two babies good-bye, she was looking forward to having other children to whom she could be the kind of mother she knew they would need.

8. *My family must like him.*

Big progress here! Needless to say, they hadn't been fond of her previous boyfriends.

9. *Must believe in the Atonement.*

Brooke felt that any guy who had remained strong and worthy in the gospel would never accept her after the mistakes she had made in her life. She knew he would have to have a strong testimony of repentance and forgiveness, the same as she had come to know.

Brooke had a nice list of qualities she was looking for in a future husband, and it was interesting to note that her prior boyfriends matched only a few items on her list. She mentioned in her defense that she hadn't actually wanted to marry those guys, that she was only dating them. She shared with me that she wasn't sure she believed a guy like this actually existed—either he would be a really good guy who wasn't attractive to her or a really attractive guy who wasn't good to her.

We spent several sessions working to change her attraction to bad guys and helping her find hope in the suggestion that she needn't settle for less. She needed to believe there actually was a good man out there who would fit all of her criteria, and then we moved on.

We next looked at the qualities she presented to others that might draw the wrong type of people to her. She was completely at a loss. It remains fascinating to me that she couldn't see the image she was presenting to men, even then. But so often it is easier to see something from the outside looking in than the other way around. Let me describe her for you.

Brooke was an attractive young woman. She was very thin and shapely, despite delivering two children in as many years. She dressed fashionably, and I assumed (correctly) that she came from a wealthy family who supplied her with money. But her dress was not only fashionable, it was also provocative. Brooke did not dress in a sleazy or cheap way; however, without being technically outside the lines of immodesty, she did wear very tight-fitting, suggestive clothing. Her hair was modern, and she wore a small but noticeable diamond stud in her nose.

I struggled to explain to Brooke the message she was sending. It was difficult. At this point in her life she was very strong in her testimony of the gospel and in her desires to live happily ever after as a wife and mother, serving in the Young Women's presidency or being the wife of the bishop someday. Indeed, she was an amazing young woman, strong in her beliefs and in her convictions. And yet she was continuing to attract bad men. "See," she had said many times, "that's all there are out there!" I asked her to consider what type of girl the guy on her list would be looking for, and her second list of qualities looked something like this:

1. She would be attractive—thin, neatly dressed, and healthy in her manner.

Brooke surmised that if he were attractive, he would probably marry someone who was also attractive.

2. She would be active, not lazy, with a lot of interests and motivation.

She would be the type, she said, who could whip out a Primary program while baking bread and helping the kids with their homework all at the same time.

3. Definitely an active member of the Church.

Brooke worried that this might refer to someone who was waiting to have her first kiss over the altar.

4. Would have set strong boundaries for the sake of morality. She would not be the type to tempt him into situations he knew he didn't want to be in.

"She would probably listen to nothing but hymns," Brooke added with a smile.

5. She would be honest, kind, giving.

6. She would think the world of him and would always let him have the final say in all their family decisions.

7. She would want many children.

8. His family would adore her.

9. She would have a limited knowledge of the Atonement because she would have never done anything to cause her to use it.

Or at least, she conceded, she would have fully repented of any mistakes she might have made in her past.

Brooke had to come around to the ideas that, first of all, there were actually good guys out there, and second, she could be the type of girl they would want to marry. She began to think of her own image in terms of that good guy she was going to someday marry. She worked hard to change many aspects of her image, including the way she acted when she was out with her friends. And she began to notice a difference in the men who were talking to her now. But as she was preparing to begin dating again, she wondered how she would know the good guys from the bad ones. She had been fooled before, and she was only beginning to trust in her judgment about these things. So we began looking at red flags in behavior.

She started a second study of the men around her, this time looking at a variety of men for signs of healthiness or unhealthiness. She watched her father, her friends, the members of her bishopric, neighbors, and co-workers. And she evaluated characteristics they exhibited that were either healthy or unhealthy.

She noticed that her neighbors, a couple she admired a great deal, seemed happy because of the husband's unending support of his wife. She noticed that one of her friends was very nonjudgmental of people and never talked badly about others. She noticed her father's kindness as he spoke with her on the telephone from so far away.

She also noticed many signs of unhealthiness, or red flags. She observed that for all the kindness her father showed towards her, he sometimes was very controlling of her lifestyle or choices. She saw in another friend how suggestively he spoke to the girls he met. And she noticed how belittling her best friend's boyfriend was to all women, specifically to her best friend.

Brooke was becoming a discriminating judge of the guys she was willing to allow in her life. She began to believe not only in her worth as a person but also in her ability to choose better men to date. We discussed how some men might have a red flag behavior here or there, because we are all imperfect. It would be when she saw many red flags in one man, or specific red flags, that she would choose not to date him. And so she began from that point to date better men.

Brooke made progress in creating healthier patterns of behavior for herself. As she did so, she increased her self-esteem by building feelings of selfworth: she was taking control of her life, learning to trust her own ability to make good choices and do good things. She went from repeating a terrible mistake to dramatically progressing and becoming more the person she was meant to be.

* * *

I am told that the Chinese symbol for *crisis* is made up of a combination of symbols meaning both danger and opportunity. A crisis is a dangerous time in a person's life, something that pushes us out of a comfortable place and into the unknown. We can feel frightened, sad, or hopeless; however, it is also an opportunity to learn and grow, both individually and in our relationships with others. A crisis will almost always change us. We must be actively working so that the changes that occur are changes of growth. I was glad Brooke did not simply close her eyes and wait for the pain of this crisis to pass. Instead, she opened her eyes, came to realize the patterns that had brought her to pregnancy out of wedlock, and then developed new ways of looking at herself and others. These healthier patterns of behavior would certainly lead her to better relationships and a happier life.

I saw Brooke again about a year ago. She looked wonderful. She was single and attending Brigham Young University, and when I saw her I had to smile. She was still the Brooke I knew and loved so well. Yet I could almost picture the apron she would be wearing while writing some future Primary program and baking bread. It would probably match the tiny diamond studs placed discreetly in the lobes of her ears.

FUTURE RELATIONSHIPS

Developing strong personal relationships is never easy, and for those who have been involved in moral sin, especially if this involvement has led to pregnancy, it can be difficult. Even if the person in question has fully repented and has gained valuable insight by working through this crisis, he or she will continue to face the consequences of those prior actions. These matters affect many peoples' lives, both before the birth and long afterwards. We have discussed in depth how having a baby out of wedlock affects those involved during the pregnancy. These issues can continue to affect lives long afterwards.

When a young woman who has placed a baby for adoption looks at developing new relationships with men, she will certainly be reminded of the painful results of poor choices made in her past. Nonetheless, provided she has thought through her experience in the ways I have suggested, she will now have some positive experiences to draw upon in facing the challenge of a new relationship. She has a chance to make far better dating decisions—decisions that are framed in terms of genuine preparation for temple marriage. She will have to be brave, however. Not everyone will believe she is a changed person, even if she is. Not all men—even very good men—can deal with the fact that a potential mate has had prior sexual experience and has given birth to a child outside of marriage. Consider Mallory's story.

MALLORY'S STORY: WHEN THE PAST HAUNTS THE PRESENT

"I finally just said it. He knew I had something serious to tell him, but I couldn't get the words out for the longest time. So I finally just said it. 'Last year, I had a baby and placed him for adoption.'"

She was shaky now, sitting across from me, and I could imagine how she must have been last week as she told the young man she had been dating about her baby.

"How did he react?" I could see she was struggling to talk about it, and I encouraged her to continue.

"Well, he didn't say anything for a really long time, and then he just said, 'Oh.' That's it, just 'Oh.'"

I watched as Mallory cried once again—this courageous girl who had cried in my office through pregnancy, delivery, and placement of her child for adoption. I felt a pang of sadness for her that she should still be crying after she had done so much to change her life. She had come so far personally and spiritually; it seemed she deserved just a little bit of peace. And now the one thing she wanted more than anything else in the whole world—to meet a worthy young man who treated her right and marry him in the temple — seemed threatened by her past. It is true there are consequences for our behavior, sometimes far-reaching, and Mallory was feeling the effects still; she would probably feel the pangs for some years to come. Still, I wanted her to find someone good.

This hadn't been the first time Mallory shared her past with someone she was dating. She had seen mixed responses. Some young men were supportive of her decision and felt that that was a mistake for which she had repented. Others could not get past it and chose to end the relationship. But this guy was different. Mallory had been seeing him for some time, and they had discussed marriage. She had very strong feelings for him and had been concerned for some time about how he would feel. She had finally felt they could not progress further without his being aware of this very big part of her life.

"He dropped me off at my house without saying much. I asked him how he felt, if he was angry or what, and he said no, just that he needed to think this through. He told me it was a shock for him, and he didn't really know how to feel about it. He said he'd call me later and left." At this final statement her lip quivered. "I haven't talked to him since."

She didn't know what would happen next, and it seemed as if she was going through a loss all over again.

I have asked many young men with whom I have come into contact how they would feel if they learned that a woman they were dating had had a child out of wedlock. I have asked many who are already married, "Would you feel differently about your wife had she shared with you during your courtship that she had broken the law of chastity and conceived a child out of wedlock?" I am often surprised by their answers. Some feel they would have had the maturity and understanding to accept it, and others admit that they would have had a very difficult time with it.

During a group session a couple years ago we were hearing from a panel of birth mothers who, after placing their babies for adoption, had gone on to meet wonderful men and marry in the temple. Each of them shared her experiences with the young men and women listening, and many had brought pictures of their children—both those they had placed for adoption and those they had had after they married. They also brought along their husbands, who shared their experiences. Each husband told what it had been like to learn his girlfriend or fiancée had placed a baby for adoption. It was very touching to hear and clearly very personal for those couples to share. All of the husbands on the panel shared their experiences, some having taken longer than others to accept what had happened. But one of the husbands stood out in my mind by a single comment he made. He said, "When my wife told me about her past, the only thing that I could think was, 'She is the person she is today because of the experiences she has had in her past.' Her character and her testimony have been deeply affected by her going through those experiences. I wouldn't want to change who she is for anything."

What a beautiful statement of support and love. Though it is wonderful that the sin and crisis of an out-of-wedlock pregnancy can eventually lead to strength of character and deepened testimony, it is important to note that this husband was not celebrating what his wife had done in becoming an unwed mother; he was celebrating who she had consequently become in the course of replacing bad choices with good ones. While he knew full well that she had made grave mistakes that caused pain for herself and so many others, he also saw that she had made significant changes in her own life, becoming stronger spiritually and personally through repentance. The baby and her experiences with him are a part of her life.

Mallory was seeing the continuing consequences of earlier choices. But I knew that she wasn't willing to settle for anyone who couldn't accept her with her prior experiences.

Interestingly, Mallory sometimes mused that knowing about her pregnancy was a litmus test for guys, a way to weed out any man who perhaps didn't fully understand and accept the Atonement of Christ. Unfortunately, it weeded out some she had hoped would stay. And despite her hopefulness for her life overall, I knew she was again feeling great remorse for the decisions she had made in breaking the law of chastity.

Some weeks after telling her boyfriend about her pregnancy, Mallory told me they had talked again and decided to "slow things down a bit." He was feeling very unsure about things, and though Mallory was in a lot of pain because of it, she expressed understanding.

"It's my problem and my mistake. Even though I wish he felt differently about it, I can't really blame him for his reaction. I need to marry someone who is okay with my son and with me. Even though my son isn't with me, I will always love him and he'll always be important to me. I need to be married to someone who is okay with that."

And there are such men, one of whom was the husband who came to our group of birth mothers and reported the love he had for his wife, knowing full well what she had done. Part of the faith that unwed mothers must develop is not only faith in themselves and in the Lord but also faith that others will also believe in the changes they have made for the better in the face of adversity.

THE INCREDIBLE WAYS ADVERSITY CHANGES US

An out-of-wedlock pregnancy can seem a debilitating blow to those involved. There is no question that it brings adversity into the lives of many. Adversity brings change, and change can be painful. Yet I wish to emphasize how many young women and young men I have known who have faced the adversity of an out-of-wedlock pregnancy and its consequences and have then made remarkable transformations. I have also seen many parents of unwed parents make remarkable personal changes as they dealt with their child's pregnancy. That is not to say that everyone who faces these experiences will become better people because of it. How we respond to adversity is a choice that we make. But if we do respond well, adversity can prove to be the catalyst for much-needed changes.

Sometimes a young woman or man who seems oblivious to the pleas of concern from parents or to the impassioned counsel of Church leaders needs a powerful opportunity to change. Of course, getting pregnant out of wedlock is not to be sought out in order to effect change. But the consequences of sin, like all adversity, can sober individuals into transforming their lives.

An out-of-wedlock pregnancy is sobering in ways that open possibilities for change.

Adversity can be a blessing if we respond to it with humility. It can allow us to become different, better people despite the setbacks it seems to present. Unlike many other forms of adversity, an out-of-wedlock pregnancy involves a child, and the love that child evokes can bring a powerful and positive motive for change into the lives of his or her parents. Consider how the love Natasha felt for her son made it possible for her to deal first with the adversity of her pregnancy and later with other disappointments.

NATASHA'S STORY: THE REDEEMING LOVE OF A CHILD

Natasha dropped by my office one day. She asked if I had a minute, and after I closed the door, tears quietly rolled down her face. Natasha proceeded to tell me a story of what seemed to her an example of perfect injustice.

I already knew much about Natasha's life, having worked with her over the past year as she dealt with an unwed pregnancy and placed her newborn son for adoption. Natasha had a rough start. As I said in Chapter 1, even from the beginning I considered her a beautiful example of maintaining hope. Now, as she sat in my office, it was three months after the birth of her baby; the pain of saying good-bye was very fresh to her still. Through the help of her family and through sheer personal strength she had broken away from a controlling and physically abusive boyfriend. She had spent several months praying and contemplating her options, finally coming to the decision that placing her baby for adoption would give him the best chance for happiness. She loved this baby and had wanted to raise him; however, she felt that adoption would give her child stable, married parents (her own were divorced), and this way her son could not be influenced by his biological father.

Although these months had been difficult, Natasha continued to feel strong in her conviction that she had done the best for her son and for herself. She still had painful days when she desired only to hold her beautiful baby or smell him one more time. Instead, she looked through pictures of him being held by the smiling mother and father she had chosen and being kissed by his new and proud big sister. She settled for peace now and prayed for happiness eventually in her own life.

Today, however, she had received the news that brought her into my office. Her former boyfriend and the father of this baby boy was now in a relationship with her friend, a friend who had surely seen his mistreatment of her and the pain he had caused. Her friend, she learned, had just given birth to his second son, and they were raising this baby together.

For Natasha it seemed that she had made all the sacrifices and suffered through all the pain, while her former boyfriend was now holding a newborn son and "living happily ever after." She questioned where the justice was in this life that she should sacrifice in doing the right thing while he went on seemingly without consequence. She was upset with the injustice that he could avoid any of the physical or emotional pain involved throughout her pregnancy. She was upset that he had never seen, never even expressed a desire to see, his precious son. She was angry that he felt none of the pain in making a decision for the sake of the baby and laying this infant in someone else's arms, only to say good-bye and walk away. She was angry that she had faced all this without his support and that she was still alone while he had gone on to another relationship. Most immediately, she was upset that he was holding his new son now and her arms felt more empty than ever before.

We talked for some time, and her expression of emotions helped her to see her life and his in a clearer perspective. She began to express gratitude that she was not with him and still tangled in that unhappy part of her life. She was grateful that she had learned through this experience a greater under-standing of her Heavenly Father's plan for her own life and the life of her pre-cious son. He had not had the experience of holding and loving this child, as she had, or of realizing how very perfect and incredible their baby was. By escaping the responsibility of her pregnancy, she realized, he had also lost an opportunity to change his own life. True enough, he had not gone through all of the pain, but he had also not experienced the spiritual confirmation that Natasha had felt. He had forfeited the experience of touching his son's skin, smelling his hair, or kissing his cheek one last time. As painful as these expe-riences had been, Natasha realized that they were among her most valuable and treasured experiences.

For Natasha, the sacrifices were certainly worth the later rewards she received. She went on to meet a wonderful young man who accepted her past as a part of who she is. The last time Natasha dropped by my office, she was married to her sweetheart and expecting a baby girl in the near future. She talked about their plans for the future and her hopes for both her new daughter and the son she had placed some years ago. Her wedding announcement had read, "Dreams really can come true," and with Natasha, I suspect this is still the case.

*　*　*

Some of the most incredible people I have ever met are people whose lives were forever changed by an out-of-wedlock pregnancy. They are people whose experiences of pain and heartache have molded them into strong, faithful examples of how to live our lives. Adversity changes us. Our lives are shaped and our character is built through the challenges we must confront along the journey of our lives.

This book is a tribute to the many whose faith has allowed not only the families of others to be built but their own families to be strengthened through adoption. It is a tribute to all those who have made sacrifices in their own lives in order to give life, hope, and happiness to their children. It is a celebration of the people who were, are, and will be in the future strong enough to be guided by their Father in Heaven to do what is best for themselves and the precious children whose lives were entrusted to them.

To the many other individuals and families whose experiences have been shared in this book, either by me or through their own narratives, I say thank you for letting me share in your experiences and for showing me your examples of strength. Those who overcome adversity through faith—especially the adversity of a pregnancy that takes place outside of marriage—are truly awe-inspiring people, people I am grateful to have known.

*　*　*

JUNE 22—

What an amazing day! Nathan hit his first home run in Little League, and his father and I were so proud. Adam was even more excited than we were—he seems to think his older brother can do no wrong.

As I was watching my two boys celebrate with their daddy, I was thinking about how differently my life has turned out from what I originally planned. I know I never expected that it would take some of the turns it has taken.

Gracie is eight years old now, and she is still as beautiful to me as the day she was born. She was my first child, and I will always love her. But she has her own family now, parents and siblings who love her as much as I do. And I have mine.

Would I change anything about my life? Absolutely. Choices I made early in my life caused me and my loved ones far too much pain. But I would never change Gracie, or the joy she has brought to my life and so many others. I would not change the person I am today because of her. I have questioned many things about my life, but I have never doubted my decision to place her for adoption.

Gracie saved me. She'll never know how much her birth changed my life. I give thanks every day for the life I have now. And I give thanks that I was able to share hers. We were together for only a short time, but her life has influenced mine forever.

PART 2
STORIES OF ADOPTION

Introduction

Gideon O. Burton

People have often asked me why I became involved with this project. "Have you and your wife adopted a child?" they ask. We have not. Neither have I worked in the adoption field, as has my co-writer, Monica Blume. No, adoption became of compelling interest to me because a young woman, a student of mine, had the courage and candor to write the story of placing her baby for adoption.

Jennifer (I will call her) was a pleasant, quiet student who sat in the back of the Mormon Literature class I was teaching at Brigham Young University. We had been studying personal essays, a genre of writing that Latter-day Saints take to quite readily because we are accustomed to writing about our lives in journals and to speaking frankly about our beliefs and feelings in testimony meetings and missionary settings. I invited students to try writing their own personal accounts.

So Jennifer came to my office with a draft of her essay. Hers was a long, difficult story that started with letting her guard down and led to a broken relationship and the heartache of an unexpected pregnancy. There was tragedy in her story—foolishness, and sin, and many tears. But there was redemption, too. Jennifer found herself surrounded by loving help: a spiritually insightful mother, two patient bishops at home and at school, plus home and visiting teachers specially assigned to her as she experienced the awkwardness of being a single pregnant woman attending college.

My student's story was compelling to me—not because of the drama of her sin (which was certainly sad) but because of the way that, with help, she redeemed her bad experience. And the baby that was the result of her transgression became the catalyst for remaking her life. No, not because she then became a loving mother raising a daughter alone; she was ill prepared to provide all that her child deserved. Rather, she became a loving mother through the act of offering her baby to a family who could give her child all that she could not.

Jennifer's story moved me profoundly. As a teacher of literature I saw in it all the elements of dramatic tension and resolution that make for compelling reading; as a Latter-day Saint I saw the miracle of repentance and witnessed again how the love of a child has transforming power. I was humbled and grateful to see the gospel in action. Jennifer's suffering was sobering, but it was relieved by parents, Church leaders, and fellow Church members who each acted well their part. I was equally amazed to learn about the system the Church had set up to help unwed mothers. I suppose that I vaguely knew that social services were offered by the Church, but Jennifer's personal essay taught me about a whole world I'd known nothing about (but have since come to value immensely in my role as a bishop).

I learned, for example, that LDS Family Services provides trained counselors with degrees in social work and marriage and family therapy for such young women and young men, as well as for their family members. These professionals are also committed members of the Church, and they work alongside parents and bishops to prepare these struggling young people for the difficult choices and additional heartache they will yet go through. They are not alone.

Jennifer's caseworker at LDS Family Services was named Monica, and as Jennifer described everything that Monica had said and done, it made me think very highly of LDS Family Services and the trained professionals working there. Monica respected Jennifer at a time when Jennifer's self-esteem was very low. She carefully outlined to Jennifer both the choices and the consequences of either single parenting, marrying, or placing her child for adoption, and she also invited her to attend group sessions. There, others who are facing the same choices come to support one another and hear from people who come back to tell about how their choices and lives have worked out.

Jennifer chose to place her child for adoption. What an emotional experience! But Jennifer's essay did not suggest that this was a tragic time; rather, it showed me that she had been prepared and that this experience was actually one of enormous loving sacrifice—tearful, but good. Jennifer titled her story (included in Part 2) "Her Birth Mother, Forever."

What a great story. Even if it were fiction, I reasoned, it would be compelling. But it was not fiction. Jennifer's candid words drew me in until I identified with her plight and felt great sympathy for her situation—even though I am neither a woman, nor her age, nor had I experienced anything like she had. As in great literature, the vivid realism of Jennifer's experience sobered me into an awareness of human suffering that I could relate to vicariously. Though her journey was not easy, it was edifying for me, just as it was redemptive for her. I was so pleased that she had been brave enough to tell it. As I later expressed to Monica, I was delighted to see how my student had not endured a bad experience but used a difficult experience to become spiritually stronger, and she became better prepared to be a mother when the time is right.

Monica, who has had much more experience in observing this amazing process, was quick to point out to me that not everyone has such a good experience and that no one purposefully gets into such serious difficulty to find spiritual growth. Indeed, there are many who are unlike Jennifer—who never get professional help, or don't rely upon gospel principles or prophetic counsel regarding these situations, or are misdirected by the very people who should be helping them. But Monica reinforced my earlier realization that people can choose to make this crisis an opportunity.

My work as a bishop has introduced me to many kinds of suffering that Latter-day Saints endure in their private lives, and I now see adoption as the uniquely redemptive miracle that it is—by coming together through adoption, the adopting family and the birth parents replace their suffering with love. True, it is not right for every unwed mother to place her child for adoption, and true, not every adoption works out perfectly. But story after story has convinced me that God has made a way for two hurting parties to contribute to the healing of one another, and, quite beautifully, this redemption takes place through the love of a child.

When I discovered that Monica and her colleagues regularly invite the birth mothers and family members they work with to write about their experiences as part of the healing process, I was delighted. Writing is a way not just to communicate, but to heal.

It has long been my experience that narrating one's life is therapeutic. I have known this from years of journal writing, and from teaching writing, I have seen that writing about one's life is not just creating a chronicle for future generations; it is an act of faith for us now, a vehicle for making sense of our distress, a way of measuring God's influence, a bandage on our souls as we unburden ourselves through honest personal expression. Writing is not the only way, but it is one very powerful way to help make us whole. Like adoption, honest personal writing is about sharing a life, about turning over to someone else something precious that you have created. There is risk involved, but good readers, like good parents, recognize the offering that is made, and both are edified together.

I invite you to follow the same journey that I have had both in empathizing with others as they tell their moving accounts and in learning the wisdom of the Lord in establishing a Church that can truly serve the difficult temporal needs faced by unwed mothers and infertile couples. As usual, we discover that in temporal affairs there are tremendous spiritual possibilities, and nowhere is this more manifest than in the journey these travelers take along the incredible path of adoption.

I Knew What Needed to Be Done

by "Elizabeth"

I was pregnant. Twenty years old, single, and pregnant. A flood of questions tore through my mind. "How could this have happened to *me?* How am I going to tell my family? Is my life over? How will people look at me as a single, unwed mother-to-be?" I had done something that I could not reverse. Immediately following the confirmation of my pregnancy, I felt a strong impression that I should place the baby in another home better prepared to receive this sweet blessing. I then knelt down to ask Heavenly Father for His help and guidance in following His prompting and coping with this painful decision. Pleading with my Heavenly Father became a source of abiding strength and comfort.

I wasn't raised in the Church. In fact, I had only begun regularly attending meetings a few months earlier. Despite possessing only a tiny shred of testimony, I knew that temple marriage was essential and still possible. I naturally pondered the possibility of spending the rest of my life with the father of my baby. The idea of my very own family seemed wonderful and exciting; however, the warning voice of the Spirit came strongly, telling me not to pursue that direction. I had hoped he would take me to the temple. Deep down, though, I knew he would not.

I sought the first possible opportunity to speak with my bishop. While I shared with him my experiences, the influence of the Spirit was felt, and tears flowed freely from his eyes and mine. Throughout the weekly meetings that would follow, this sweet bishop never lectured me or condemned me. He simply offered loving counsel in a much-needed spirit of hope and encouragement.

One day, the bishop asked if I would like to speak to someone from LDS Family Services. I agreed and made an appointment. It was awkward, at first, to speak with a representative of LDS Family Services. I was so emotional and felt so embarrassed to be including more strangers in this very personal process. I could sense, though, that it was important for me to work with them. I understood the road ahead would be long and difficult, but for some reason I was not afraid.

LDS Family Services proved invaluable. I was grateful the Church had established this inspired program. From the first meeting I felt that Dale, my assigned caseworker, had only my best interest in mind. He asked me a few background questions about where I grew up, my family circumstances, and my feelings about the coming baby. I was experiencing such a flood of different emotions that crying seemed to be my only method of expression. We discussed at length the options available to me. If I chose to continue with adoption proceedings, we discussed how the baby, my family, the father, and the baby's future family would be affected.

This was what I needed. I needed to talk about my feelings with someone who would sincerely listen. I also needed someone to simply cry with. I yearned for an environment where the supporting and consoling influence of the Spirit could be felt on a consistent basis.

During this time, my desire to be close to my Heavenly Father and receive forgiveness greatly increased. I could feel Him daily, granting me the strength and confidence that I wouldn't have otherwise had. I was given the opportunity of selecting the future family of the new baby. What a sacred and significant privilege this was! I was so humbled to bless a grateful and worthy family with such a treasure. I immediately recognized the family the Lord had chosen to raise the sweet baby. I felt myself becoming anxious to deliver. I could feel, in a sense, this experience drawing to an appropriate close.

The day finally arrived. Dear friends were by my side lending comfort as the nurses began preparing me for the delivery. The long needles and strange equipment were a horrible sight. Every painful and fearful emotion Heavenly Father had spared me to this point was blazing forth with a terrible brilliance. Doubt crept in. I didn't know if I could do it. I wanted to go home. The contractions came harder and harder. Within a few hours, a sweet baby girl was born. I will never forget my kind doctor saying to me with tears in her eyes, "You did it, Elizabeth. I am so proud of you!" She was a mother herself, and her compassion and simple words meant so much.

When my baby girl was brought back to my room, feelings of love seemed to flood into me. I loved to hold her as she drank from the bottle. I loved to see her look up at me, as though she recognized me and needed me. I loved how soft and sweet she felt in my arms. I wrote in my journal that day:

"Oh my, this has been a marathon two days and it is almost over. I have a little baby here beside me. She is finally here and so perfect. Every time I look at her I love her more and my heart seems to break. How will I do this? How will I say good-bye? I won't feed her anymore; I won't feel her little body and soft cheeks after tonight. I didn't know it would be this hard. I would love to just run away with her. We could be so happy together. We could play, and I could stare at her beautiful face all day and all night. And I would cry because she wouldn't have the priesthood in her life or be sealed to a family in the temple for eternity. I could never take those things away from her. Oh, this is the most terrible feeling to have her go. I know that tonight will be over soon and tomorrow my sweet little angel will be gone. Her parents are so excited. Everyone has been so nice to me, so many have brought me flowers, so many have hugged me, been there for me, and understood. This has been a bittersweet experience. And I have been so blessed."

I will never forget the bond I felt with her. I will also never forget the sadness I felt as I realized her new mother was missing this sacred moment. My heart broke thinking of the new mother and how desperately she must have wanted to carry this child. How many tears she must have shed knowing she would never experience this moment.

Heavenly Father's hand was clearly evident every step of my journey. I knew He had led me to those who would love me and a bishop that would cry with me as we worked together to fully understand the Atonement. It was not easy to have everyone know that I was single and pregnant. It was not easy to have to explain every detail of my life to a social worker as we mapped out my feelings and made plans for the delivery of the baby. It was not easy to feel as if every aspect of my life had to be painfully dissected time and time again. My patience was tried as I dealt with so many different people. I didn't like feeling the shame I felt each week when I went in to meet with my dear bishop. I didn't like that I was a walking stream of tears. I didn't like being a twenty-year-old, unwed mother-to-be meeting people my age who immediately doubted my testimony and future dreams. My pride hurt, and my tears never seemed to end.

I knew myself, though, and I knew what needed to be done. I knew the process I was going through, though painful, would seal my heart unto my Heavenly Father. I knew that my first and foremost obligation every day would be to mend my relationship with Him and progress, never losing the precious perspective I was gaining. I had gained a solid testimony of prayer, of the scriptures, and of the love our Savior has for each one of us. I was humbled to a point I never could have imagined.

I had a favorite scripture during this time: "I, the Lord, am bound when ye do what I say; but when ye do not what I say, ye have no promise" (D&C 82:10). This scripture taught me everything I needed to get through this trial. The lesson is simple. Study the gospel, learn the principles, and do what you know to be right. Live righteously. What a simple answer to life's very difficult problems and circumstances. Do what is right, and the Lord is bound to bless you.

Almost two years have passed now as I write this. I still vividly remember those sweet days with the angel baby girl I carried. I remember the painful difficulty of placing her in a stranger's arms and leaving the hospital feeling so empty and alone. I remember crying for months as I struggled to regain a normal life.

Gradually, I learned to laugh more often, and my heart seemed to heal a little more quickly. A short time later, I met a wonderful person who became a sweet friend to me. The kindness he showed me during that difficult period has left a permanent impression on my heart. I am so grateful for him and his ability to love as Christ does. Recently, we have realized our dreams of a temple marriage and have embarked on our eternal journey together, full of hope, faith, and confidence in our future.

Elizabeth has been married in the temple, and she and her husband now have a child of their own. Her husband is very supportive of her experience with adoption, and she keeps in touch with the daughter she placed.

SLOW MIRACLES: AN ADOPTIVE MOTHER'S STORY

by "Charlotte"

When I was a little girl, my family went on an outing to Mount Timpanogos. I remember looking up to the top and thinking how huge the mountain was. We started out on the trail, and I started out with a lot of energy and was excited about the climb. The trail became harder and longer. The winding trail seemed to last forever, and I kept thinking that our destination would be around the curve. "Are we there yet?" were my words. The trail became higher and harder, and most of us needed to be carried for part of the way. You get to the top only after all of the effort. This is like our lives. The Lord promises it will be worth it, and then all the struggles and fighting will be as but a moment.

Shortly after Evan and I were married, we found out that our chances for conceiving a baby were slim. We realized we had a journey to take and a mountain to climb. The trail was difficult, and turning the corners and not finding the desired result was devastating. When we were living in Utah, we felt led to go to Montana. We didn't know why. Evan had better job offers elsewhere. When we got there, Evan's company changed its health policy to cover infertility treatments. But our treatments reached an end. For years we climbed the mountain of childlessness, and we finally felt our opportunities had been exhausted. Something drew us to Wyoming, and we turned to LDS Family Services for adoption. I kept thinking, "Are we there yet?" How long would we suffer from not having a child? We had gone so long already. Suddenly I turned the corner, and there was a phone call, and a miracle.

Evan was away on a business trip when our stake president called. He said there was a baby that needed a home. It was a baby boy with blond hair and blue eyes. I could not believe what he was saying. Could it be my miracle? I called the foster home. A planned adoption had fallen through for this little boy the day before. The foster mother wanted this boy to grow up in the Church and serve a mission. She had e-mailed all of the stake presidents in the area with a plea for this boy. It was a miracle the stake president and his wife thought of me. She told me I could come in the morning and see him. I pictured how cute he was. I heard him cry in the background, and tears streamed down *my* face. Waiting to meet him—oh, my night was filled with tears, smiles, and grateful prayer. I never did sleep. On the way to meet him my heart was racing in anticipation. I walked into the home and saw him sleeping. He was so precious. I instantly fell in love. I spent hours holding him, looking at every finger and sweet thing about him. He smiled. My heart and joy were full. Since I had finished my paperwork and the needed home studies through LDS Family Services, I was able to start the proceedings to bring him home. The agency he was placed through had fees that were much higher than what we had saved for adoption through the Church. But here is the other miracle. On Valentine's morning, my mother had called. That was also the morning of my call from my stake president. She said that a trust from my grandfather, who had died, had come in the mail for me and she had sent it that day. The money we saved along with the money that was sent was the amount we needed to adopt our sweet baby boy.

It took us less than a day to get up to the top of Mount Timpanogos. As a child, it seemed like forever. The time it took for my trials to be resolved was a miracle for me. Sometimes I cried out and wished that my trials be removed from me. But it was during this time I grew and gained a strong testimony of faith. Elder Boyd K. Packer said that some of us think a miracle is a miracle only if it happens instantly, but miracles can grow slowly; patience and faith can compel things to happen that otherwise never would have come to pass (*Ensign*, February 1972, 71). Although it took us eight years to have a baby, I forgot the time, and it was as but a moment.

Charlotte and Evan report that when their second son arrived biologically, they felt the same sense of that child belonging to their family as they did with their first, adopted, son. They still write to the birth mother of their first child.

An Adoptee's Story

by Chris Michalek

While the 1960s were a decade of dramatic change in moral attitudes and cultural mores, single mothers had not yet become accepted. It was in this situation that my own mother found herself in a rural farm community. She went away to live with her sister to distance herself from the intense relationships and stigma in her own small town. She declined a marriage proposal and chose instead a much more difficult path . . . alone.

She discussed the idea of adoption with her family and pondered it much in her own heart. It was decided that she would place the child in the home of her sister's friend with the assistance of an attorney to file the necessary paperwork. This was a difficult decision for my mother, but she loved me deeply even then and wanted the best for me. As was the custom at the time, there was to be no correspondence or relationship between her and the family she had placed me with. She knew that some information would likely be available to her through her sister, but there would be no formal avenue of communication, much less any expectation for a later reunion. Again, she chose her path . . . alone.

Since both my brother and I came into our home through adoption, it is a topic that is at the heart of our family. As long as I can remember, we have been very open in talking about adoption as a process. My parents would tell us of the great desire they had to have us be a part of the family. This made me feel wanted. What could make a child feel more special than to know that he was "hand picked" to be a part of a family?

We were told of birth mothers who cared so much for us that they were willing to give us the best even though they would miss us. I was able to feel secure knowing that I was loved from the moment of conception and that there was someone, even outside our family, that cared for me deeply.

Though adoption was an open subject in our family, it was not central to my nor my brother's identity. I was never introduced as an "adopted son" or anything of the sort. My parents were very good to discuss the subject if we wanted but did not make it a constant reminder. Likewise, the limited information they had regarding my birth parents was available if I asked but not discussed otherwise.

There were times, as with most adoptees, when I wondered and fantasized about what my biological parents were like and the circumstances regarding my adoption. These occurrences were brief and never sprang from a desire to be "rescued" from my family but were instead ways of incorporating a significant aspect of my life into my own self-image and identity.

I always held an almost magical vision of my birth mother. Growing up, I imagined her as beautiful, caring, and strong. My parents had shared with me that she was an active LDS woman and that she continued to be concerned about me. With this as my only guide, it was almost like having a guardian angel with me when troubles came. Due to the great love and support that my family always offered (and bolstered by a perception of adoption as a blessing that afforded me this support), I had strength to smoothly navigate most of the challenges of childhood and adolescence.

I never felt the need to seriously question my identity nor a longing for reunion with my birth parents. I was asked on numerous occasions by friends about my adoption and some were taken aback that I didn't want to know about my "real" parents. I often replied that I knew my "real" family. They were the ones I had grown up with and shared my life's experiences with. This was true, but somewhere deep inside I was also aware that seeking out the real person could mean shattering the wonderful image I had come to hold so dear.

My personal story gave me strength during the tumultuous period of adolescence and into adulthood. I had married and begun preparing for my career before I fully understood adoption. I was thirty years old when I received a call from my mom. She had just received a call from an old friend. She told me that my birth father's family had made contact with her and they wanted to meet me. At that time, all I knew about my birth father was that he had died in Vietnam. I responded that I was interested but that I was concerned about my mother's feelings as well.

She told me of the friendship she had with my biological aunt and how my placement had been arranged. I was surprised to learn how closely my birth mother had followed my life from afar and of her ongoing desire to reunite. It continues to astound me the level of respect that they showed for my agency in not pursuing a reunion earlier despite their perennial proximity.

I was able to meet members of both my maternal and paternal biological families in the same weekend. It was a humbling experience to realize the impact and meaning that my birth had for people I had never met.

The most personal aspect of the reunion was coming to know the woman who brought me into this world and then let me go in hope of a brighter future. She was and is everything I had imagined her to be. I discovered that she had found love and married shortly after my birth. Despite a myriad of losses and challenges in her life, she continues to be a strong example of faith and devotion to others.

In the eight years since our initial reunion, we have continued to stay in contact with one another. We talk occasionally on the phone and visit each other when possible. I have attended family reunions and feel great affection for my half-siblings. It is unfortunate that we now live so far apart.

My experience with adoption does not end there, however. My wife and I have had the joy of adopting our two daughters. We came to know two more wonderful women who had the courage and love to bring our children to our home. Through letters, gifts, and pictures, we have been able to feel of their indomitable spirits and great charity.

Much as my parents did, I strive to be as open and grateful as possible when discussing adoption with my daughters. I want them to appreciate the great blessings that have been afforded them. I want them to know how much we wanted and longed for them to be a part of our family and of the women who made that possible. I strive to give them the same sense of worth that I was given.

Chris Michalek, who was adopted as an infant, has adopted two daughters. In addition to his full-time work as a therapist, he works part-time for LDS Family Services and continues to be an advocate of adoption.

A Pregnancy Timeline

by "Heather"

January 2002—

* I'm working two full-time jobs and live in a house with a bunch of roommates and two dogs. Why on earth am I so stressed out? Why can't I make it through a single night without making several trips to the bathroom? I swear I'm gaining weight.

* I find a sample pregnancy test that must be a year old. On a whim, I decide to take it; after all, I really haven't felt normal for a while. The problem is the box is gone. What do the two pink lines mean? I call a married friend of mine to ask. She says I'm pregnant.

* I quit every bad habit I have—even caffeine. I go to bed early and try to keep up a healthy diet that will be most beneficial for your health and growth.

* I can't handle working both jobs anymore. I get way too tired all the time. So I drop the first one and decide to work extra hours at the second job during the Olympics.

February 2002—

* Though I never get morning sickness, I can't handle strong smells. I don't wear my girly lotions anymore. I eat turkey sandwiches from Subway every day—they're the only food that doesn't make me sick. I have my very first doctor's appointment and everything is going well. She gives me some vitamins.

* I saw you on an ultrasound. I can't believe there is a perfect tiny person inside me. I spend all my free time sleeping—mostly at my parents' house. My apartment is too depressing and smelly.

MARCH 2002—

• I pack up all by myself and move to our new house. Thank goodness I am leaving that horrible house, bad roommates, and smelly dogs.

• My cousin gets married and I go to the luncheon. It's the first time I've spent time with any relatives since I became pregnant and I try to suck my stomach in extra hard so that they won't notice the extra weight around my middle.

• I go to aerobics with my mom every Monday, Wednesday, and Friday. I'm not a milk drinker, but I know it's important that I get enough calcium so I drink a huge glass of Nestlé's Quik every morning. I need to have a good break-fast, too, so I take up cereal eating. I don't put milk on it though; I hate soggy stuff! I carry baggies of Cheerios everywhere. The hospital offers free ultrasounds, so I get one. You are very active at this one. I'm just in love with you.

• I speak to a case worker at LDS Family Services. I'm not interested in considering adoption at all, so I figure this will be my only visit.

• I decide to give the birth parent group a try. It's actually pretty in-credible. I'm learning a lot about adoption, but it's still not for me.

• I go to my cousin's missionary homecoming and tell one of my cousins that I'm pregnant. She's my only extended family member to know.

APRIL 2002—

• Still going to aerobics (plus taking walks every other day) and eating cereal (Golden Grahams—yummy). Oh yeah, lots of chocolate milk. I get a job at a daycare. That way I won't have to leave you when I go to work. I watch all the two-year-olds while they take naps. I feel bad for all the kids who have to spend 8–10 hours there a day. It's actually pretty depressing.

• I switch doctors and start seeing the one my mom had when she was pregnant with my brother. He's super cool.

• I think adoption isn't such a bad idea. But if I decide to place, I'm going to disappear out of state for the remainder of my pregnancy. That way no one will have to know and I will come back and resume life as usual.

• I talk to my caseworker. She helps me see that running away will make it harder for me to heal. I can see that she's right, but I still feel so embarrassed and ashamed. I am so scared to tell my extended family. They will be so disappointed. It won't be long before I start to show so I'd better tell them soon. My mom and I decide to invite my aunts and grandma over for lunch. My mom makes an awesome meal. I tell everyone while we eat and wait for the awkward pause and looks of disdain. But as soon as I'm done speaking, one of my aunts says, "You look so good! We love you!" I cry with relief. I am overwhelmed by their acceptance. My grandma asks me if she can cry, too. I will never underestimate my family again.

• My mom and brother go with me to my third and final ultrasound. You are being pretty modest so we can't tell if you are a boy or a girl. They bring in an ultrasound specialist to see if he can get a better look. Sure enough, you're a boy! I wanted a boy!

MAY 2002—

• I have definitely decided that you were not sent for me. I am learning so much about adoption and realize that there is a family out there that needs you. I know this, even when I don't want to know it. It's very sad for me, but at the same time, I feel at peace.

• I go to Birth Mother's Day at LDS Family Services. The room is filled with birth mothers. I am one of two women who are still pregnant. Everyone shares their experiences and pictures. Everyone is emotional. I'm amazed to see birth moms with the same emotional intensity five years after placement as those just months after. Those who have moved on, married, and are raising their own children were still as emotional, if not more so, than anyone else. I get a plant there and name it Artemis, after the goddess of unmarried women, youth, and childbirth. I start looking at adoptive parent profiles and fill out my paperwork.

• The real Mother's Day is not so happy. I lose it in the middle of sacrament meeting. Never have I ever cried like that. Face red and soaking, I run out of the meeting and race home. No one in my ward even knows I'm pregnant, so they all think I'm wacko.

JUNE 2002—

• We leave for a little family vacation. My new maternity swimsuit looks like a nightgown, but the water is *so* nice I don't even care. I get a dandy sunburn.

• You move around quite a bit now. My tummy isn't huge, but you can tell I'm pregnant.

I am getting pretty sick of looking at adoptive parent profiles. They're all starting to look the same. Maybe I'm not quite ready to make it completely official by choosing your family. I want you all to myself still.

JULY 2002—

• I feel great. I must be the luckiest person to have such an easy pregnancy. I go hiking and swimming and walking all the time. I don't crave anything weird. Everyone else must be crazy for thinking my macaroni and cheese omelet is a bad idea.

• I am not going to look at family profiles anymore. I have three set aside and I feel like your parents are among them. For the life of me, I have no idea which ones, though. I get a blessing and have everyone pray with me to choose the right parents for you. On the 31st I write a letter to your mom and dad to let them know they're going to have a baby.

AUGUST 2002—

• I eat bags and bags of mini marshmallows. I think mac and cheese with hot dog chunks is scrumptious. I mix Golden Grahams with Multi-Grain Cheerios and Alphabits. This must be the hottest August in history. I have the hardest time sleeping. I stay up late. It is so hot.

• I meet your parents for the first time. I already love them so much and I am so excited for them!

• I have another face-to-face meeting with your parents and bring my parents along this time. I couldn't be more certain that they are meant to be your family.

• I take a job watching the kids of an aerobics buddy. Maybe lifting her toddler all week will put me into labor!

• Okay. I'm not ready to have you yet. You need to just stay put. What am I going to do after you're born? Life is pretty good right now. I get to sleep in, I get out of doing yard work, and I am pretty comfortable here. I don't want to get a real job, I'm not ready to go to college, and I DON'T WANT TO DATE!!!

SEPTEMBER 2002—

• I start going to the doctor on a weekly basis. I didn't really mean that about you staying in there forever, but you seem to be taking it to heart.

• All that castor oil, jumping on the trampoline, and jalapeños were not such a great idea.

• I am really frustrated. Every day I go overdue feels like a lifetime. Your grandparents and aunts write me letters. That makes me feel better. They are so amazing.

• You finally arrive—my beautiful, precious angel.

Heather is currently a full-time college student in the process of starting her own business. She still keeps in touch with her baby's family and reports that they are like an extension of her own. She remains actively involved with volunteer programs promoting adoption awareness.

A Grandmother's Testimony of Adoption

by "Evelyn"

I remember my oldest daughter asking me at a young age what happens when a single girl in the Church gets pregnant. I told her of the counsel of the prophet regarding adoption. Little did I know that I would be faced with that situation.

When my unmarried daughter came to me in her early twenties and told me she was pregnant and that marriage was not an option, I knew what should be done. But saying it and doing it are two very different things. When I asked her what she was planning to do, she looked me in the eyes and said, "I am going to do what you have always taught me to do. I am going to see that this child gets sealed."

The day that my daughter told me about her pregnancy, the Spirit spoke to me loud and clear. "This baby does not belong to your family. He is not to be in your family. He belongs to someone else." There was no mistaking it.

Still, my daughter was having second thoughts. Even though she knew what the counsel was, she was hesitating. Her father and I shared our thoughts and feelings on the matter but told her the decision was hers. We knew that the prophet had given clear counsel on this matter. He has not, and never will, lead us astray, but the decision needed to be hers. We asked that she meet with the Church social services before making any decision, and she agreed. After studying, pondering, and praying, she decided on adoption. When she told us of her decision, we felt the peace that comes from making the right decision. I knew that the parents of that baby were patiently waiting somewhere. We counseled her that she was literally about her Father's business, as her job was to make sure the baby was healthy and to find the parents that this baby was supposed to go to. We felt the Spirit more strongly than ever before. It was truly as if she were being carried by forces beyond the veil.

As we prepared for the birth and adoption of this child, we did so as a family. My daughter continued to work to find "the" family for the baby. She read and prayed about each profile she was given. She then called us all together. We opened with a prayer, and she shared the profiles with us and asked us to choose which one we thought would be the best. As each of us read the stories and letters of these prospective parents, we were deeply touched; however, there was one family that stood out to all of us. It was not a surprise to us that this particular family was the one that our daughter had chosen also. Even though the final decision was our daughter's, the Spirit confirmed to all of us that it was the right choice. What a sacred experience that was.

In preparing for the adoption, my husband and I also met with the caseworkers. We found them to be so loving and caring with our daughter and with us. We were encouraged to prepare for the adoption along with our daughter. I chose to prepare a basket much like the one that Moses' mother placed him in as she sent him off to preserve his life. I felt that my daughter was sending this child off to preserve his eternal life. I also crocheted a baby blanket, and that was what he was wrapped in when he left us.

We now have six grandsons, all of whom are very precious and dear to me, but I will never forget the day this child was born and the days of the week following his birth. I was in the delivery room with my daughter and could feel the angels attending to her and the baby as he entered his earthly life. The days that followed were ones of great joy and sadness. We loved him so much. I watched my daughter hug him, kiss him, rock him, hold him, change him, feed him, all with such tenderness and love that only a mother could give, and then, a few days later, I saw her send him to his family that had been anxiously awaiting his arrival.

We took pictures, hugged and kissed him, said good-bye, and placed him in his basket. Were we sad? Yes. Were we happy? Yes. Did she do the right thing? Yes.

If we could feel what it is like in the premortal existence to say good-bye to our loved ones as they come to earth, this event was the closest we could ever get. The mixed feelings of joy, sorrow, and great love were beyond anything that I have ever felt. What a great experience. What faith it took on the part of my daughter to trust the Lord enough to do what has been counseled by the prophet of the Church. That experience taught me a lot. Mostly it taught me that courage, faith, and obedience precede the miracle.

What started out as a major crisis ended up being one of the most spiritual experiences of all of our lives. All of us were strengthened in ways we had no idea would ever happen. I know that we have a prophet and that when we do what he counsels us to do, the blessings come abundantly. I have a strong testimony of this process. I hope that all parents who are faced with this situation can have the strength, courage, and will to love that child enough to give it what it came to earth to get, an *eternal* family sealed in the holy temple by the priesthood of God for all time and eternity.

Our courageous daughter was sealed in the temple herself, one month ago, to a choice young man for time and all eternity. What a blessing that was to see her kneel at the altar of God in His holy house, again doing the right thing, in the right way as counseled by the Savior through His prophets.

Evelyn and her husband are currently serving a stake mission in an inner-city branch of the Church. Their daughter is doing well and often speaks to LDS groups advocating adoption. Evelyn shared her story because "sometimes," she reports, "the grandparents are the last ones to get with the program."

HER BIRTH MOTHER, FOREVER

by "Jennifer"

I took a year off from Brigham Young University just after the end of my second year and lived with relatives in a new city. There, I met a man I thought I loved. It was a whirlwind with Glen. I knew it was a dangerous relationship, but I continued anyway. One night, in a moment of complete weakness, I agreed to give him what he wanted in hope that I would be free from the spell he seemed to cast on me.

As my bishop helped me put my life back together again, I knew I had to get away from Glen. But could I ever go back to BYU? My repentance was recent and still so new, but I needed to start again, and I felt sure that school was the place to do it. I prayed that Heavenly Father would let me return and that I could prove to Him I was ready for it all again. I only wanted a second chance.

My bishop thought it would be all right for me to apply back and he checked the box that said I was working on something. My interview with the stake president was interesting. I expected a conversation about what I was repenting about and what I wanted to major in at BYU. Instead, through the whole interview we spoke about my becoming a mother one day. He wanted to make sure that a family was my number one priority and not a career. I didn't know how powerful that conversation would prove or how inspired he had been at the time.

Time passed, and I was accepted back to BYU in the fall. My life was turning around and it could only get better. There was so much to do and things were too crazy for me to think about why I wasn't feeling all that well. At night, I began to worry.

School started, and I knew I had to be pregnant, but I just couldn't accept that fact. After all, I wasn't the type of girl to get pregnant unmarried. I had a head on my shoulders. I prayed fervently each night that Heavenly Father would not let this happen. I knew the Lord had other plans for me, but I didn't know what. I had to tell my mother I was pregnant, but how? How could I, her only girl, disappoint her?

Living at home made it difficult to hide a secret. My mother noticed little things—my heartburn, for example. Each night I was in tears in bed wondering what I was going to do, how I was going to reveal this news. I had worked so hard to be at a spiritual place in my life again, but now I felt alone and scared. "Jennifer, just tell me what's wrong," my mother pleaded. "I will try to understand, whatever it is," she murmured through streams of tears. We sat in tears as I told her what Glen and I had done, how I had repented and was still working each day on it, and how I was trying to accept what I had suspected earlier. It was so overwhelming for me, and she told me of an experience she recently had in the temple. She knew I was pregnant. The Spirit had revealed it to her to break the initial pain of it all. She just didn't want to accept the truth—like mother, like daughter.

I knew I couldn't keep this child. But what was the next step? My mother became my friend, and with her I started to assemble my support for the long journey I knew I had ahead.

The next Sunday on campus I met with my BYU bishop and once again revealed in tears that I was pregnant and due fairly soon. He was surprised, but we went right to work on what to do. First things first: I had to see a doctor right away. The rest of that afternoon was busy with calls from him. That night I met a few people who would be my strength and carry the burden of my secret: my visiting teachers (specially assigned, as they were the Relief Society presidency), and my home teacher, the elder's quorum president. I felt taken care of despite my fears.

The ultrasound confirmed that all was okay and the baby was healthy. I was going to have a girl. I felt a great relief. She was going to be okay. I had become, it seemed, like so many mothers whose only concern is for their child. I knew this baby was special and I had to do the right thing, whatever that was.

My bishop set me up with Monica from the local LDS Family Services. I was afraid to make decisions about my own life, let alone someone who wasn't even born yet, but Monica calmed my fears and told me my options. I was glad to know I could pick the family I wanted to give my child to. Heavenly Father was looking out for me, and I knew this had to happen this way.

I was invited to the weekly group meetings, usually held after my appointments with Monica. At first I avoided these sessions, making excuses to avoid seeing people who in no way could relate to me, a pregnant, single, twenty-one-year old woman. I finally decided to go, and learned I was wrong. Most of the girls were my age or close to it and had stories just like mine. It happened to many, I discovered, and my heart opened. How often I had pre-judged young pregnant women! But now, I felt at home among all of these mothers.

On the other hand, school, work, church, and friends were all more difficult now because I kept my pregnancy secret. Afraid of possible prejudice toward a pregnant single girl at BYU, I hid my growing belly as best as I could. I couldn't really look pregnant, so all of the cute clothes that showed off a rounded belly were out of the question. It was hard to fight the urges to scream out, "I am not this fat, I am just pregnant!" But I couldn't. I was distracted in classes by my protruding stomach and my need to go the bathroom every ten minutes. It seemed so unfair that others (who were married) were allowed to be pregnant on campus; I felt so out of place.

Church was similar. I would come in and sit down and be protected by the support system of my visiting teachers. I didn't go to many activities for fear of discovery, and I didn't get to know many in the ward. I kept my secret. Work was the same story, just sit and answer the phones, no talking with others.

After helping me make a list of all the potential characteristics I wanted in my family someday, Monica set out to find families that matched the same descriptions. I read through several letters and looked at scrapbook pages of families. I took three of them home for the week to read and decide on. This was it—crunch time to find a family for this little girl. I read all three files several times during the weekend and prayed constantly that I would know the perfect family for my baby. One couple, Joey and Danielle, would not leave my mind. I knew it was the Lord's way of saying they were the right couple. My mother agreed with my decision on Sunday night, and that week the couple was asked if they wanted to have a baby soon.

I truly felt like Joey and Danielle were family. I sent a homemade card announcing that they were going to have a baby very soon and telling a little bit about me. I couldn't concentrate as I waited for their reply. It came right away, filled with their excitement yet also their slight trepidation in taking on their first baby. Danielle revealed she knew in her heart a few days before my announcement that she was to be a mother very soon. I couldn't help but think at that moment of how wonderful the gospel is. The baby kicked with acceptance of her new family that had waited seven long years for their first child.

Time was running out. We set up an appointment one cold Tuesday night for me to meet the couple. I had worn a dress to look nice and not so huge at that point. My mother was with me. It was awkward and strange, but exciting. We talked freely, sharing family traditions and stories. The time went by so fast. I wished it could have lasted forever, but that still wouldn't have been long enough. They hugged us good-bye, and I knew this baby was happy. In her journey to this life she wound up in me, but she was meant for them.

Eleven days after my due date I was told I could have the baby that week-end. I went to the hospital, but after two days the baby didn't come. Joey and Danielle sent me beautiful, fragrant flowers, praying I would be all right. Their family had changed the name from "birth parents" to "Jennifer" on the temple prayer list, and I knew I needed those prayers right then. I was still in labor Sunday afternoon when members of a local ward came around and delivered the sacrament. What a blessing to feel a little bit of the Sabbath in the hospital. My bishopric came later and gave me a blessing. I felt the power of the priesthood as I lay in my bed with their hands on my head. I was told that I would find love and happiness in a righteous manner and that I was doing the right thing in the Lord's eyes. I had been blessed throughout the whole journey, yet why did it have to be so hard at that point?

She was born Monday morning. She was beautiful and sweet and I couldn't keep my eyes off her. How could I have created something so pure and perfect? She was all bundled, and I held her tight, admiring every little inch of her small body. My mother stood beside me taking pictures, hiding her tears at the sight of her first granddaughter.

Her name was to be Janiece, a combination that Joey and Danielle had created from both grandmothers' names. I cared for her for two days. I loved feeding her and changing her. I watched her sleep and make the greatest faces. I knew I was meant to be a mother, but my time was just not yet. She was my baby for that short time, and then it was time to give her to her new parents. That last day was hard and full of tears and prayers. I held her tight in my arms as I signed papers releasing me as her parent. I was now her birth mother, forever.

Time has passed now. Janiece is nearly two and certainly different than she was when I saw her so long ago. She now has an eternal family, something I might never have been able to give her. This was why I placed my baby girl.

Having Janiece changed me, gave me strength I never knew I had, faith I didn't know existed. I feel like a more complete person as I have gone through a very strong refiner's fire. I wonder who else out there is facing the same fears I did. I want them to know I survived. Everyone's situation is different, but for me, I knew Janiece was special, meant for me to touch only for a short time but to carry in my heart forever.

Jennifer went on to graduate from BYU. When her daughter turned three years old, she asked her adoptive parents to tell her the story of "being in Jennifer's tummy." Jennifer is grateful her child has been raised knowing she has a birth mother who loves her, and she adds that Janiece will be in her heart forever.

A Bishop's Perspective
on Adoption

by Wayne Schneider

Nikki had always been one of those members of my ward who was very easy to be around. This young woman was bubbly and happy and made you feel good just to be in her presence. It was always pleasant for me as her bishop to visit with Nikki, as she was willing to talk openly and honestly. Our contact was positive and hopeful. Then came the interview that was different.

It was a busy Sunday afternoon. When Nikki came through the door, I was almost immediately concerned. It was apparent that something was amiss. Nikki was not open and sharing. Instead, she was defensive, closed off, and even angry. Tears welled up in her eyes as my questions came closer to the real problem. She finally broke down—she had broken the law of chastity.

Over the next several months we met regularly, weekly at first and then biweekly. Although there were weeks when things did not go so well and she struggled to feel worthy of answers to her prayers, her life steadily improved. After several months, I could see a change in her countenance and a renewed commitment to live the gospel and keep the commandments.

Nikki graduated from high school and moved on to college. Things seemed to be going well. But one day Nikki came to me again to confess transgression. This time was different. She was pregnant.

Having worked together before, we understood and trusted each other. I invited the young man to meet with me, and he agreed. We discussed the option of marriage. These young people revealed a maturity that contrasted with their situation. The young man was willing if that was required of him. But Nikki did not feel that their relationship was strong enough to weather the challenges ahead.

I encouraged both of them to meet with LDS Family Services. There was much that we did not know about how this pregnancy would affect them. The professionals at LDS Family Services had knowledge and experience in areas that I did not. It was a relief to me to know that I could help Nikki with repentance, LDS Family Services could help her with the pregnancy, and we could both guide her in the tough decisions that were to come.

Nikki involved her parents early, and they were very helpful and supportive. In particular, they refrained from making her decisions for her. Although it was very difficult for all of them, they supported Nikki in her decision to place the baby for adoption. I've seen parents of the birth mother want to keep the baby and even raise it as one of their own. Nikki's family chose to let this baby go so she could have the kind of life she deserved.

As the pregnancy progressed, so did the repentance. Nikki had chosen to live at home during the pregnancy, and her parents were able to lend their support. Her friends and ward members offered support as well. There were a few negative reactions from ward members who felt that their own children would be influenced negatively. These parents needed to trust their children to recognize Nikki's situation and to witness the trials she was facing. Their children could also show compassion to Nikki and help her through the pregnancy. Nikki was well on her way through repentance before her pregnancy became obvious. The birth of a child was not the sin.

By the time the baby came, Nikki was well prepared. She had regained her spirituality and felt worthy to receive answers to her prayers. Presenting the baby to the adoptive parents was very difficult, but Nikki and her parents knew it was the right decision. Not only was I able to share in this humbling experience but her Relief Society president was there offering support as well.

I learned many things as I shared this experience with Nikki. I came to appreciate the many others who shared their expertise, recognizing that I needn't have all of the answers myself. I discovered wise and loving counsel given by the Brethren to use with those facing an out-of-wedlock pregnancy. I learned to trust in the Spirit to guide me as I worked to help Nikki.

Several years have passed, and Nikki is now married and has a beautiful daughter. She and her husband have been sealed in the temple and are growing in the gospel. I respect her and value the strength of this daughter of God.

Wayne Schneider has been released from being a bishop and reports it was a difficult but fulfilling calling. While he misses those experiences, he is grateful to have been a means through which the Lord could help others.

My Family Helped
Me Choose

by "Darcy"

During my senior year in high school, I met a boy I fell head over heels for. He eventually became my life, and I spent all of my time with him. I guess it wasn't such a good idea to always be together because our relationship became very serious and neither one of us was prepared for what was about to happen. After only four months of being together, I became pregnant. It was so scary for me. I never thought that at age seventeen I would be pregnant. You always think that it won't happen to you. I remember telling my boyfriend a while back I thought I was pregnant, and he used to joke around saying that I was just being paranoid and to wait things out. One day after he picked me up from work, we passed by a store to buy a pregnancy test. I took the test in a gas station while my boyfriend waited in the car. I remember not even looking at the test because in my heart I already knew the answer. I brought the test out and just handed it to him. He sat there quiet and then asked, "What does the plus mean?" I looked at him and said, "It means that I was right."

On the way home we didn't say anything to each other. We both walked into my house as if nothing was wrong. My mom was in the kitchen, and we sat there talking to her. I then walked him outside, and he just looked at me and said, "What are we going to do?" He began to cry, and I couldn't console him. I just kept thinking, "What am I going to do?" Finally, I hugged him, and we talked things out. He wanted to tell my mom everything, but I wouldn't let him. That night I couldn't sleep. So many things were going through my head, and I was thinking about all my options; yet none of them seemed good enough to me.

For a while I couldn't decide on what to do, and I didn't tell anyone. Only my boyfriend and I knew. We were both alone and very scared. He later asked me to abort the baby, and it hurt me so much to hear him say that. I could not kill my baby. He used to tell me, "It's just a little blob right now"; however, I knew better. The sad part is that in the beginning it crossed my mind, too. I felt so guilty for that. He begged me like you couldn't imagine to take the "easy way out." He made an appointment for me to get an abortion. Two nights before the appointment I spoke to my best friend and told her what was going on. She told me to talk to my sister because she would understand and help me out. My sister and I weren't really close at that time, but I remember that as soon as I hung up the phone with my best friend, my sister walked in. I just looked at her and asked her to hug me. She hugged me, and I just broke down. She begged me to tell her what was wrong, and I finally told her. She just looked at me and began to cry. She then looked up, smiled, and said, "I'm going to be an aunt!"

The next day she bought me a pregnancy test, and it came out positive again. Later on that night she found out from my friend that I was considering abortion so she decided that the best thing to help me was for her to tell our mother. She gave our mother the news that same night. I knew that our mom knew the next morning because when she woke me up for seminary she was more gentle than usual. She looked at me and a tear fell. I felt so horrible. I was hurting my mom. That night my boyfriend came over, and my mom and sister set up a family meeting in which I had to tell my father. It was so hard to do, but I also remember feeling so relieved that my sister had told our mom because in a way she saved my baby and me. After talking to my father and boyfriend, we came to the conclusion that I would get married. I really wanted to keep my baby, and I was beginning to feel such a special love for that little person that was just starting her life inside me.

My mom made an appointment for me to go to the doctor, and my dad made an appointment for me to meet with LDS Family Services. I was beginning to see things in a better perspective. I thought everything was going great, and I was going to marry the guy I loved and be able to keep my baby. I thought I had it made, but then came the hard part. I was with my boyfriend 24/7. I realized then that I wasn't ready to get married. I ignored those feelings for a while and continued to look for a place to live and plan our budget. I began to realize it was not going to work out, and my baby was going to live a life of deprivation. Her parents would always be working, and she was going to be handed around. I wanted a better life for my baby and myself. I didn't want to marry a guy I knew wasn't right for me and then end up getting divorced sooner or later. That's when I really looked into adoption.

Choosing adoption was very difficult because it was the hardest route to take. Adoption would mean having to carry my baby for nine months and then just letting her go. But I wanted my baby to have everything she deserved, which I knew I couldn't offer her. I would not be able to provide her with both a mother and a father to whom she could be sealed. I wanted a lot more for me, too; I wanted her to be proud of me.

I decided to go through with an open adoption. Now almost two years later, I find myself working hard and going to school. I am trying to reach my goals and make things right in my life. Meanwhile, I have received letters and pictures from my baby's parents. I have never seen such a happy baby, and that helps to reassure me every day that I made the best decision. Seeing her grow up so healthy and happy makes it all worth it. She is my life and my number one love. I love her to death. She is the reason that I keep going and wanting to be a better person. My goal is to make her as proud of me one day as I am of her. I think of her every day, and I have no doubt in my heart that she is being well taken care of and loved.

Darcy is currently attending college to become an accountant. She reports that she still thinks of her precious child often and thanks God for her. She describes her as "my angel and inspiration to always reach for the stars."

THE LITTLE BROTHER
I ALWAYS WANTED

by "April"

The day was perfect. I'd been looking forward to the event of that Thursday for most of my time on earth. Driving two and a half hours was a small price to pay for the joy and happiness that was soon to enter my life.

A little brother. As an only child, I'd always dreamed of a little sister, but when the news came that my family had finally been chosen to adopt a little boy, I didn't care that he wasn't a she. He was going to be mine. Someone for me to play with, to hold, to cuddle. Later he'd be someone for me to show off to my friends, someone to love and to cheer me up when life isn't going my way. Even though my soon-to-be little brother would be twelve years younger than me, I didn't think life could get any better.

As my parents and I drove, we decided that we needed to finally settle on a name for the new spirit joining our family. After much deliberation, we settled on the name of Gavin. That name became music to my ears. It meant that I wasn't going to be lonely anymore. No more days of boredom, sitting inside, alone, when none of my friends could come out to play. We discussed what changes we'd have to make in our lifestyle to accommodate a newborn baby in our family. We stopped at Denny's for a quick lunch and then bought some flowers to give to Gavin's birth mother.

When we pulled up to LDS Family Services, I started to feel a little nervous. I was used to having my parents to myself. Whenever I had wanted attention, it was there. If I was ever hurt, I didn't have to stand in line for treatment. I was far from spoiled—my parents wouldn't allow that. But life was pretty good. Was I really prepared for the huge change in my life about to take place? Despite my brief doubts, I was again quickly filled with excitement and anticipation, remembering the times when I would lie on my bed, wishing I had someone of my own to play with, to care for, and to love. My dream was coming closer to being fulfilled.

We met his birth mother. You could see pain in her eyes and how hard it had been for her to give up her child, but she told us a little about her life and why she had made this difficult decision. She wanted her baby to have a better life and more opportunities than were available to her. I was so thankful to her for being willing to sacrifice for this child so that I could be happy. She told us that she loved him but that she knew she had made the right decision in choosing us to raise her son.

After this dramatic scene was over, our social worker brought a baby into the room we were sitting in. Not just any baby, but my baby—the soul that was to become the light of my life, the person I love most. He was so beautiful. I started to cry, and when it was finally my turn to hold him, I could feel my love for him burn inside. I had known this boy for less than five minutes, yet he had already brought me the greatest joy I had ever known. He looked up at me. Not just a glimpse, but a concentrated look. It was almost as though he was approving of my being his new sister. After a minute, he closed his eyes, and we both let out a sigh of complete contentment.

Since that day, my life has changed. It seems as though he's been a member of our family forever, yet sometimes I think back and I can still remember the days of being an only child. I love all of the members of my family, but there will always be a special place in my heart for Gavin, the one that changed my life forever. He's getting older and doesn't always want to sit on the couch and snuggle with me at the drop of a hat like he used to, but he'll always be my baby brother.

April was active in music during high school and has gone on to attend BYU. In the summer she enjoys managing a children's day camp. Her adopted brother, Gavin, will turn eight next year and looks forward to being baptized. April and Gavin are still as close as ever.

Placing My Baby:
A Spiritual Decision

by "Laura"

W hen I first found out I was pregnant I would not even think about adoption. I didn't want to talk to anyone about adoption and was very defensive when someone mentioned it. I wanted to keep this baby. I was, after all, the mother. To make matters worse, there was a chance that I had the beginning stages of cancer and might not be able to bear another child. I wondered if this was the only child I would ever have.

I decided I would start doing the right things in my life. I wanted to be the perfect mother for this innocent child. So I started going to church, praying with real intent, and reading my scriptures. At first, I read the scriptures just because I was supposed to. Then I desired to really learn from them, so I studied them. It wasn't long before I loved reading the scriptures.

I counseled with my stake president. I shared my concerns with him. He gave me a blessing, and in that blessing the Lord reassured me that if I chose to place for adoption, nothing would be kept from me and I would be able to have more children. He spoke with so much power that I was confident in this promise and my concerns about my having more children decreased.

I met with my bishop often. He advised me to receive counseling through LDS Family Services regarding my pregnancy. I agreed and met with a counselor every other week. With my bishop and the counselor I discussed the First Presidency letter from July 2002 that offered counsel to those in my situation. The First Presidency encouraged marriage first and foremost. I knew marriage wasn't an option for me. If marriage was not a possibility, the First Presidency counseled, the baby should be placed for adoption.

The counsel in the First Presidency letter came to my mind one day while I was studying 3 Nephi 28. Verse 34 struck me when I read, "And wo be unto him that will not hearken unto the words of Jesus, and also to them whom he hath chosen and sent among them; for whoso receiveth not the words of Jesus and the words of those whom he hath sent receiveth not him; and therefore he will not receive them at the last day." I thought, "Then I don't have a choice to keep my baby!" I talked to my bishop about it, and he told me I still had my agency and could choose. At that moment I resolved that I would make the right decision, whatever it was. I committed to do everything in my power to receive an answer as to what I should do.

Slowly, I began allowing myself to consider adoption. It seemed that every time I tried to get an answer about whether to parent my child or place for adoption neither of them felt right. I was getting so frustrated. Although my mother said she was very supportive of any decision that I made, my dad was all for adoption. He even went out of his way to try and find a family for the baby. He had a friend who knew a couple that wanted to adopt a fourth child. This family sent an introduction letter with pictures. I thought it wouldn't hurt just to look at it. When I did, I had such a wonderful feeling. Their oldest child, Jocelyn, was a light to me. She looked familiar. I told myself, "If I ever decide to adopt, this would be the family." I was in love with them after reading the letter and seeing the pictures they had sent. I had a feeling of closeness toward them even without meeting them.

Still, I decided I would keep this baby. I even moved to a different state to keep all the pressure of my family and friends to a minimum. While living with my aunt and uncle and their family, I saw every day how an eternal family should be. Four months later I had a dream, a dream so sacred that I shared its details with no one until after I gave birth. In my dream I saw my daughter at five years old and she was sobbing. I didn't know why, so I went up to her and tried to comfort her. I asked her what was wrong. Through tears she cried out, "Mommy, Mommy!" I couldn't understand why she was calling for her mother when I, her mother, was standing right there! Only when she looked up at me and said, "No, I need my mommy. Why didn't you let me go?" did I understand. She wasn't crying out for me. That night I was up at 2:00 A.M. praying and asking Heavenly Father if adoption was what

I was supposed to do. It was revealed to me in a way I could never deny that I should place my daughter for adoption. I had committed to do the right thing. Now was the time for me to do my part.

I called my parents to share my decision with them. I found out that my parents had been in the temple praying for me the night that I had the dream. Later my dad told me that earlier it had been revealed to him that I would make the right decision to place her for adoption. I called my counselor. She asked if I was scared. I told her I wasn't scared. I felt so much peace and confidence that I knew adoption was what the Lord wanted.

Everything fell into place after that. The moment I saw her for the first time all I could do was cry. I couldn't help myself. Everything was just too beautiful. To be able to create life is such a sacred power, and to share the gift of a child with another family has been a great blessing. I believe that my baby and Heavenly Father knew long ago which family I was to choose.

I could not have done it without my Heavenly Father. He has revealed to me that He has a better purpose for us both. He knows more than I do about the road ahead, and I put my full trust in Him. While words can never explain all the pain and heartache I've felt, neither will words ever capture the love and joy I have experienced knowing that I did what was right for both of us. Making the right decision has given me the most comfort.

She gave me the chance to be the mother to bring her into this world and to get her to her eternal family. I love her. It was so hard to let her go. I can't help but think of what Heavenly Father went through when He had to give up His Only Begotten Son for our sake. It was for a greater purpose that Heavenly Father gave up His Son, a sacrifice that blesses all of us.

Laura reports that her life has been blessed by her child and that she believes with all her heart that she has given her daughter a better life.

TO MY CHILD'S
BIRTH MOTHER

by "Steve"

Dear Stephanie,

I feel the need to share some of my own feelings and experiences of the past year. It's hard to believe that Jake has been with us a year. The time sure has flown. Before Jake came, Summer and I had many fun times and enjoyed each other's company (we still do). But we had been married long enough to know that in order for our happiness to reach the next level we needed a baby.

After many doctor's visits and tests, we didn't know why we couldn't get pregnant. We decided to consider adoption. I was not too thrilled about the idea at first. But as I thought and prayed about it, I realized it was the right thing to do. There were many unknowns and uncertainties, so it was a trial of faith. I can't count the number of blessings this adoption has given me. What an incredible experience.

After we met you for the first time Summer and I reflected on our visit with you. I remember saying to Summer, "I also wish that we could adopt Stephanie." I was so touched by our visit. The Savior's unconditional love filled my heart. I really don't know how to explain it. My heart went out to you because of the situation you were in and also because of your tremendous courage, love, and desire to do what was right. I felt extremely excited that I was going to be a father and at the same time terribly heartbroken at what you were going through.

When we met again at the hospital, I wasn't sure if I was going to make it. You probably noticed that by me being so nervous. Jake seemed so tiny and fragile I didn't want to break him. About a week before Jake was born I was trying to come up with something to say to you, knowing we might not see each other again for a long time. The only thing I remember saying to you as you walked out was, "We love you forever." I feel just as strong now as I did a year ago about that statement. It's times like these that I am grateful for the gospel and the knowledge that we will see each other again some day.

Jake has been the main attraction since the day we brought him home. Both sides of our families continue to love and adore him. He is obviously one of the cutest babies ever, especially with those "chipmunk" cheeks. Jake has always been a happy baby. He loves to laugh and play. He seems to be so content. I like to think he knows how much he is loved and this is the reason for his mild behavior. It has been so fun to watch Jake grow and develop this first year, even when I stayed up with him all night on a few occasions.

The court day and temple were both special experiences. It was neat to see the excitement on the judge's face and in his voice. He said he spends a lot of his time legally splitting families apart, but he was so excited to be able to legally put a family together. We even got a picture with the judge for Jake to see when he gets older.

The temple day was quite special. I didn't know the temple had a nursery. Jake did wonderfully well with the temple matrons while Summer and I went off to do some paperwork and get ready for the sealing ceremony. When we walked into the sealing room, it was hard to hold back the tears. The sealer had us put Jake on the altar facing me, while my mother and Summer's mother steadied him so he wouldn't fall off. Jake watched attentively as the sealer started the ceremony. It was the most amazing thing watching Jake and listening to the sealer. Jake seemed to know exactly what was going on and at the same moment the sealer said "Amen," Jake let out a cheer. It is just wonderful how our spirits can be in tune with the other side of the veil sometimes.

Jake is now big enough that he and I do some wrestling and play hide-and-seek. We also play a little baseball and basketball. He just laughs and has a great time. He is learning to obey, and it amazes me that he understands so well when we talk to him. He loves to be outside, and sometimes gets very upset when we bring him inside.

I am forever grateful to you for your courage and love, which has allowed me to become a father. Thank you! I am so grateful for our Heavenly Father's plan and the blessings that come from it. I am anxiously awaiting the day when all of us will meet again. What a happy and joyous occasion that will be. Please never forget that I have a special place in my heart for you. There is no way that I can ever forget what you have done for me. I love you very much, and I pray for the Lord's choicest blessings to be upon you.

Love always,
Steve

Steve and his wife have adopted another son since their first adoption. Their two children are the best of friends, and even though they have different birth mothers, he reports that some people think they are twins. He considers adoption a great miracle and blessing in his life.

A Single Mother's Candid Advice

by "Catherine"

I would like to share a little of what I have learned, having once been in the same position where you are now. I hope you can benefit from my experience and see with greater clarity in order to make your own best choice.

First of all, I commend you for thinking through your options. You have some tough choices to make that will affect not only yourself but also many others for a long time. You are obviously trying to make the best decision for your child. You are showing maturity and wisdom to seek counsel and explore your options, no matter what your end decision is.

I got pregnant before I was ready, and I was in a bad situation with the child's father. I had always known I could not have an abortion, so I went to find out about adoption. I went to several counseling sessions. I did not like the idea of giving my baby up, but I knew it would be better for the baby and me. She would have a home with parents who had eagerly waited for her, and I could put my life in a better situation. I want you to know that raising a child on your own is probably the hardest thing you will ever do in your life. I say that even with all the extra help I had that many people don't have—being twenty-nine when I had her, I was more mature, had financial help, and supportive family and friends—and yet many times it seemed nothing but impossible.

One thing that you will quickly give up is your own life. I do not mean that you cannot work, pursue an education, and spend time with friends or date. You can, but it will never be like it was before. You will find less time to go after your own interests, will most likely be very exhausted doing so, and when you are doing those things, you will feel guilty for the moments you aren't with your child. As for any dreams or plans you might have had for yourself, you can still pursue them but they will have to be amended.

You may wish to imagine how you would answer some of the following questions: Do you know what it is like to feel you are missing out on your baby's childhood because you are out trying to prepare for a better future for the both of you? Do you know what it is like to put this child you love in a daycare where they don't love her—because you have to? Do you know what it is like to realize all your dreams you had about raising children won't come true because you have to do it alone? Do you know what it is like trying to do the work of two parents and to still feel it is not enough? Can you imagine how heart wrenching it is to not be able to give your child the life you dreamed for her? Can you imagine how you will answer when she wants to know why she doesn't have the kind of family, home, or life that her friends have? Can you imagine not being able to sleep through a whole night for a year and a half or not taking a shower till noon? Can you imagine *every single moment* you need to spend away from the child having to make sure you have someone to watch her and make sure you can afford it?

Those are just some of the practical matters on why it is so difficult. Your life will never be the same, and it is not easy. You must know raising a child is a drain on your energy, time, life, opportunities, and finances. Having said that, I do not mean that it isn't 100 percent worth it. Children are a great blessing and worth every bit of the effort and sacrifice it takes to raise them. However, don't deceive yourself into thinking it is easier than it is.

Now, let me tell you about what is really difficult about keeping your child. You will want to give that child the world and when you can't, it will break your heart. Your child will be sweet and innocent and deserving of everything good. You will want to provide it for them and when you can't, because of your situation, it will tear you up inside. I can't tell you how many bucketfuls of tears I have cried over this. Be prepared to fill up your own buckets.

Another thing you should know is that by keeping your child, your past colors more of your future. Obviously, having a child is one way that the past shows up in your future, but that is the good part. I thought that if I changed myself, got out of a bad situation, took on the challenge of single motherhood and persevered the best I could, that I could forget the unpleasant parts of my life and go forward, having turned something bad into good. However, that is not completely true. When you have a child you form a link with the other parent for a lifetime. Not only with them, but often with their family and friends also. This could be fine if it was always pleasant, but if not, it can be a living nightmare. If they are not good for you, they can be detrimental for your child.

Surprisingly, the other parent may be very uninterested in both you and the child in the beginning or for periods of time and you will feel as if they are fading out of your life. (That in itself is another painful issue—when it feels as if the other person doesn't care as much as you do about the child.) However, when you least expect it, they can come into your life, decide to be included, and make demands. That is their right legally, no matter how unfair it may seem. It is not just the child who is affected. Legally, they can prevent you from moving; they can make decisions on how to raise the child, where you can live, what schools the child goes to, what holidays are spent with whom, and when and where you can travel. They can even affect your marriage and job opportunities! They are not only involved with the child you have together but with any children you have in the future.

Speaking legally, hopefully you and the person you got pregnant with will be on amicable terms during your child's lifetime concerning custody, visitation, and support. That is sometimes the case. But often, as it was in my case, it is not. If there are disputes over custody, that is another unpleasant aspect to deal with. I have spent almost $20,000 in legal fees and am not even close to coming to an agreement. I have several friends whose legal fees have exceeded $50,000 to come up with arrangements they are not even happy with. While I know many people resolve things far more reasonably, you should also know that there could be legal battles to fight. A lot of time and energy can be spent on attorneys and in courtrooms, taking even more time away from your child. Furthermore, if you can't agree, you will have "experts" and others who do not know you or your child tell you how to raise your child and when you can and cannot be with them. If you ever want to feel sad, spend a day in family court. I don't think anyone ever wins, and there is a sense of pain and sadness all around.

I would love to find someone who is the kind of person I should have been with in the beginning, someone who would love my daughter so that she could have the kind of family life she deserves. Only she could never be adopted by that father; her biological father will never allow it. I have to bring my past with me.

I want you to know I love my daughter. While the road has been difficult, she has made it all worthwhile. There are amazing single parents out there, and there are many resources. Each situation is different, and only you will know in your heart what is right for you. If you do decide to keep your child, you should know that there also will be many happy moments to help balance out the sad. While it is hard, it is not impossible, and you can get help. I only shared some of the painful issues with you so you could be more informed and wiser than I was.

Now, if you are considering adoption, I also have some words for you. I have often wondered, as I have gotten to know and love my daughter so much, could I have placed her for adoption? While I can probably never know for sure, my inclination is that I might have been able to. While she is my greatest joy and I treasure the time I have with her, I think it is because I love her so much that I might have been able to let her be adopted. While I know I have been a good mother, that she loves me dearly, and that she has benefited from the love I have given her, sometimes I feel I have cheated her. The most difficult part is to realize you have this precious person and yet be unable to give them this happy family life you know they so much deserve. I think how I would have felt to deliver someone so wonderful and to give her to a family who had been praying and preparing to be the kind of parents and family she deserved to have. As her natural mother, I love her with all my heart, but I was unprepared and not in a situation at that time in my life where I could give her the family I wanted her to have. When all is said and done, that is the part that hurts.

I believed that no one could ever love my child as much as her natural parents. I have since learned that that is not true. You contribute your genes to have a child but must contribute love to be a parent. Everyone has a different capacity to love and that is what makes a good parent. I have been fortunate to be around some adoptive parents with their children and have thought, "If only *every* child could be so lucky!" The care a child receives is based upon the parent's ability to love and not upon blood relation.

If you do end up doing adoption, I know that will be one of the most heart wrenching decisions you'll ever make. If you do it, it will only be because you feel someone else can provide a better future for the baby's life than you are able to now. It will also be the most unselfish gift you will ever give—to parents who need a child and to a child who needs parents. And to you, who need a second chance and more time to prepare for having a child.

I cannot think of a more Godlike action, and it makes me feel that you are doing something almost sacred. I think of how wonderful it is to take a hard situation that at first seems so difficult and to make something so loving out of it! Turning one person's pain into three people's gain! From a painful past to a bright future—for you, the child and the adoptive parents. Cannot God always make good out of any situation?

Pray, study, and learn about all your options so you can be informed on how to make your best decision. Then go deep within yourself and listen to what you feel is right in your heart. Once you know what that is, have the courage to act on it. You will find inside that you have strength you do not yet know exists.

Also, know that you have a bright future ahead of you. No matter what you decide, there will be joy, happiness, and opportunities that you can't imagine yet! Remember your value and how priceless and precious you are. I have found much comfort in Emerson's wisdom: "Whatever lies behind us and whatever lies in front of us are but tiny matters in comparison to what lies within us."

I hope that the things I have shared with you can help you in the future. I pray that you can make your own right choice and be comforted with your decision. The best is still yet to come!

Catherine continues as a single parent, working full time while trying to be as involved as possible with her daughter. She reports that although both she and her daughter have made many sacrifices in their lifestyle, she feels good about what she has been able to give her. She says that they have much support from her family and friends, and her daughter is thriving.

A Birth Mother Finds Peace

by "Therese"

My life changed the day I placed my little girl with her parents. It was a most difficult day because I knew it was the last day I was going to see my little girl. I remember leaving the hospital to take her home for a short time before I had to go to the agency. I wanted to spend some time alone with her in an environment that was more comforting than the hospital. The things I shared with my daughter while I was with her during that short time will forever be treasured in my heart. I wanted to read Faith her first book, so I read her the book *Guess How Much I Love You*. This is one of my favorite books because it expresses, so innocently, the love one can have for another. I then told her why I made the decision to place her, and I explained to her that she was going to have the most wonderful life with her parents.

Wanting one more special moment with her, I knelt down in prayer with her in my arms. I can't recall the words that were expressed, but I know that my heart was full.

When I got to the agency, I spent some time with the new parents before placing Faith in their arms. Our time together was wonderful, and I didn't want it to end. I knew it was time to give Faith to her parents, but I wanted just a few more precious moments with her.

I went out with Faith to say my good-byes. I told her again that I loved her and that I knew she was going to have the most wonderful life with her family. I also told her that I knew this was the best thing for her. I remember looking down at her and asking her if she was ready to meet her parents.

At that same time a smiled appeared on her face. I knew at that point it was time. I hugged her and kissed her and told her that I loved her.

We walked into the room where her parents were, and I handed my little girl to her mother. I stayed in the room only a short time after that because I knew that my time with her was over. She was now with her parents. I hugged and kissed her parents and bent down to give Faith one more kiss and whisper "I love you" in her ear. I remember leaving the agency feeling very sad and upset, but I felt comforted at the same time. I knew that my daughter was with her parents, and I knew that I made the best decision for her.

The strong confirmation I received that day through the Spirit is a blessing that forever touches my heart. Looking back on that day brings me heartache and sorrow, but remembering the confirmation I received is what gets me through those hard times when I wish I could be with my daughter again.

Therese went on to receive a graduate degree in social work. She is currently working with children and is making plans to establish her own private practice.

STRAIGHT TALK FROM A
HIGH SCHOOL PRINCIPAL

by Michael C. Hicks

It is a unique experience to work as a high school principal. I have seen teenagers excel in their lives, but I have also witnessed experiences of sadness and tragedy resulting from foolish decisions made by teenagers. Joan was one of those teenagers.

Joan was a ninth-grade girl. She came to the high school with stars in her eyes. In junior high school she had been a cheerleader and was very popular. Soon the older boys began to take notice of her. She had many dates. Joan got pregnant about halfway through her freshman year. When the school found out, they had to drop her from cheerleading and take her off the basketball team. Joan was tough, or so they thought. She made the decision to give birth to the baby and raise him herself.

The baby came, and Joan and her mother began the task of raising her little boy. She brought him to school to show him to her friends. It was exciting for all concerned. Interestingly enough, however, the novelty soon wore off. She was told to leave her baby home as he was a distraction at school. All the girls were still polite but avoided Joan.

Her life quickly changed. Dirty diapers and late-night feedings soon took their toll. Joan dropped out of school. Her mother tried to help, but it seemed this baby complicated both their lives. Life got pretty tedious for this family. Happiness seemed beyond reach.

It was about this time, just before she quit coming to school, that Joan came to my room at the school and told me her story. It was too late now to change much. Joan tried to finish school by correspondence but finally gave that up too. How sad.

I have been a school administrator for twenty-five years, nineteen of those years as a secondary school principal. I have also been involved through Church service with young people for many years. Most recently I served five years as a bishop. Please allow me to share some observations.

Most of the time, when a girl gets pregnant, the boy refuses to accept any responsibility. I have seen this happen far more often than I have seen the boy step up and act with honor and responsibility. Too often the girl is on her own in these sad situations. It is the girl who has to face the consequences after the pregnancy occurs.

The many pregnant teens I have seen in my career have still been in school when the pregnancy occurred. Seldom, almost never, is a teenage girl mentally or physically prepared for the nine months of pregnancy or the life-time of responsibility that comes with becoming a mother. Being pregnant is not an easy thing. The girl goes through months of stress, watching her body change and increase in size and shape as the baby develops. Then, after the baby is born, she is certainly not prepared for what happens next. Raising a child is a twenty-four-hour-a-day commitment that lasts for years.

A new baby usually brings some excitement. I have often seen young mothers bring their new baby to school to "show him off." I have been dis-mayed to see this. Young girls who don't know any better treat this baby like a toy or a status symbol of some kind. Soon enough, however, the novelty wears off, the child is no longer a "neat thing to have," and the work and heavy responsibility become increasingly apparent. Many times it turns out that the girl's mother, grandmother, or some other person takes on this duty and the young mother goes on with life. This type of arrangement is almost never good for the baby. These little children all too often grow up with feel-ings of confusion, not really knowing who their mother is or who really loves them. How sad this is for these little children who are becoming more and more numerous in our schools and society.

I have observed that at those times when a girl makes the decision to "keep my baby and be a good mother," an interesting thing happens. After a few weeks or months the drudgery of childcare begins to take its toll. The young mother is no longer invited to parties, dances, social events, etc. Her former peer group disappears. The kids back in school don't know how to treat their former friend and classmate, and they really don't want to deal with it. They just want to go on with life. The new young mother is left alone, out of the loop she was previously part of. High school kids do not want a girl around who has a baby. She might be treated politely, but things are never the same again for her as long as she has that baby. For example, after the big game everyone goes for a soda and burger, but the mother goes home to her baby. Life is and will forever be different. The heavy load of changing diapers, feeding time, washing clothes, bathing the baby, staying home with a crying child, and wondering where the fun in her life went begins to weigh pretty heavily on her. Oftentimes resentment begins toward the baby and certainly toward old friends and others who seem to have forgotten her.

Some time ago a mother and her daughter came to my office at the school. This sweet, beautiful girl was on the school cheerleading squad. She was popular and involved in the life of the school. They informed me that the girl was pregnant. The boy was a jerk, and they did not want him involved at all. They asked what to do. Since I was also a bishop, I was aware of some options to suggest to them. We talked and cried together and finally, after much prayer and consideration, they made the decision to place the new baby for adoption through LDS Social Services [now LDS Family Services]. When the baby came he was immediately placed in a strong LDS home where there were two loving and committed parents who wanted this child, and he was given a wonderful home. Surely, that baby is being raised the way the Lord meant him to be. Now I know that this was a huge decision for this girl and the prospective grandmother to make. But in my opinion, it was the most loving and unselfish gift they could have given this tiny new baby. The girl was soon back in school and mingling with friends who took her in, and her life went forward with high hopes for a happy future. I am sure that for the rest of her life, she will have tugs at her heartstrings from time to time. But I also know that there is a little boy out there somewhere who will grow up healthy and happy with two parents who will love him and nurture him and give him the best they have.

I could go on and tell more stories like these, as I have many of them, but let me say this. In my years in education and as a bishop in the Church, I can tell you that the stories that turn out happy in the end are the ones in which the girl has courage enough to bless the life of the child by placing the child for adoption. There are many couples who have the desire and the means to adopt and raise a baby as their own, with love. I do know of one or two exceptions where keeping the baby turned out okay, but even then, it was only after many trials and much tribulation.

My counsel has always been to stay pure and not get involved in premarital sex. Period! But if a girl ends up pregnant, she should not compound her mistake by trying to take the parent route at any cost. It sometimes works out, but very seldom. She should love the baby enough to give it a home where it can grow up in joy.

Michael C. Hicks has spent more than thirty years as an educator, nineteen of them as a high school principal. He has also recently served as a bishop for five years, and another ten in other bishoprics. He and his wife have eight children and thirty-eight grandchildren.

Mariah's Story:
The Birth Mother's
Perspective

by "Natalie"

W hen I was twenty years old I got pregnant. I told my parents a few days after I found out. My parents were disappointed but became very supportive. My dad told me he loved me and would support me in my decision. Then he told me that he strongly believed in the Church and was quick to listen to the prophet's counsel. I asked him what the Church's stand was about my situation. He told me that they first counseled marriage, and if that was not a good situation, they counseled for adoption. This hit me like a ton of bricks. At that moment I knew that I was supposed to place my child for adoption. I knew it, but I didn't accept it until later.

At LDS Family Services a woman named Audrey told us how adoption works and explained all the steps. Before we left she told me about a counseling session they have called "group." At group I felt very awkward—what would the other people think of me? Then I saw a girl that I knew from high school and that made me feel so much better to know that there were other people out there who knew what I was going through and also to see those who had gone through it and survived. One of the girls had recently placed her child and was telling us her experience. I cried the whole time. The girls at group were such a strength to me. We would talk about problems we had to deal with, about birth fathers, family, high school, work, grieving, and spirituality. Nurses came in and talked about labor. Single mothers came in to shed light on what that was like. We had panels when adoptive parents came in and talked about their children and their birth mothers. Group was my biggest means of support besides my family.

I had put it off, but I needed to choose a family for my baby. Audrey gave me six files of families in a blue folder. How was I supposed to know who would be the right parents for my child? My bishop later told me not to worry because he knew that I would know when I came to the right one. I told him I had difficulty listening to the Spirit and that I was afraid that I would make a mistake. He told me that if he felt that I was doing the wrong thing in placing my child he would tell me. He told me that he strongly believed that I was making the right decision. As I left his office I felt a reassuring comfort that I would be able to find the right parents.

After Sunday dinner I got up from the table and went down to my room. I kneeled down and began to pray to Heavenly Father to help me to find the right parents for my child. I prayed for what seemed like forever. I sat up with constant tears running down my cheeks. I picked up the blue folder and I opened it. The very first packet was Darrell and Cherie's. I picked up the letter written to the birth mom. As I began to read their letter, I felt this overwhelming peace and comfort. I stopped crying, and I felt this huge weight lifted off my shoulders. I felt as though they had written the letter just for me. By the end of it I knew that they were to be the parents of my baby.

When I told Audrey that I had chosen Darrell and Cherie, she told me that their caseworker had said that Darrell and Cherie were having feelings that something was happening and they kept calling asking what was going on. I quickly wrote a letter to Darrell and Cherie, introducing myself and telling them all about my wonderfully spiritual experience picking them. They wrote me beautiful letters expressing their love for my sacrifice and for the little baby that I was carrying. We continued to write every week. We got to know each other and had this sacred bond that helped prepare for our face-to-face meeting later. When that happened, they gave me flowers and presents and we hugged and talked. They told me they would name the baby Mariah. The Spirit was so strong, continually testifying to me that I was doing the right thing and that all would work out.

My beautiful, perfect angel was born at 11:35 P.M., weighed 8 pounds 2 ounces, and was twenty and one-half inches long. She was so beautiful. I just stared at her in amazement. They brought her over to me and I held her and just cried. She had big, beautiful eyes that were wide awake and looking right at me. She had the most beautiful big lips and round chubby cheeks.

My dad came over and put his arms around me. I held him so tight, and I asked him how I was ever going to be able to do this. He had tears streaming down his face, and he told me it would be okay. My mom stayed with me the whole time. She slept in the big chair in my room. She was such a support to me; I will be forever indebted to her for her service.

The next day Audrey came to the hospital and brought the papers that I would sign. When it came to the part where I was to relinquish all of my rights to her, I physically couldn't get myself to sign. I just sat there for the longest time sobbing. Audrey asked me if I wanted everyone to leave, and I said yes. They all left but my parents. Then my dad gave me the most beautiful blessing. In his blessing he related my experience and sacrifice to Christ's suffering in Gethsemane. He spoke of my love for her and my desire to give her a better life and the blessings of the sealing covenant. He spoke of Christ's love for me and how He knew what I was going through. He told me that just as I loved this baby, Christ loved me and sacrificed for me as I was doing for her. When he had finished I felt that undeniable confirmation that I was doing the right thing and signed the papers.

When the day came that I would give Mariah to her parents, Darrell and Cherie gave me a hand-stitched quilt that they, their families, and friends had stitched for me. They had also written me a poem that explained the quilt. It said that everyone that had stitched it would be those loving Mariah for me, and that every time I felt lonely or sad I could just wrap up in it and feel the love that they have for me and for her. They also gave me a beautiful necklace of sapphire, her birthstone; I still hardly ever take it off.

I told Mariah how much I loved her and how much I would miss her. I told her that I loved her so much that I needed to give her the best life possible, and that was with Darrell and Cherie. I asked her to please understand that I loved her and to forgive me. I sat there crying so hard that I was shaking. I held her so tight I didn't want to let go. I knew that I had to. A saying we had in group was, "I would rather suffer than have my baby suffer." This kept echoing in my ear. I kissed her, told her I loved her one more time, and got up and placed her in Cherie's arms.

My dad came and held me. I hurt so bad that words can't come close to describing the pain that I felt. My arms were so empty; I hurt in the depths of my soul. I couldn't stay in there any longer. I said I was sorry but I had to leave. I walked out the door without saying good-bye and just fell into the corner of the wall, hurting so bad that I wanted to die. My dad rushed out and grabbed me in his big, safe arms. He carried me out and down the stairs.

But the moment we walked out of the building I started to feel that sweet peace that I was so accustomed to feeling, and I stopped crying. It was the most amazing feeling I have ever felt. Later I told my family that I knew what Christlike love was, and in time I began to heal. Darrell and Cherie still write back and forth with me. They keep me informed about Mariah and how she is progressing. I still have my good days and my bad days. I still miss her, and I still love her. I still cry, like I am as I write this, but that unbearable pain is gone. I have no regrets, just a lot of respect for birth mothers, adoptive parents, and their children.

When Mariah was ten months old, they came to visit me. We met at the temple and had a nice visit. This was such a good experience. I loved being able to see them again. I felt very good with the visit. It was emotional but not bad. I felt good, and I know I did the right thing. I know that Mariah is where she is supposed to be. She just turned one last week, and I still have no regrets. This experience has made me so much stronger than I ever was and brought me back to my Heavenly Father. I could not have done this without His help and love for me. Mariah was sealed when she was six months old to her parents. She has a mother and a father who love her more than anything. She also has my family and me, her birth mother, who loves her more than life itself.

A lot of people do not understand adoption; they see it as purely selfish. I know the truth, for I have experienced it. I know that adoption is about pure, selfless love. I love Mariah more than words can adequately say. I hope that one day she will understand and thank me for the hardest decision in my life. For now, I take it one day at a time.

Natalie placed her baby three years ago and reports that she is very happy. She is attending college and aspires to one day counsel other birth mothers through LDS Family Services. She adds that her experience with adoption has made her the person she is today, and she will always be thankful for that.

Mariah's Story:
The Adoptive Mother's
Perspective

by "Cherie"

Both my husband and I served missions, both of us graduated from college, and we were married in the temple. So I thought we had all our bases covered. I just assumed our children would be coming soon because that's what we'd planned for. Who would have known that *becoming* parents was to be our trial?

After years of infertility, some surgeries, and constant discouragement from the wave of unsuccessful medical results, adoption was our answer. We began the paperwork process, and we were often encouraged by good family members and friends. We found it helpful to talk with other couples who had already made this journey. As we completed our paperwork and submitted it for approval, we felt a peace of mind that we hadn't felt for a long time. It was true: we had done all we could do, and now we put it in the Lord's hands. Both my husband and I were busy people with work and Church callings. We went out of our way to serve those around us, so that we could keep our minds busy. We learned that it is important, although not always easy, to be happy for others, when their ability to become parents occurred seemingly more easily than ours. We learned that it is okay to feel sad at times, but it is also perfectly well and good to share in others' joy and to let nieces, nephews, and other children fill your heart with love. That way, the void doesn't seem quite as large. It helps to make the waiting bearable.

A year and a half after our paperwork was completed, we received the news that we'd been chosen by a birth mom. She was having a baby boy. To make a long story short, she changed her mind after giving birth. She couldn't part with her child. I could understand that, even though my heart ached. And both my husband and I found comfort in each other and also in family and friends who cared about us and weren't scared of the complex circumstances we found ourselves in.

I learned two things after this adoption fell through. First, I found that I was more concerned for the welfare of a newborn baby—a child I'd never seen nor held—than I was about myself. What I mean is, my husband and I hurt and felt grief, but we were more concerned about that baby boy and what his future held. I felt sad because I was convinced it was going to be tough for him and for his mother. But I also knew that it was her choice to make as the baby's mother. The second thing I learned was that when you feel like you probably won't ever want to get out of bed the next morning, it is possible that prayers will help hold your heart up. And when it is the right time, regarding the child that is meant to be yours, it will work out.

About four months after that experience, we received another letter. This time, it was really from our birth mom. You see, even though she is the biological mother of our daughter, she is, to us, *our* birth mom. She is our angel, our miracle, our answer to prayer.

When we met our birth mom and her parents for the first time, I was amazed at how natural it felt and how much love I felt for them and *from them.* I hugged our birth mom right away and I could feel her little pregnant belly between the two of us as we embraced. This baby between us would be the link between us for eternity. I loved her and her parents right off. I did not feel as though they were strangers, even though this was our first time meeting. It was an emotional, incredible visit. A lot of the things we talked about in that meeting were so special—for instance, the spiritual confirmation that our birth mom and her parents had experienced concerning Darrell and me being the parents for this expected baby girl. Most of it was so special, almost too sacred to share too much.

There was something our birth mom said to us that pierced me to the heart and gave me a glimpse into just how sweet this little expectant mother was. When she found out she was pregnant, she had no doubt that she would be keeping her baby. But, she told us, a friend of hers who is also a birth mom said to her, "Either you suffer or your baby will suffer." And that was that; she knew she would place her child for adoption. Our birth mom loved her baby girl so much that she couldn't let her suffer, so she would let her go to a mom *and* a dad. And with tears in her eyes, yet with a steady resolve, she said, "So I will be the one to suffer."

She didn't say it as though she was asking for sympathy or pity; it was just coming straight from her heart. I have never felt so humbled in all my life. In that moment, she taught me more about charity and love than I had to that point known. I knew that, without a doubt, she did love, and would continue to love, her baby forever. As we all talked, the hours passed by in what seemed like minutes. It was hard to go home after that. But it was another stretch of our incredible journey.

Back home, we continued to get things ready—everything that we felt a baby girl needed. It seemed like the Spirit touched every aspect of our preparation. From what to write in letters to our birth mom, to selecting a name for our baby girl, to piecing and stitching a quilt for our birth mom—the Spirit seemed to be guiding us along our path. It all just felt sacred. I started to think that other moms who carry and deliver their newborns wouldn't trade that experience for anything. But I wouldn't have traded my experience of how I became a mom, either. Not for the world.

Like anyone who's been involved in the placement of a baby, it is hard to express the emotions that take place. It is a sacred, bittersweet time. I haven't felt any kind of emotion like that in my life. And it isn't possible to adequately describe it or share it. I could write thirty pages about it! But still, I can't give those feelings to anyone who wasn't in that room that day. I will have to just say, it was incredible. To watch this baby girl's birth mom and family hold her and hug her and whisper good-bye in her tiny ear, with tears streaming down their faces, was the most humbling and heart-wrenching experience. I quietly told our birth mom that I knew I couldn't take the pain out of her heart. I told her, though, that I would do everything possible, everything in my power, to do right by this child, for her. I knew I would be responsible for giving this baby girl the love of two mothers' hearts.

All of a sudden, the birth mom's family was gone, out of the room. My husband was holding our daughter. He had red, puffy eyes. He looked at me and said, "That was the hardest thing I've ever done."

We fed, changed, and buckled up our little sweetheart. We gingerly got her into the car and called home to waiting family and friends. They wanted to know everything about her right then and told us to drive quickly, but safely, home. I sat in the back seat with our new beautiful baby and let my husband chauffeur us home. I kept looking over at her in her car seat. I couldn't believe she was finally here. I'd known her less than an hour, yet I was in love. So was her daddy! It was a tender time. We were elated to have our baby here, but our hearts certainly were soft and tears still came easily, as we were the recipients of an amazing act of love that our birth mom had so courageously rendered.

It's been a little over a year since that day. We were sealed in the temple when Mariah was six months old. That day was the culmination of countless prayers being answered. Mariah wore two bracelets on her wrist and, in the layers of her white dress, a handkerchief sent to her from her birth mom. After the sealing, I sent the handkerchief I had held that day, and also one of the bracelets and the baby shoes Mariah had worn that day, to our birth mom.

We love our Mariah, and she is the light of our lives. She is my world, and I would do absolutely anything for her, as I know her daddy would. Our baby girl's journey here on earth, with us as her parents, was only made possible because of a decision. That decision was one of selflessness and an eternal perspective—of her birth mom, *our* birth mom.

Mariah is now two and a half years old. She keeps busy coloring, visiting cousins, and building snowmen. One of her favorite things is to help Mommy unload the dishwasher. She also loves when Daddy comes home so she can get a horsey ride.

Cherie and Darrell have completed the paperwork to adopt a baby brother or sister for Mariah.

WAITING TO ADOPT

by Travis K. Manning

I think I know where, if not precisely when, I first entertained the notion of adoption. Years ago on a cool April morning in South Salt Lake, I faced a class of kindergarten children and told them I was Superman. It was easier than getting them to pronounce my real name. The children whom I substitute-teach know I am role-playing when I take on the persona of a comic book hero like the blue-tighted, x-ray-vision-equipped Man of Steel; still, some kids' countenances brighten into even wider smiles, and I know I've gotten them believing in the fantastical, the surreal.

The idea of being parents has seemed surreal to my wife and me, despite our efforts to become such. Then, as now, Ann and I are attempting to have children of our own the old-fashioned biological way, but to no avail. We've had tests done, and all systems are go. There is no valid medical reason that justifies our infertility.

I think often about my great-great-great grandfather Absalom Woolf and his two wives, Lucy Ann Ambleton and my great-great-great grandmother, Harriet Wood. They did not need in vitro fertilization or ovulation medication. Absalom—"Appy," as he was fondly nicknamed by his two wives—fathered eighteen children, six sons and twelve daughters. I would that we were as fertile as they, though I cannot imagine myself with two wives. Nor can I imagine providing for twenty-one mouths! Appy, Lucy, and Harriet have thousands of progeny now. Ann and I have none.

Unlike many teachers, I do not accept the notion that my students are my kids. I want to father my own little family with children that I can train up to make a difference in the world after I die, with solid testimonies of the Savior Jesus Christ, to continue fighting for just causes, to raise kids of their own but better than Ann and I will have done. I want children who can visit me on holidays, who will send me e-mail photos of my grandkids, who will remember the eternal truths I have taught them and act accordingly, who will send colorful scribbled refrigerator art regularly.

Students in elementary school are not my surrogate progeny, though I'm tempted after days like this one in April to embrace such a stance. Diego asked me if I could fly for him at first recess because I had said, after all, that my name was Superman. I said I would, knowing he would forget. But Diego did not forget. Fifty minutes later I galloped around the playground, cruising through the woodchip-laden kindergarten play area, arms stretched wide, sneakers kicking up shavings and dust like a rooster tail behind a speedboat, weaving in and out of red plastic slides, a fireman's pole, and black swings with long chains, bending from side to side, articulating swooshing and drowning sounds. Diego did not buy my comic book hero routine entirely on that spring morning. So he suggested that I couldn't actually fly because I wouldn't show the "S" on my chest. Though I didn't understand his reasoning, I told him that I never let people see my "S" while at school.

I still don't let most people see my "S," let alone students, and several summers after substituting in this Title I south-side Salt Lake City kindergarten class, after tying seven-and-a-half pairs of shoes and singing the Barney cleanup song six times—"Clean up, clean up, everybody do your share"—I wonder who I really am. I know I am a child of God—at least, I have a pretty good feeling about it—but when will I begin to raise children, too? Maybe the invented "S" on my chest represents "scared" and not "Superman." Scared to have children of my own. Or maybe it represents "self-absorbed," which is what my life is for me now to a certain degree without children to nurture, my extra energy wrapped up in personal hobbies such as mountain biking and basketball.

When we do have children, I will have to better learn how to clean up my own messes. My friend John came over recently and said, right off, "Your house is not childproof!" With two children of his own, he knows of what he speaks. I suppose I will learn to shut the door to my office and lock it, and I will learn that leaving stacks of books and papers out on the coffee table and living room floor is asking for trouble. Like billions of human beings before me, I suppose I will adapt.

Teaching children is physically and emotionally exhausting. The exchanges between me and the children siphon my patience like chocolate milk through a straw. I hope to be in top physical and emotional condition for our future children, as it will try my resolve at all levels. But I know I will never be that ready. I am told no amount of training can successfully prepare future parents, as the real training is largely on the job. Baptism by fire. Do or die. I asked my own mother a few years ago how she and my father successfully raised seven children. Her guileless response: "Well, Travis," she said after giving it some thought, "we took them one at a time."

If Ann and I don't conceive soon, we will adopt. We are going through the paperwork process which, though necessary, is not an easy task. We find ourselves having to indicate what race, gender, and age will be acceptable for our adopted child. We can opt for a baby or an older child, one with a disability, pink-skinned, brown-skinned, or otherwise.

Parenthood requires that parents comprehend the fundamentals of raising a child. But like Robert Fulghum, I just comprehend the seed in the styrofoam cup. The roots go down and the plant goes up and nobody really knows how or why, but we are all like that. Teaching children has provided me with repeated opportunities to evaluate my own child-rearing desires, my own strengths and weaknesses of character.

As a teacher I've never been hugged by anyone as much before, even by my wife. I can be standing, watching, or helping students, and out of nowhere a kindergartner will latch onto my leg, right about my knee, a double-handed tight squeeze of affection (sometimes a runny nose leaving a wet spot somewhere near my thigh). Or, while I'm walking down the hall, little girls or boys spontaneously reach up and grasp the hands of a stranger—mine. Sometimes children reach for each of my hands simultaneously. Their loving spontaneity and meekness are qualities I have rarely seen in myself. I long to hold the hands of my own children, father with daughter, father with son. Adopted or not, it makes no difference.

Travis K. Manning is a freelance writer and a graduate student who enjoys mountain biking. He and his wife continue to pursue building their family through adoption.

My Miracle

by "Tamara"

I still don't really know how I left that night—how I was able to go home and wake up in the morning. Or how I am still here today, living and breathing. I don't know how I was able to see tomorrow. I know that I will never forget that day or the months that preceded it—especially those last few days, the ones when she was there, when I was actually able to see her for the first time, to hold her, to smell her. Those memories are engraved in my mind so deeply that even when I am gone, they will still be there. It really is amazing how someone so small, so innocent, so perfect, could come and completely change me. I don't know where I would have been without her, and I don't ever want to know. But now I know why we call babies miracles.

"I'm not going. It's probably just another false alarm."

It was real. I was in labor.

I had gone to the hospital twice already and been sent home both times; there was no way I was going back until I knew for sure that I would be staying. But after a few hours I gave in. Adele, the woman who had been helping me through this time, said if I couldn't get through the contractions without crying it was time to go in.

When we got to the hospital, they made me wait in a cold room. The room was stark, no pictures on the walls, no furniture—just monitors and a bed. But they were letting me stay; that's what mattered. This was the last day I would have to be pregnant.

Finally, they moved me into the real delivery room. As they rolled me

221

into the room I saw a TV, a phone, long pink curtains, and a few little tables. There was even a recliner in which Adele made herself comfortable as soon as we got in there. As soon as I got the painkillers, I was asleep. Most people tell me it isn't fair that I slept through my labor. I see women on TV who make it look like the worst thing in the world, and I laugh; I couldn't feel anything, so I slept.

Hours passed. When the time finally came, it hit me: all the months I had spent feeling her kick me, being awake at night wondering what she would look like, hoping I was making the right decision for her—it was all coming to an end. Soon Megan would be here. Soon I would have to be stronger than I ever thought was possible. Soon I would have to face the one thing I had feared for so long. I would have to say good-bye.

I started to think about all the other mothers there preparing to deliver. I thought about the men who were probably with them, holding their hands. I thought about the friends and family who were anxiously waiting to welcome their new baby, and I thought about them taking their baby home, forever. And I hated them. And then I hated myself.

I started to push, and in a matter of minutes she was there. They put her in my arms. Shocked and amazed, I looked down on her for the first time. I felt tears roll down my face and didn't even know I had started to cry. They were tears of joy because she was so perfect, so beautiful. But they were also tears of deep sorrow. I knew that I would not be taking her home. I remember seeing her tiny little face, flushed from delivery but content. Her little almond shaped eyes were open and looking up at me, as if she had known me forever, as if she were as happy to see me as I was to see her.

Her feet were so small, and her toes were curved under, like mine. I showed them to everybody who came to visit. She had little chubby rolls under her chin and on her arms and more dark hair than I have ever seen on a baby. She looked so much like her dad. I wish he could've seen her.

My family arrived and friends came by to visit. But I wouldn't let them stay long. My dad's heart melted when he held her that first time. I had never seen him cry before. And I'll never forget the way it made me feel. I knew, then, that I wouldn't be the only one to miss her. The first night we were together she slept across my chest. She just lay there curled up, happy. Every once in a while she made the little squeaky noises that I love so much.

For hours we lay there together. I told her everything. I told her about her dad and why he wasn't there. I told her about my family, the people she would never know. I told her about me, what I liked, what I would do with my life. I told her how I loved her. And I promised her that one day she would be proud of me. I didn't want her to ever say she didn't want to know me or that she had a birth mother who only made mistakes. I told her I was afraid I would never see her again and how it broke my heart. And I told her I was sorry. Sorry I wasn't ready for her. Sorry I couldn't give her all that she deserved, sorry I wasn't able to be the kind of mother that she needed.

We called the adoptive couple and told them she was born. I let them hear her cry over the phone. They cried with me and sent me flowers. And we made plans for when we would meet. The three days I had with Megan went so quickly. I wanted to freeze time. I took hundreds of pictures and hours of video, hoping to preserve what I could. But they'll never be enough.

Sunday morning we left the hospital, and I took her home for a few hours. My mom and I gave Megan her first bath and got ready all of the things I was sending with her. I wrapped her in the blanket I had made for her and held her all day.

That night we went to the agency, and I had to go inside. When I walked into the room, a room that had once seemed so friendly, so warm, I only saw the ugliness of it—the way the couch fabric didn't match anything, the empty chairs that other girls had sat in at our group meetings. I wondered how many girls had seen their babies for the last time here and how many couples had been made a family because of it. They handed me the papers and read them aloud to me. Upon signing them I terminated all my parental rights to her. *Terminated*—such an ugly word. When I think of it, I think of death. I think of the end of something wonderful that can never be replaced. And that's how I felt. I was dead inside. All the strength I had was gone. I had used it all to sign the papers.

The family came in, and I showed Megan to them. I showed them the gifts I had for her, and they gave me theirs. I gave them my child; they gave me a necklace. How can that ever be fair? Then the time came, and I had to leave. I had to get up and put her into their arms. When I showed Megan to the woman and told her that she would be her new mom, Megan cried. I wanted to tell myself it was because she only wanted me, but I was afraid it wasn't true. I gave her one last kiss and went out the door. I couldn't walk, and I nearly collapsed. My mom and dad held me up as we went to the car.

We drove away. I gave Megan to strangers and drove away. I could see the light through the curtains in the window as the building disappeared out of sight. The night seemed so empty, the world so lonely. She was gone, and now she'll never know me as her mother. I was going to go home and die. There was no possible way I could ever live again. But the next day came. I woke up.

I won't see her when she takes her first step or on her first day of school. When she gets her heart broken for the first time, she won't turn to me to comfort her. When I think of these things I try to remember that now she has a father, a man who won't run away from her when things get hard, someone she can look up to and love. She has stability. She has a family. The only way I could give her what she deserved was to give her away.

Every day I wonder what she is doing, how big she is getting now. I wonder if she is sleeping, or being held, or eating. I wonder what her first word will be and how she will sound when she says it. I wonder if she will know just how she changed my life.

Because I gave her life, I was given back mine—a second chance to be who I know that I am, to live out my dreams and make her proud to have come from me. When I look back on who I was and who I have become because of her, I can only be grateful. I can't say I wish I hadn't made a mistake, because she is here, and she taught me how to live again. All I can say is I wish I had been ready for her.

Now I know why people call babies miracles. She was my miracle, and because of her I can live.

After Megan was born, Tamara went back to college, where she met the man she would marry a year later. They now have a baby son. Tamara adds, "I thank God every day for the opportunity I have to be his mommy."

A Birth Mother's
Correspondence

by "Cami"

Letter from Adoptive Parents

MARCH 10—

Morgan is such a beautiful baby. Our families just love him. He is so good. The only thing we have a hard time doing is getting him to sleep at night. He seems to have his days and nights mixed up. I try to keep him up in the early evening so he will sleep at night. I have only managed to keep him up one evening for a few hours. I learned that I need to sleep when he does during the day. It has been hard to reverse my schedule, but I am actually adjusting to this pretty well now. He always makes me laugh, even when I am exhausted. It always makes those nights up with him even more worth it. During the day, he sleeps pretty well. I can vacuum, have a friend's screaming kids over, or just make as much noise as I want and he doesn't wake up. A few times he will get startled, but I think he actually sleeps better with a lot of noise.

Letter from Birth Mother

MARCH 13—

I am so happy to have heard from you! I was worried that Morgan might not take a bottle very well, but it sounds like he has been fine. I know he has a little trouble straightening out night and day. Before he was born, his "playtime" was from about 1:00 to 3:00 A.M. I guess not much has changed.

I have been working hard on his scrapbook. I have sorted through about

225

a thousand pictures. A few pages are finished and several more are laid out in my head. I am so glad you made this book for me. I was also very glad to get to meet the two of you. That was a very comforting experience. I am so happy that you chose to keep Morgan's name. It was very difficult for me to give him a name because I thought it would be changed. The name Morgan was special to me and I didn't know if I really wanted to give it to him, knowing he wouldn't keep it. I was much relieved when both of you felt it was a fitting name for him. For me, that was just one more confirmation that all would be fine. It was so wonderful to speak to you and get to know you better.

I need to go, but I can't end before I thank you again for what you are giving Morgan. I thank God that I found you. I know I was led every step of the way. I am so grateful that Morgan will have an eternal family. I can never thank you enough for living righteous lives and being good examples for my little man. I love you all. Please give Morgan a big hug and a kiss for me.

LETTER FROM ADOPTIVE FATHER

APRIL 24—

There are a couple of experiences I thought you would like to hear about. When Heidi and I got back into town, the place where I work surprised me by putting together a baby shower for us. Although Heidi couldn't be there, it was really neat. Together they gave Morgan about twenty-three outfits, a stroller, a portable crib, diapers, formula, a blanket, and much more. I was overwhelmed by the kindness shown to us. They also gave us some cash. In fact, some people who contributed had never met me, but they wanted to help Morgan. It was kind of nice, because as I went around to thank people, I had the opportunity to talk to several of them about the Church. Morgan really seemed to open some doors. Hopefully as I get to know the people at work better, some will want to join the Church.

LETTER FROM ADOPTIVE MOTHER

AUGUST 13—

Recently we have been reflecting over the past six months since we have had Morgan. As we looked at pictures taken in March, it is hard to believe he has grown so much. He is such a handsome little boy with such a big spirit. It seems like wherever we take him, people comment on how handsome and cheerful he is. Sometimes we feel bad because other couples who have babies his age don't get the comments we do. He always seems to steal the show.

We were also looking back on the time before we decided to adopt. It took us a while to come to this decision. I went through surgery, fertility drugs, and other medically necessary things to get pregnant. After nothing worked, we both began to feel that we should look into adoption. It took several months of praying and going to the temple before we knew that adoption was the right choice. After this decision was made, everything just fell into place. We know that Heavenly Father has truly had a hand in all that has come to pass in the last months. We are so grateful you were in tune with the Spirit and made this all possible. You have given us the greatest gift anyone could ever give us. Without you and Morgan our family would have never been complete. Morgan is the light of our lives. You have blessed our lives more than you may ever know or that we could ever express.

We are so grateful for your sacrifice and for the decision you made. We love Morgan so much. We are looking forward to taking him to the temple to be sealed as an eternal family. I know it will be one more experience that will make this year one of the most memorable. Thank you again for everything.

LETTER FROM ADOPTIVE MOTHER

DECEMBER 3—

Morgan took his first steps the other day. It was so exciting. He now tries to walk everywhere. He usually doesn't take more than four or five steps before he falls, but he does try. I am sure he will get better every day. Morgan is pretty coordinated. He also likes to babble a lot. I think he really thinks he is talking to us, or at least it seems like he is. He will repeat a lot of sounds that we say. I think Morgan will turn out to be a pretty intelligent little boy. We are now also finding that Morgan is a daddy's boy. Anytime he is upset about anything or crying, all I have to do is take him to Karl and he will calm down. He also gets so excited when Karl walks through the door from work. It is so neat to see. I hope Morgan will always stay close to Karl and follow his example.

I hope all is going well for you. I will probably write you right after Christmas. I should have some more photos for you then. Have a wonderful Christmas!

Letter from Adoptive Parents

March 12—

I have kept copies of all of the letters I have sent, and they have been a record of what Morgan has been doing during each month. This last year has gone by so quickly. I started thinking back on the day that we met you and your parents. It was such a neat experience that we will never forget. Morgan has brought us so much happiness. His little spirit brightens our home.

Morgan is really on the move these days. He runs around everywhere and is into everything. He loves to climb onto and into anything he can. One day I even found him in the dryer playing! Morgan has recently taken a great interest in reading. We had previously tried to read him books, but he wouldn't sit still long enough for us to reach the first page. Now he brings us books, points to something, and waits until we tell him what it is. He has also begun to tell us exactly what he wants. If he wants something in the kitchen or he wants to go outside, he will take our hand and drag us to what he wants. I just can't wait until he can talk. I am sure we will have some interesting conversations then.

Morgan just had his one year checkup. He is now twenty-one pounds and twenty-seven inches long. It is amazing to think that he has more than doubled his weight in just a short time. I have sent along some pictures from Morgan's birthday. We took him out to eat and then came home and had cake. As you will see from the pictures, he ate most of the cake himself. We had a lot of fun, and I know he did too. There are also some pictures of Morgan when he was two or three months old that we had forgotten to send you. The little photo album that the pictures are in has Morgan's hand and footprints on it. They didn't turn out perfectly because he doesn't hold still for very long. We were lucky to get them. We had paint all over us and the room by the time we were done. It was a mess, but I thought you might like to have them.

We want to thank you for bringing Morgan into our lives. You will always be a special part of ours. Thank you for everything. We love you!

Letter from Birth Mother

April 17—

This is the last letter I can send you for a while. I certainly will miss hearing from you. I can honestly say that I love you all. I have no regrets about giving Morgan up. I know I made the right choice for both of us. At times, it has hurt a lot. But I always knew we would both be blessed. Thank you for being so diligent in writing and sending pictures. They mean so much to me. I pray that you will all be well in the years ahead. I can tell by the photos that Morgan couldn't be better!

Thank you so much for caring for my dear child. I miss him terribly, but it makes it better to know he's with you. I know you are finally an eternal family. What a joy! It is just what I wanted him to have. Thank you for living worthy of the temple's blessings. He will benefit so much from your example.

I am excited to tell you that Richard and I have decided to start trying for a baby in April. I am so thrilled! I can't wait to have a baby to raise with my husband. I am sending along a gift for Morgan's birthday. Richard and I picked it out together. We agreed that it is perfect for a little man like Morgan. I thought the handles would make it easy for him to drag or push around. Richard just liked the fact it was a truck!

We'll be missing all of you. Take care of yourselves! I'll send a picture as soon as I can get my hands on one!

I love you. Give Morgan a kiss.

Cami reports that she can never calculate the good that has come into her life as a result of her decision to place her baby for adoption. Now married, she has two beautiful boys and recently went to the temple. "I still think of Morgan every day."

Karl and Heidi have been joined by another son and daughter. Morgan is now seven, a loving big brother, and a great example to his younger siblings. He loves baseball, soccer, and animals. He cannot wait to be baptized.

Saying Good-bye:
A Family's Letters to
"Cassandra"

My dearest Cassie,

I can't believe you are finally here. Now that you are, I can't believe that you are going so soon. This is the hardest thing that I have ever gone through. I hope and pray that I never have to do something this hard again. I just want to hold you and never let you go. I wanted to tell you *our* story.

In January, I realized I was pregnant. I was extremely scared and didn't tell anyone. I was somewhat in denial. I never did a pregnancy test or went to the doctor. I kind of just let it be. I have never been so afraid in my life.

Your birth father and I had been dating for about a year and a half. He is not a member of the Church, but he was my very best friend. We are still very close friends. I didn't know if I was going to keep you or place you for adoption. I just didn't know what was going to happen from that point of time in my life. I was scared to tell your birth father because I was afraid I would lose him. I felt I needed him so much at that time in my life. When I told him, I was so scared. He was calm, and I quickly learned he was just as scared as I was. We talked and decided that we would place you for adoption. We knew that we couldn't provide the right life for you.

You were a kicker! You loved moving up into my ribs. That was really uncomfortable! I decided that I wanted to stop hiding, and so in July I went to see my bishop. While attending college, my testimony had grown so much. I prayed more for you and for me about the decisions I was going to have to make. My bishop helped a lot, and I finally told my parents.

230

They were scared and disappointed in me. But love was the overall feeling that they showed. We knew that there was a lot that I needed to take care of. I went home after the next couple of days, and we started to work things out. I prayed often for you. Cassie, I know without a shadow of a doubt that placing you for adoption is the very best thing.

I read the letter that your parents had written in hopes of adopting. It was great. I read a lot of other letters, too, but I kept coming back to your parents'. I prayed so much because I didn't want to make the wrong decision. I wanted you to go to the right family because I love you so much.

I ended up being a lot further along in the pregnancy than I thought. I gave birth to you on August 11. You were such a beautiful little girl. I held you close to me and never wanted to let you go.

Cassie, I want you to know how much I love you. That is why I am placing you with your parents. I feel through the Spirit that you are supposed to be with them. I am at peace with my decision right now. Tomorrow morning I will place you in their arms and say my good-byes. I can't even start to express how much I love you. I want what is best for you. I can't provide you with a mommy *and* a daddy. I can't be sealed to you. Your parents are taking care of all of that. I gave you life, and now your parents will raise you and teach you. I want so bad to be married in the temple some day, and I want the same for you. Listen to your parents. They will know what is best for you. I trust them completely.

Honey, I love you so, so much. I can't believe how much I do. You were with me for nine months and that is so special to me. I cherish every single minute that I have been able to spend with you. I don't want to go to sleep tonight for fear I will miss spending those last hours with you. I love you!

> Your birth mother,
> Madeleine

* * *

Dear Cassie,

I'm having a very hard time writing this right now. All sorts of feelings and emotions are running through me, and I really don't know how to express my feelings towards you in writing. The one thing I know for sure, though, is that I love you very much. Your birth mom and I really want you to know how much we love you.

I'm sure your mom and dad will explain to you why we chose to place you for adoption, but I want you to hear it from me, too. We chose to place you for adoption not because we don't love you enough but because we *do* love you so much. Cassie, I want you to know that if there was any way your birth mother and I could care for you as well as your mom and dad, then we would, without hesitation. But we know that your mom and dad are wonderful people, and even though we love you just like they do, right now they can do a much better job of caring for you and looking out for you, and that's what matters most. Your birth mom and I love you so much, but we want what's best for you, and we know your mom and dad can give you that.

I know you don't remember, but your birth mom and I had a wonderful two days with you before we gave you to your mom and dad. We took countless pictures of you, held you, fed you, and (believe it or not), I even changed your diapers!

Your birth mom and I are giving you to your parents tomorrow, and I'm looking at you in your little crib right now and listening to you make all sorts of funny little noises as I'm writing this. You're not even two days old right now, and I feel like I've known you forever. We were both awake last night at 3:38 A.M., your one-day birthday! You and I celebrated together, which consisted of you opening your eyes, sort of smiling at me, and gripping my finger with your little strong hands.

Cassie, I would love to be the father that you grow up with. But I know I can't be as good a father right now as your dad can. I want you to know how much we both love you, and we only want what's best for you—which means you being with your adoptive parents. In leaving you, I want you to know that we are both hoping you have the best life and that we will never forget you. I love you, Cassie!

> Love,
> Your birth dad, Zach

* * *

My dear little angel Cassandra,

Today, your grandpa held you in his arms and gave you a blessing. I just want you to know I love you with all of my heart. I will always remember holding you in my arms and talking to you while giving you that blessing.

I told you that your birth mommy loves you very much. She wanted you to have a wonderful life and felt that she could not give that to you at that time, so she went to her Father in Heaven and asked for His Spirit to help her do the right thing. I told you of my love for you and of the love your grandmother has for you. You will always be a wonderful part of our lives! We will pray for you daily and think of you often.

I want you to know that the past few days have been the hardest of my life, seeing your birth mother go through the most difficult thing in her life. I love your birth mother, and I know that Heavenly Father has helped her in this decision. I met your mommy and daddy today. They are great! You are very blessed to have them. They already love you!

Well, your grandpa is not always good at saying all the right things. I just want you to know that I have held you close in my arms. My tears have fallen on your blanket—tears of great love for you. I'm sure there will be many more as I talk to my Father in Heaven, and I hope and pray you will feel this love throughout your life. Take care, my sweet little angel.

> I love you so much!
> Grandpa Aaron

* * *

My precious Cassandra,

There is so much I want to tell you but am not sure where to start. I want you to know how much you are loved. You will grow up with the love of your adoptive family, but you must also know how much you are loved by your birth family. Although we know this placement was the very best for you, it was very difficult for all of us. I hope and pray with all my heart that someday you will realize the tremendous sacrifice your mother made for you.

I want you to know how courageous your mother was. So many people were opposed to the idea of placing you for adoption. It would have been easy for her to cave in and keep you. I'm sure she thought about it many times, but she just kept praying and asking Heavenly Father for guidance to do what was right and to choose the right family. The minute we met your parents I knew our prayers had been answered. I felt an instant love for them and knew that they would take care of my precious granddaughter.

I must have kissed your precious face a hundred times in the last two days, and I will kiss you over the next few years in my mind. I am so thankful that your parents prayed for your birth mom as well. She has felt Heavenly Father's help in this and will continue to need His help.

I hope that someday when you are ready that you will have the desire to meet us and let us be part of your life. We love you—please always know that. You have a very special place in your grandma's heart.

God bless you, my precious girl,
Grandma Shannon

* * *

Dear Cassandra,

There is something very special about you—you were adopted. I know your parents were thrilled to have the opportunity to adopt you. I haven't met your parents yet, but I know that is the family that you belong to.

My name is Caleb. I am your uncle. When I held you for the first time today and looked into your beautiful face, I was crushed. I was hurt because I knew that I wouldn't be able to be your favorite uncle. I wouldn't be able to watch you grow up. I am having a hard time with this.

From the day I was born I loved sports. I would sleep with my bat and my ball. When I was two I would wake up in the middle of the night and wake up my dad to play baseball with me. So he would wake up and pitch to me right there in his room. I love baseball almost more than anything.

I hope that you have a love for sports. (You certainly do have the genes for them!) If I can give you any piece of advice, it would be to never go far away from the Church. It is the one thing on this earth that can help you through anything. We wouldn't be able to make it through this without it.

I want you to know that I love you very much. And I hope that one day maybe I can see you again.

Love,
Your Uncle Caleb

* * *

Dear Cassandra,

A lot has been happening these last few weeks. When I got to hold you in my arms, I wished my sister had made the right choices before she got pregnant. You are such a beautiful little girl. I know that she is letting you go to the right parents.

Here's a little about me. My name is Kylie. I am your aunt. The sports I play are soccer, basketball, and softball. I used to play football. It was really fun. I played for three years. I was the kicker, running back, and safety. My parents have not let me play since I started my freshman year of high school. I am a freshman right now.

I just want you to know that everything is going to work out just fine. I realize that the Lord can help you get through anything. He gives us these trials to help strengthen us and acknowledge our blessings. I love you, and you will always be in my heart.

Love,
Your Aunt Kylie

* * *

Dear Cassandra,

You were so cute when you were a baby. I was so happy that you came to us. I loved holding you. I wanted to be holding you every second when I wasn't.

I'm going to say some stuff about me. I'm eleven years old right now. I play basketball—I love it! That's the only sport I play right now.

I bet when you get older you will be very beautiful! I love you so much!

Love always,
Your Aunt Allison

Three years after placing her baby for adoption, Madeleine was married in the temple. She is now a student at BYU-Idaho. She recently traveled to Ecuador to volunteer in orphanages for several months. She reports that she would not be where she is today if she had not chosen to place her daughter for adoption, and she is grateful that Cassie has an eternal family of her own.

THIS IS MY REAL FAMILY

by Brittany Jones Beahm

My best memories are white ones. The red box of Ritz crackers is the only thing of color that I remember, but everything else is white: the carpet, the chairs, the ladies' hair. I was two, and I was crying. Friendly faces that weren't my parents' tried to calm me, and the red box was the only object in the dressing room that momentarily captured my attention. My memory then skips to another room where I didn't recognize the two people dressed in white kneeling at the altar. I remember reaching for my grandparents who were seated nearby, and my fussing finally turned quiet when they let me hold my baby brother. And I remember the mirrors.

I have always been glad that my first memory was made in the temple, however fuzzy around the edges that recollection may be. I grew up knowing that every good thing in my life—my family, my opportunities, my testimony—centers around that one sacred day. This knowledge, impressed upon me like the whiteness of the temple, has always been the foundation of my security.

My parents had been married for eight years when Dad had his dream. He saw two tow-headed children—first a girl and then a boy. Dad knew we were coming, but my mother wept, telling him his dream was a desire of his heart which was medically impossible. When the telephone rang on a blue November day, Dad didn't ask if the baby was a boy or a girl because he already knew.

It was two years later when my parents strapped me in the car seat and drove around the city all night, hoping that I would fall asleep. I was too excited for my brother to be born the next day. We named him Jameson, and I claimed him as my own. Mom would enter our room in the dark of morning to find me lying in his crib, singing to him and teaching him his first word: *sister.* As soon as he could walk, I stood him on the back of my tricycle and sped down the sidewalk, his arms around my neck. Wearing matching Osh-Kosh overalls we looked like twins, and when people asked my mother where we got our blond hair, she always responded, "From heaven."

From the time we were young, Jameson and I knew we had been adopted and, more important, sealed. For me it made no difference—my family was close to perfect, and we would be together forever. My mother had explained that we were meant to be a family, but since she couldn't have children herself, some special people had helped us get here—people who loved us enough to choose what would be best for us.

Jameson and I posed more questions as we grew older. We asked about our birth parents and the adoption process, and Mom and Dad always answered openly. If our friends found out we had been adopted, their questions invariably were: How old were you? Are you biological siblings? Do you know your birth parents? Sometimes the questions were ridiculous: What's an orphanage like? Do you call your "parents" by their first names? I usually responded with a laugh, thinking to myself that my family probably exemplified "family" better than theirs. "After all," I'd say, "we probably don't qualify as a typical family, anyway. Not only have we been sealed in order to be together for eternity, but we're happy about it!" Even when my friends didn't understand, I knew that I *was* with my real family.

My real mother, my real father, and my real brother. Because we are promised that "whatsoever ye shall seal on earth shall be sealed in heaven" (Helaman 10:7), our family is as real as anything can possibly be. As true as this is, Jameson and I hold different attitudes about meeting our birth parents. He is curious and will most likely seek them out one day, but I am content and have no desire to know who they are. I feel nothing more than gratitude towards them. Someday I will thank my birth mother for the life she gave me—not only physically but also by her adoption decision, which must not have been easy to make. I will assure her that it was the right choice, although I would hope she knows this already.

That we were meant to be together is reaffirmed each time we kneel in family prayer, discuss the day over the dinner table, or laugh so hard we cry. Not only are we a family but we're all best friends, a fact not easily forgotten. Mom often reminds us, "We prayed you here." Dad always says, "I'm lucky to be your father." And at night Jameson and I sit on the floor and talk for hours. After spending time at my house, a friend recently remarked, "It's nice to hear people actually say they love each other and see they really mean it."

During one of our late-night talks when I was nine and Jameson was seven, we discovered that we could possibly leave on our missions at the same time. We had always done everything together, and I didn't want to be left behind! Our mission calls did arrive on the same day, and we entered the Missionary Training Center together. At the moment of separation, when families walk out one door and missionaries exit another, Jameson and I waved good-bye to our parents and began our missions side by side. It was comforting to walk next to my brother and my best friend. After several years of anticipation and preparation, we were anxious to teach about eternal families and to testify of the blessings of the temple. Not only had we been taught but we also understood from personal experience what it means to have "a house of prayer, a house of fasting, a house of faith, a house of learning, a house of glory, a house of order, a house of God"—a home of love (D&C 88:119).

Jameson and I experienced the MTC together and left on the same airplane. As special as these memories are, the most meaningful was made a few months before. This memory, too, is white: it was my first time in the celestial room of the temple, and my earliest memories flashed with the brilliance of the mirrors. As my parents and I waited for Jameson to come through the veil, I experienced the same feeling of anticipation that had kept me awake the night before he was born—the anticipation of being complete as a family. When Jameson joined us, the four of us cried and rejoiced, thanking a loving Father who, in His great plan, had allowed us to be together. In the familiar penetrating whiteness, we were grateful.

Brittany Jones Beahm and her brother, Jameson Jones, were both adopted. Recently both of them were married in the temple. Brittany is pursuing graduate studies in English at BYU and teaches French at the MTC.

INDEX

ABOUT THE AUTHORS

Monica L. Blume, a licensed clinical social worker, has counseled birth parents and adoptive couples for more than ten years. She speaks to Latter-day Saint audiences across the country and has lead various support, education, and training groups on the topic of adoption. She and her husband, Dennis, are the parents of six children.

Gideon O. Burton is an assistant professor of English at Brigham Young University and the associate editor of *BYU Studies.* He and his wife, Karen, are the parents of four sons. Gideon serves as bishop of his Springville, Utah, ward.